After H E G E L

After

GERMAN
PHILOSOPHY
1840–1900

Hegel

FREDERICK C. BEISER

PRINCETON UNIVERSITY PRESS
Princeton & Oxford

PUBLISHED BY PRINCETON UNIVERSITY PRESS

41 William Street, Princeton, New Jersey 08540

IN THE UNITED KINGDOM: PRINCETON UNIVERSITY PRESS

6 Oxford Street, Woodstock, Oxfordshire OX20 1TW

PRESS.PRINCETON.EDU

Jacket Images: Image of Karl Robert Eduard von Hartmann from the Benjamin R. Tucker Papers/Manuscripts and Archives Division, New York Public Library, MssCol3040; Image of Eugen Dühring from Eugen Karl Dühring, Dühring-wahrheiten: in Stellen aus den Schriften des Reformators, Forschers und Denkers, nebst descend Bildniss. *T. Thomas, 1908; Image of Hermann Lotze from Richard Falckenberg,* Hermann Lotze. *Stuttgart, 1901; Image of Friedrich Adolf Trendelenburg from a photo album owned by the Mathematische Gesellschaft (Hamburg), Oberwolfach Photo Collection, © Archives of the Mathematisches Forschungsinstitut Oberwolfach gGmbH (MFO).*

All Rights Reserved

Library of Congress Cataloging-in-Publication Data

Beiser, Frederick C., 1949-
After Hegel : German philosophy, 1840–1900 / Frederick C. Beiser.
pages cm
Includes index.
ISBN 978-0-691-16309-3 (cloth : alk. paper) — ISBN 0-691-16309-X (cloth :
alk. paper) 1. Philosophy, German—19th century. I. Title.
b3181.b45 2014
193—dc23
2013050419

BRITISH LIBRARY CATALOGING-IN-PUBLICATION DATA IS AVAILABLE

This book has been composed in Adobe Caslon Pro

Printed on acid-free paper. ∞

PRINTED IN THE UNITED STATES OF AMERICA

1 3 5 7 9 10 8 6 4 2

for MICHAEL MORGAN

CONTENTS

CONTENTS

PREFACE

The second half of the nineteenth century in Germany was one of the most creative and revolutionary periods of modern philosophy. It has been, however, little studied in German, even less in English. The aim of this book is to introduce the Anglophone reader to the philosophy of this period. To ensure wide historical coverage, and to maintain a philosophical focus, the book is organized according to controversies rather than themes or thinkers.

There is no pretension to completeness in this work. I claim only to have introduced the Anglophone reader to five major controversies of the period. In discussing any one of these controversies much more could have been said; but for reasons of space I had to be selective about which material is most important and interesting. There were other major controversies in the period; but even an adequate treatment of their main episodes would have gone beyond either my word limit or my time frame. A proper discussion of "the crisis of historicism," or the debate between logicism and psychologism, would have taken me well into the twentieth century.

While I have been severe in setting myself stopping points, I have been more liberal about starting points. In some cases a full understanding of a controversy required treating its origins before 1840, and in those cases I could not so easily restrict myself.

All translations from the German are my own. Because almost all of the writings cited in this book are untranslated, all titles appear in the original German. For the sake of consistency, even translated works are left in the original.

For the stimulus to write this book I am very much indebted to Rob Tempio, philosophy editor of Princeton University Press, who proposed to me the idea of a short history of nineteenth-century philosophy in the spring of 2013. For the encouragement to write it, and other books, I am especially grateful to my friend Michael Morgan, to whom this book is dedicated.

SYRACUSE, NEW YORK
November 2013

After H E G E L

INTRODUCTION

I. A REVOLUTIONARY HALF CENTURY

This book is about German philosophy from 1840 to 1900. All periodizations are artificial, and this one is no exception. But there are still good reasons for choosing these dates. 1900 is the beginning of a new century, one more complex, tragic, and modern than any preceding it. 1840 is significant because it marks both an end and a beginning. It is the end of the classic phase of Hegelianism, whose fortunes were tied to the Prussian Reform Movement, which came to a close in 1840 with the deaths of Friedrich Wilhelm III and his reformist minister Baron von Altenstein.[1] 1840 is also the beginning of a new era in German philosophy. In that year Adolf Trendelenburg published his *Logische Untersuchungen*, and Hermann Lotze finished his *Metaphysik*,[2] two works which broke utterly with the Hegelian heritage and which pushed metaphysics in a new direction. Shortly thereafter, in 1843, Ludwig Feuerbach published his *Grundsätze der Philosophie der Zukunft*,[3] settling his accounts with Hegelianism and initiating a new materialist-humanist tradition in philosophy.

The chief focus of this book is, therefore, German philosophy in the *second* half of the nineteenth century. It is an unusual topic, since most books on German philosophy in the nineteenth century concentrate on the *first* half century. And with good reason. The first three decades of this century were some of the most creative in

1   On the significance of this date for the Hegelian movement, see my *Hegel* (London: Routledge, 2005), pp. 311–13. On the important ties between Hegelianism and the Prussian Reform Movement, see John Toews, *Hegelianism: The Path toward Dialectical Humanism, 1805–1841* (Cambridge: Cambridge University Press, 1980), pp. 95–140.

2   Adolf Trendelenburg, *Logische Untersuchungen* (Berlin: Bethge, 1840); and Hermann Lotze, *Metaphysik* (Leipzig: Hirzel, 1841). Lotze wrote his book from May till December 1840; it appeared in early 1841. For an analysis of both of these works, see my *Late German Idealism* (Oxford: Oxford University Press, 2013), pp. 28–68, 153–64.

3   Ludwig Feuerbach, *Grundsätze der Philosophie der Zukunft* (Winterthur: Fröbel, 1843).

modern philosophy. They coincide with the formation and consolidation of the idealist tradition and with the growth and spread of Romanticism, two of the most influential intellectual movements of the modern era. By contrast, the second half of the century seems less creative and important. Idealism had fallen into decline, and Romanticism was a rapidly fading memory. No intellectual movements of comparable stature grew up to replace them.

The common opinion about German philosophy in the second half of the nineteenth century, even among German contemporaries,[4] was that it was a period of decline and stagnation. The great creative "age of idealism" had passed away with Hegel's death, it seemed, only to be succeeded by "an age of realism," which was more concerned with empirical science and technical progress than philosophy. The little philosophy done in this period—so it was said—had been conducted either by idealist epigones, who were not original, or by materialists, who were not really philosophers at all.

All this leaves us with the question: Why write about the second half of the century at all? What of philosophical significance transpired in this half century that it deserves to be treated in a monograph like this one? The short and simple answer to this question is that the common opinion is just false, and that the second half of the century, though written about much less, is more important and interesting philosophically than the first half. There are several reasons why this is so.

The second half of the nineteenth century was a period dominated by crises and controversies, whereas the first half was one of consolidation and consensus. The idealist and romantic traditions had already come into their own by the first years of the nineteenth century, and it was only a matter of establishing themselves in universities and the public consciousness. The decline of the idealist and romantic traditions by the 1840s, however, led to a period of

---

4 See, for example, Friedrich Albert Lange, *Geschichte des Materialismus*, Zweite Ausgabe (Iserlohn: Baedeker, 1875), II, 64–65; Eduard Zeller, "Ueber die gegenwärtige Stellung und Aufgabe der deutschen Philosophie," in *Vorträge und Abhandlungen* (Leipzig: Fues, 1877), II, 467–78; and Rudolf Haym, *Hegel und seine Zeit* (Berlin: Gaertner, 1857), pp. 5–6.

disorder, confusion, and ferment. This disorder and confusion was also the womb of creativity and rebirth, the start of a new era of philosophy.

Normal times in philosophy are those when there is a settled and agreed definition of philosophy, when philosophers have a general consensus about the nature of their discipline and the tasks it involves. Revolutionary times are those when there is no such definition, when there are many conflicting conceptions of philosophy. Following these definitions, the late eighteenth, early nineteenth, and late twentieth centuries were normal times. The latter half of the nineteenth century, however, was revolutionary. For this was an age when there was no settled or agreed definition of philosophy, when there were many conflicting conceptions of the discipline. Philosophers asked themselves the most basic questions about their discipline: What is philosophy? How does it differ from empirical science? Why should we do philosophy? We will have occasion to examine some of the answers to these questions in chapter 1.

The second half of the nineteenth century was revolutionary for another reason: the rise of historicism. It was during this period that historicism came into its own as a self-conscious intellectual movement in German life and letters. "Historicism" has many meanings,[5] of course, but not the least of them is the thesis that history is a science in its own right, independent of art, philosophy, and the natural sciences. This thesis was a new development of the nineteenth century, one of its characteristic doctrines. For millennia, history had been regarded as more art than science, more pastime than discipline, because the paradigm of science had been strictly mathematical. Only mathematics, it seemed, could achieve the universality, necessity, and certainty required of science. But if this were so, then how could history, which concerns particular and contingent events from the past, about which nothing is certain, be a science? Never before was this question posed so explicitly, and never before treated with such depth and finesse, as in the second half of the nineteenth century, which not for nothing be-

5 On the many meanings of the term, and for a general introduction to the topic, see my *The German Historicist Tradition* (Oxford: Oxford University Press, 2011).

came known as "the age of history." We shall consider some of the central debates about the scientific status of history in chapter 4.

The second half of the nineteenth century is revolutionary for still another reason: namely, it marks the greatest break yet with the Judeo-Christian heritage. It was the most secular age in two millennia. When Nietzsche famously declared that God is dead in the 1880s, he was only articulating an attitude that had already become commonplace decades before. It is surely telling that some of the most famous philosophers of this age—Feuerbach, Stirner, Büchner, Marx, Schopenhauer, and Nietzsche—were atheists. The first half of the century, however, was far less secular; it still clung to the remnants of religion. While theism and deism had declined by the end of the eighteenth century, they were replaced with pantheism. During the first decades of the nineteenth century, pantheism enjoyed a renaissance. It was reborn because it seemed the most viable solution to the latest conflict between reason and faith, the conflict which had emerged in the 1780s during the famous "pantheism controversy" between Jacobi and Mendelssohn.[6] Spinoza's famous phrase "*deus sive natura*" made it possible to both divinize nature and naturalize the divine. Following that dictum, a scientist, who professed the most radical naturalism, could still be religious; and a pastor, who confessed the deepest personal faith in God, could still be a naturalist. Pantheism thus became the popular, unofficial religion of the *Goethezeit* and the *Vormärz*.

It is a token of the greater secularization of the second half of the nineteenth century that it questioned the pantheist synthesis of reason and faith held during the first half of the century. The materialism controversy of the 1850s, which we will examine in chapter 2, assaulted the old via media of pantheism. This controversy posed once again, in the most dramatic fashion, the age-old conflict between reason and faith; but it did so in a more radical and uncompromising manner than ever before, one which forbade any religious solution, not even pantheism. The dilemma is now between a complete materialism or an irrational leap of faith,

6 On that controversy, see my *The Fate of Reason: German Philosophy between Kant and Fichte* (Cambridge, MA: Harvard University Press, 1986), pp. 44–126.

where not only theism and deism but even pantheism is regarded as a form of faith. "Pantheism," as Feuerbach once put it, "is *theological atheism* . . . the *negation of theology* but from the *standpoint of theology*."[7] It was now time to push over that standpoint of theology, which was wobbling and ready to collapse. Rationalism no longer meant just a complete naturalism but also the critique of all forms of hypostasis, which appeared in *any* belief in the divine, even pantheism. For the materialists and radicals of midcentury, pantheism was just another form of religious hypostasis, the alienation or surrender of human powers to the divine. The process of rationalization, the culmination of criticism, was therefore a complete humanism and atheism.

We do well to remind ourselves that, in the modern movement toward secularization, Germany was in the very forefront of modern Europe. One reason for this is the rise of modern biblical criticism in the 1830s and 1840s. The criticism of the Old Testament by Wilhelm Vatke (1806–82) and the criticism of the New Testament by David Friedrich Strauss (1808–74) and Bruno Bauer (1808–82) had undermined more than ever before the authority of the Bible as the source of Christian Revelation. Another reason for Germany's leading position is the rapid rise of a native materialist tradition, which played a prominent and dramatic role in intellectual debates beginning in the 1850s.[8] A final reason for Germany's leading position was the rapid ascent of Darwinism.[9] Though Darwin was an English import, his doctrines found a much quicker and friendlier reception in Germany than in England and the United States. This is partly because the ground had been prepared for him by the German materialists, and partly

---

7 Feuerbach, *Grundsätze*, §15.

8 On this tradition, see Frederick Gregory, *Scientific Materialism in Nineteenth Century Germany* (Dordrecht: Reidel, 1977); and Annette Wittkau-Horgby, *Materialismus* (Göttingen: Vandenhoeck & Ruprecht, 1998).

9 On the reception of Darwin in Germany, see Alfred Kelly, *The Descent of Darwin: The Popularization of Darwinism in Germany, 1860–1914* (Chapel Hill: University of North Carolina Press, 1981); Eve-Marie Engels and Thomas Glick, eds., *The Reception of Charles Darwin in Europe* (London: Continuum, 2008); and Robert Richards, *The Tragic Sense of Life: Ernst Haeckel and the Struggle over Evolutionary Thought* (Chicago: University of Chicago Press, 2008).

because of the advanced state of physiological and biological research in Germany.[10]

The rapid and radical secularization of Germany in the second half of the nineteenth century had, of course, profound philosophical consequences. It meant that some of the most important philosophical questions were now given, for the first time, a completely secular meaning. For millennia the questions of evil and the meaning of life, which had dominated philosophy and theology, reflected the Judeo-Christian belief in providence. The existence of evil was a problem because it seemed to contradict the existence of a wise and beneficent deity; and the meaning of life was a mystery because it was determined by an inscrutable divine design, by one's place in the providential order. In the first half of the century, these age-old questions were still interpreted in a pantheistic sense; by the second half, however, they were reinterpreted in completely secular terms, so that they were free of any assumption about the existence of God, providence, and immortality. Now that there was no divine providence to give meaning and value to life, the question arose whether it had any meaning or value at all. As always, evil and suffering were real and omnipresent; but their existence could no longer be explained away by divine providence, which had once redeemed all evil and suffering. And so the question inevitably arose: "Is life worth living in the face of evil and suffering?" From the 1860s until the end of the century, not only philosophers but also the general educated public in Germany became obsessed with this question. We will examine in chapter 5 the controversy surrounding the negative answer to this question: pessimism.

So, contrary to its reputation, it is difficult to imagine a more rich and revolutionary age for philosophy than the second half of the nineteenth century. What is philosophy? Is science inevitably heading toward materialism? What are the limits of scientific explanation? What makes history a science? And, last but hardly least, what makes life worth living? These were some of the grand questions discussed by philosophers in the late nineteenth century.

---

10 On the advanced state of scientific research in nineteenth-century Germany, see John Merz, *A History of European Thought in the Nineteenth Century* (Edinburgh: Blackwood & Sons, 1904–12), I, 157–225.

It was their great merit that they discussed these questions in great detail, and with great subtlety and sophistication, while never losing sight of the fundamental problem underlying them. The age that cured itself of Fichtean and Hegelian jargon realized all too well the great bane of needless technicality and the great value of clarity and common sense.

2. THE STANDARD NARRATIVES

Because it was such a fecund and revolutionary age, the late nineteenth century poses great challenges to the historian. The chief problem is doing justice to so many significant developments. It is fair to say that scholarship of this half century, and indeed the whole nineteenth century, has not met these challenges. This is mainly because this scholarship has been in the stranglehold of two narratives, which have imposed a rigid canon about which thinkers of the nineteenth century deserve examination. Unless we break free from this canon, our understanding of nineteenth-century German philosophy will be historically inaccurate and philosophically impoverished.

According to one narrative, whose roots we can trace back to Karl Löwith's seminal *Von Hegel zu Nietzsche*,[11] German philosophy in the nineteenth century is essentially the story about the revolutionary transformation of Hegel's philosophy by the young Hegelians, Marx, Kierkegaard, and Nietzsche. This transformation gave rise to two major philosophical traditions, Marxism and existentialism, which are seen as the main intellectual legacy of nineteenth-century philosophy.

Though rarely read today, Löwith's narrative has been profoundly influential. It has been the chief source for many popular histories of philosophy in the Anglophone world,[12] and it has formed the syllabi for countless courses on nineteenth-century philosophy

---

11 Karl Löwith, *Von Hegel zu Nietzsche. Der revolutionäre Bruch im Denken des 19. Jahrhunderts*, Zweite Auflage (Vienna: Europa Verlag, 1949).

12 See, for example, Robert C. Solomon, *Continental Philosophy since 1750* (Oxford: Oxford University Press, 1988); and *The History of Continental Philosophy: Nineteenth Century Philosophy: Revolutionary Responses to the Existing Order*, ed. Alan Schrift and Daniel Conway (Chicago: University of Chicago Press, 2010).

in Anglophone universities. The standard course on nineteenth-century philosophy includes, just as Löwith would have it, Hegel, Marx, Kierkegaard, and Nietzsche. The guiding assumptions are that these thinkers are the most important ones and that by reading them alone students can know at least something about the most important philosophy in the nineteenth century.

Brilliantly conceived and executed, Löwith's history deserves all the acclaim it has received. It is a well-told narrative, which captures some of the most important developments of nineteenth-century German philosophy, viz., Marxism and existentialism. The problem with Löwith's history lies less with itself than its reception. It is only *one* narrative about German nineteenth-century philosophy; but it is treated as if it were authoritative, the sole or major narrative, when there can and ought to be many others. If we take Löwith's as the only or best narrative, we will have a very limited view of the field.

What would we be missing? What is left out of Löwith's narrative and the standard histories that follow it? These are just some of the major developments.

1. The rise of neo-Kantianism, which was the dominant philosophical movement in Germany from 1860 to 1914.
2. The materialism controversy, one of the most important intellectual disputes in the second half of the century.
3. The growth of historicism, which is not an historical but a philosophical movement about the logic of historical discourse, a movement so important that it has been described as "one of the greatest intellectual revolutions in western thought."[13]
4. The roots of modern logic, which begin with Frege's writings in the early 1880s.
5. The rise of pessimism in the 1860s and the intense discussion about the value of life, of which Nietzsche was only one interlocutor.

---

13 In the words of Friedrich Meinecke, *Die Entstehung des Historismus* (Munich: Oldenbourg, 1965), p. 1.

The other narrative that has dominated our conception of nineteenth-century philosophy came from one of the major thinkers of that century: Hegel himself. In his *Geschichte der Philosophie*,[14] which first appeared from 1833 to 1836, Hegel described the idealist tradition as a movement beginning with Kant, passing through Reinhold, Fichte, and Schelling, and then culminating in himself. Hegel saw his own system as the grand synthesis of all that came before it, leaving out nothing of philosophical merit. The romantics played a minor role in this self-aggrandizing tale of dialectical triumph—Hegel gave a page each to Friedrich Schlegel and Novalis—but then they fell under the patronizing rubric "*Hauptformen, die mit der Fichteschen Philosophie zusammenhängen.*"[15] Hegel's account of the idealist tradition has been remarkably influential. Although it too was only one narrative, it became the standard account, the prevailing paradigm. This is partly because of the enormous influence exerted by the Hegelian school in the first half of the nineteenth century. But it is also because Hegel's history was reaffirmed later in the nineteenth century by two major philosophical historians, Johann Erdmann and Kuno Fischer,[16] who, not accidentally, were Hegelians themselves. Hegel's history was then revived in the twentieth century by two more major philosophical historians, Richard Kroner and Frederick Copleston,[17] who, though no Hegelians, were happy to follow Erdmann's and Fischer's precedents. Recent histories of nineteenth-century philosophy have, by and large, followed the Hegelian tradition.[18] It is necessary to add

14 G.W.F. Hegel, *Vorlesungen über die Geschichte der Philosophie*, in *Werke in zwänzig Bänden*, ed. Karl Michel and Eva Moldenhauer (Frankfurt: Suhrkamp, 1971), XX, 341–462.

15 Ibid., XX, 415–19.

16 Johann Erdmann, *Die Entwicklung der deutschen Spekulation seit Kant*, Band V of *Versuch einer wissenschaftlichen Darstellung der Geschichte der Philosophie* (Stuttgart: Frommann, 1977), first published 1834; and Kuno Fischer, Band V of his *Geschichte der neueren Philosophie* (Heidelberg: Carl Winter, 1872–75).

17 Richard Kroner, *Von Kant bis Hegel* (Tübingen: Mohr, 1921); and Frederick Copleston, vol. 7 of *A History of Modern Philosophy: Fichte to Hegel* (New York: Doubleday, 1963).

18 See, for example, Hans Jörg Sandkühler, ed., *Handbuch Deutscher Idealismus* (Stuttgart: Metzler, 2005); Brian O'Connor and Georg Mohr, *German Idealism: An Anthology and Guide* (Edinburg: Edinburg University Press, 2006); and *The Age of*

that Löwith, who saw Hegel as the culmination of the idealist tradition, never questioned his history.

Although still the standard model, Hegel's account of the idealist tradition is very problematic, chiefly because of its grave omissions. Hegel wrote a history that made sense of *his* philosophical development; and he omitted everything not necessary to that narrative. All his opponents he treated superficially (e.g., the romantics) or ignored entirely (e.g., Fries, Herbart, Beneke, Schopenhauer). It is obvious that it should not be taken seriously as history; but that is exactly what has happened. All histories of German idealism end with Hegel's death, just as *"der Verewigten"* would have wanted it.

Hegel's narrative, no less than Löwith's, severely limits our vision of nineteenth-century German philosophy. It has three major omissions. First of all, though Hegel could never have known it, the idealist tradition continued long after his death. There were three major thinkers after Hegel whose chief intellectual goal was to revive the legacy of idealism: Adolf Trendelenburg (1802–72), Hermann Lotze (1816–81), and Eduard von Hartmann (1842–1906). Although Trendelenburg, Lotze, and Hartmann were sharp critics of the *form* or methods of the idealist tradition, viz., intellectual intuition, the dialectic, and a priori construction, they were very eager to defend its *content* by basing it upon the results of the new empirical sciences. The self-conscious aim of their major works was to defend a teleological-vitalistic metaphysics—what Trendelenburg called "the organic view of the world"—against the growth of materialism and Darwinism. It would be groundless to dismiss these thinkers as if they were mere epigones, minor figures of little historical significance. They were some of the most influential writers and teachers of the late nineteenth century.

Another major omission of Hegel's history is a whole tradition of idealism, one contemporary to his own and its chief competitor. This tradition consisted in three thinkers: Jakob Friedrich Fries (1773–1843), Johann Friedrich Herbart (1776–1841), and Friedrich Beneke (1798–1854). Since this tradition has been so forgotten, we might as well call it the "lost tradition." Its members were opposed

---

German Idealism, ed. Robert C. Solomon and Kathleen Higgins (London: Routledge, 1993).

to the Fichte-Schelling-Hegel tradition in several respects: (1) they upheld Kant's transcendental idealism in its original form (i.e., the distinction between appearances and thing-in-itself); (2) they affirmed Kant's dualisms between understanding and sensibility, form and content, concept and intuition, essence and existence; (3) they kept Kant's regulative constraints on teleology; and (4) they attacked the rationalist methodology of Fichte, Schelling, and Hegel, advocating instead an empirical methodology modeled on the natural sciences.

Although Fries, Herbart, and Beneke did not form a self-conscious school, an alliance with a self-conscious agenda, they had so many attitudes, values, and beliefs in common that we are justified in treating them as a distinct tradition. They shared an allegiance to transcendental idealism, a program for reforming epistemology through psychology, a firm belief in the reliability of the methods of the empirical sciences, a theory about the close connection between ethics and aesthetics, and last but not least a deep antipathy to the speculative idealism of Fichte, Schelling, and Hegel. Placing Fries, Herbart, and Beneke in one tradition is not simply a post facto intellectual construction, given that they corresponded with one another, that they reviewed one another's work, usually favorably, and that Beneke even proposed collaboration with Herbart.

The final omission of Hegel's history is the strange but remarkable figure of Arthur Schopenhauer, who finds no mention at all in his narrative. Though Schopenhauer clearly belongs in the idealist tradition, Hegel was only too glad to exclude the most vocal of all his rivals. Unlike the late idealists or the lost tradition, Schopenhauer has always found some degree of begrudging acceptance in the current canon. He is included in the relevant literature, though he is usually discussed as a precursor and teacher of Nietzsche. Löwith found it fitting to ignore him entirely. Schopenhauer has always been a troublesome figure to accommodate for the standard history, because he clearly does not fit smoothly into the progression from Fichte to Hegel. He has been treated as an eccentric, maverick, and loner—an image for which Schopenhauer himself bears much responsibility. But there is a serious problem in downplaying Schopenhauer or in placing him on the periphery of nineteenth-century philosophy. He should be front and center. The reason is this: after his death in 1860, Schopenhauer became *the* most important and influential philosopher in Germany until the beginning of the First World War. He not only set the major problem of German philosophy in the second half of the nineteenth century—the question of the value of life—but also stated the most controversial solution to that problem—pessimism. We cannot measure Schopenhauer's influence simply by those who were positively influenced by him—Thomas Mann, Ludwig Wittgenstein, Eduard von Hartmann, Richard Wagner, and Friedrich Nietzsche—we also have to take into account even those who were deeply opposed to him. The neo-Kantians and positivists not only wrote biographies of and polemics against Schopenhauer, but they also changed their conception of philosophy because of him. It was thanks to Schopenhauer that neo-Kantianism and positivism did not degenerate into scholastic movements devoted to little more than the analysis of "the logic of the sciences."

Once we break with the Löwith and Hegel legacies, our picture of nineteenth-century German philosophy begins to look markedly different. We can no longer talk about the end of the idealist tradition in 1831, but we have to extend it until the end of the century. We can no longer write about one idealist tradition, but we have to consider a second competing one. We can no longer assume that Marxism and existentialism are the chief intellectual movements in the second half of the century; we also have to include many other movements, viz., late idealism, historicism, materialism, neo-Kantianism, and pessimism. Last but not least, we can no longer treat Schopenhauer like a maverick, and we should begin to recognize him as the most influential philosopher in the second half of the nineteenth century. This means that we should consider his influence upon a host of thinkers, of whom Nietzsche is only one example.

When we take this broader view, our history of nineteenth-century German philosophy becomes richer but also more complicated; it ceases to be the subject of one narrative and becomes that of many narratives. The dramatis personae of the period increase greatly and cease to be limited to the same stock canonical figures, the old chestnuts written about over and over again. We find that we have to read many "minor" thinkers who are now unfamiliar to us, though they were major players in controversies that still interest us. But none of this should be treated as a chore to trouble and burden ourselves. Rather, it should be taken as an opportunity to enrich and broaden ourselves. As much as German philosophy in the nineteenth century has been studied, there are still large tracts of unexplored territory awaiting the young, the curious, and the adventurous.

3. METHOD

There is an old complaint that the history of philosophy lacks philosophical motivation and merit. To be told what philosophers thought in the past does not necessarily help us solve philosophical problems in the present, and it easily degenerates into antiquarianism, the study of history for its own sake. For this reason some historians of philosophy tend to rewrite the past according to our contemporary interests and problems. This approach, however, invites the objection of anachronism, so that we read the past in the light of *our* rather than *its* concerns. And so the history of philosophy tends toward either antiquarianism or anachronism.

The approach taken in this book attempts to escape this dilemma. It organizes its history not according to thinkers or themes but controversies. These controversies concern issues which are still of interest today, thus avoiding the danger of antiquarianism; but they were also important to contemporaries themselves, thus escaping the difficulty of anachronism. This approach also has the merit of broadening our horizons beyond the standard thinkers and themes. Because most of the contributors to these controversies are not well-known or completely forgotten, we learn about new thinkers beyond the standard repertoire. We can see that, even though obscure or forgotten, these thinkers are still interesting in their own right. They often made important contributions to controversies, made interesting or illuminating points about fundamental problems that are still of concern to us.

One of the worst mistakes in the history of philosophy is to assume that what exists in the standard curriculum, or what is accepted in the canon of major thinkers, exhausts what is of philosophical merit from the past. We inherit a scholarly tradition and assume in good faith that it has brought us all that is of interest and merit from the past. We think that the "major thinkers" are those we study and that everyone else is a "minor thinker," either deservedly forgotten or only "a transitional figure." In this way we foster prejudice. "*Was ein Bauer nicht kennt, frißt er nicht.*" Scholars, like peasants, do not eat what they do not know.

Scholars who make this assumption are like travelers who never venture deep into the wilderness, allowing explorers to bring them back a few token treasures from unknown territory. They never see for themselves the rich treasures buried in the inner wilderness but rely on others to explore it for them. All historians of philosophy should be explorers; only when they venture for themselves into the greater expanses and deeper recesses of the past will they see the many treasures that await them.

I

THE IDENTITY CRISIS

OF PHILOSOPHY

I. SOURCES OF THE CRISIS

Beginning in the 1840s, the decade after Hegel's death, philosophers began to suffer a severe "identity crisis."[1] They could no longer define their discipline in the traditional terms widely accepted in the first decades of the nineteenth century. So they began to ask themselves some very hard questions. What is philosophy? What is its purpose? And how does it differ from the empirical sciences?

Before the 1840s, philosophers felt no need to raise such basic questions. The speculative idealist tradition seemed to have provided clear and convincing answers to them. That tradition, from Reinhold to Hegel, had a very definite conception of the aims and methods of philosophy, and of its relations to the empirical sciences. According to that conception, the aim of philosophy is to provide a foundation for all the sciences, a basis to secure them against skepticism. Although there were within that tradition different views about the specific method to create that foundation—reasoning from self-evident principles, intellectual intuition, a priori construction, dialectic—it was generally agreed that the method would have to be a priori and deductive. Whatever the method, the philosopher would use it to construct a complete system of the sciences, an encyclopedia, which would assign each science its special place in the general body of knowledge. Philosophy was thus "the guardian of the sciences," their founder and systematizer. Such was the conception of philosophy first proposed by Reinhold in his *Elementarphilosophie*, followed by Fichte in his

---

1 The term "identity crisis" was coined by Herbart Schnädelbach, *Philosophy in Germany, 1831–1933* (Cambridge: Cambridge University Press, 1984), pp. 5, 67.

15

Wissenschaftslehre, applied by Schelling in his *System der gesammten Philosophie*, and then realized by Hegel in his vast three-volume *Enzyklopädie der philosophischen Wissenschaften*.

By the 1840s, however, this conception of philosophy had become completely discredited. Most intellectuals no longer believed it possible for philosophy to provide a foundation for the sciences through a priori means or rational excogitation alone. There was no confidence in self-evident first principles, intellectual intuitions, a priori construction, or even a dialectic. The foundationalist program had come under heavy criticism from several quarters: from the "physicalists" (Justus Liebig, Emil du Bois Reymond, Hermann Helmholtz); from the early neo-Kantians (Fries, Herbart, Beneke); and from the later idealists (Lotze, Trendelenburg, and Hartmann). All seemed to concur on one central point: that general principles and a priori reasoning cannot by themselves provide concrete results. We cannot derive substantive conclusions from formal principles, determinate results from indeterminate premises. All content, all knowledge of existence, has to derive from experience alone. The foundationalist program of speculative idealism was condemned as a relapse into the bad old ways of pre-Kantian rationalism.

This critique of the foundationalist program raised a serious question about the future of philosophy. Philosophy, it seemed, had no reliable method of its own. There appeared to be only two options: "the synthetic method" of the speculative tradition, which begins with universals and descends to particulars; or "the analytic method" of the empirical sciences, which begins with particulars and ascends to universals. The synthetic method had now been discredited; but the analytic method was more characteristic of the empirical sciences. So what should or could be the method of philosophy?

The identity crisis of philosophy arose not only from the collapse of the foundationalist program but also from another source: the dramatic rise of the empirical sciences in the first half of the century. The sciences now seemed to cover the entire *globus intellectualis*, so that there seemed no special subject for philosophy. The growth of an experimental physiology and psychology in the first half of the century seemed to make life and the mind now part of the domain of empirical science. Not only had the sciences taken over every aspect of the universe; they also seemed perfectly autonomous, capable of achieving valid results on their own without the apron strings of philosophy. So even if philosophy could provide a foundation for the sciences, they did not really need or want such a foundation anyway; their methods of observation and experiment were sufficient on their own to provide reliable knowledge. While philosophy had once been the mother of the sciences, her children had now come of age and wanted to leave their nest. This new attitude of the sciences toward philosophy was captured by the neo-Kantian Jürgen Bona Meyer: "The daughters now demand independence from their common mother, and they do not suffer it gladly when they are supervised or corrected; they would prefer that their old and morose mother lay herself to rest in her grave."[2]

Together, the critique of the foundationalist program and the rise of the empirical sciences made the identity crisis complete and inescapable. That critique meant that philosophy had no characteristic *method* of its own; and the rise of the empirical sciences meant that it had no distinctive *subject matter* of its own. Whether in form (method) or in content (subject matter), philosophy did not deserve to exist. Proper method (observation and experiment), and every possible subject matter, seemed the privilege and preserve of the empirical sciences. Philosophy now began to seem obsolete, an antiquated discipline in danger of being replaced by the empirical sciences. Little wonder, then, that the neo-Kantian Kuno Fischer, writing in the early 1860s, referred to the "*Lebensfrage der Philosophie*," by which he meant the question of its life or death.[3]

Fischer had good reason to be troubled. For, already in the 1840s, the materialists and positivists were celebrating the death of philosophy. They had identified philosophy with the defunct foundationalist program or with the metaphysics of speculative idealism; and now that these had proven bankrupt, philosophy itself seemed to be a thing of the past. All legitimate intellectual questions, the

---

2 Jürgen Bona Meyer, *Philosophische Zeitfragen* (Bonn: Adolph Marcus, 1870), p. 1.

3 Kuno Fischer, *Kant's Leben und die Grundlagen seiner Lehre* (Mannheim: Bassermann, 1860), p. 95.

positivists and materialists believed, could be solved by the empirical sciences, so that there simply was no place anymore for philosophy. Ludwig Feuerbach expressed this new attitude toward philosophy in a pregnant but paradoxical proposition: "True philosophy is the negation of philosophy; it is really no philosophy at all."[4]

It is important to recognize that there was an institutional context behind the identity crisis of philosophy. The crisis was not only a spiritual or intellectual problem but a "bread and butter" issue. Most philosophers could survive only within a university, only as members of an academic faculty; very few could live on book royalties and lecture fees alone. For their salaries, though, they were dependent on government funding, since universities were public institutions in Germany. To receive funding, a faculty had to demonstrate that its discipline was legitimate, that it had its own "scientific" methods, and that it occupied a necessary place in the academic division of labor. But if philosophers were unsure of themselves, unaware of their own methods and subject matter, how could they make their case for government funding? The issue was pressing, because government funds were limited and because there was great competition among faculties for them. In the final decades of the century, the competition between philosophy and psychology became especially intense. Psychology seemed to be making philosophy redundant, because it could treat the mind—an old preserve of philosophy—according to the methods of observation and experiment. Many philosophers resented the assimilation of their discipline to psychology, given that a psychology appointment sometimes took precedence over a philosophical one.

Given the urgency and stakes behind the identity crisis, and given the vacuum left after the collapse of speculative idealism, it should not be surprising that there were many attempts to define philosophy in the second half of the nineteenth century. Philosophy was defined in the most various ways: the logic of the sciences, critique, metaphysics, epistemology, the general system of the sciences, the science of normativity, and worldview. All of these definitions had their strengths and weaknesses; none was entirely

---

4 Ludwig Feuerbach, "Vorwort" to *Sämmtliche Werke* (Leipzig: Wigand, 1846), IV, 158.

successful in dominating the intellectual stage. Let us now have a look at these definitions, keeping constantly in mind their merits and problems, and how they intended to resolve the identity crisis.

2. TRENDELENBURG'S *PHILOSOPHIA PERENNIS*

One of the first philosophers to respond to the identity crisis, and to offer a new and original conception of philosophy, was Adolf Trendelenburg (1802–72), professor of philosophy in Berlin from 1833 to 1870. Trendelenburg addressed the crisis as early as 1833 in his inaugural lecture as *professor extraordinarius*,[5] but his most sustained and substantial effort appears in his *Logische Untersuchungen*, which was first published in 1840.[6] No one worried more about the status and survival of philosophy in the new scientific age than Trendelenburg. Feuerbach's proclamation that the future of philosophy will be no philosophy provoked and challenged him.[7] As a classical scholar, Trendelenburg was a firm believer in the *philosophia perennis*, the thesis that there has been throughout the ages, and despite all the changes of history, a single valid philosophy. Trendelenburg identified this philosophy with what he found in the writings of Plato and Aristotle; he called it "the organic worldview," the doctrine that the entire universe forms a single living organism. It was Trendelenburg's conviction that this worldview is far from obsolete; rather, its chief principles are, have been, and forever will be eternally valid, as true today as they were thousands of years ago. Trendelenburg knew all too well, however, that if he were to keep alive the classical legacy, he had to respond to the growing identity crisis of philosophy. Somehow, he had to show that the "organic worldview" of Plato and Aristotle is still relevant to the modern scientific age. This was one of the central tasks of his *Logische Untersuchungen*.

5　This lecture was unpublished and even its title is unknown. We have a summary of its contents in the work of his student Ernst Bratuscheck, *Adolf Trendelenburg* (Berlin: Hensehel, 1873), pp. 77–78.

6　Friedrich Adolf Trendelenburg, *Logische Untersuchungen* (Berlin: Bethge Verlag, 1840).

7　See Trendelenburg's reference to Feuerbach in the preface to the second edition of the *Logische Untersuchungen* (Leipzig: Hirzel, 1862), I, ix.

Trendelenburg begins his *Logische Untersuchungen* by taking issue with the conception of philosophy in the speculative idealist tradition.[8] Accepting the autonomy of the new empirical sciences as his starting point, Trendelenburg argued that there is no need for the foundationalist program of speculative idealism. Philosophy cannot provide a foundation for the empirical sciences, he argued, because thinking on its own is empty and acquires its content only from experience. Rather than attempting to provide a basis for the sciences, philosophy should recognize "the fact of science,", i.e., the fact that the sciences are autonomous, that they have proven their own success, and that there is no point in worrying about skepticism regarding them.[9] However, abandoning these foundationalist aspirations does not mean, Trendelenburg insisted, that there is no task or place for philosophy at all. On the contrary, philosophy should now become "a theory of science" (*Wissenschaftstheorie*), a discipline whose special business is to investigate "the logic of the sciences." There is still a need for philosophy, he stressed, because the particular sciences are more interested in applying their methods than investigating them. Because they do not reflect on their most basic concepts and presuppositions, such reflection should be the special task of the philosopher. The philosopher should then become, Trendelenburg recommended, a second-order scientist, a logician whose special concern is "the methods of the special sciences."

Trendelenburg's reorientation of philosophy around the logic of the sciences was very strategic. In a single stroke it not only abolished the foundationalist program but also guaranteed philosophy a necessary place in the academic division of labor. As the logician of the sciences, the philosopher performed an invaluable task that scientists themselves could not perform. Trendelenburg's strategy would prove influential, the precedent for some of his talented students, among them Franz Brentano, Hermann Cohen, and Eugen Dühring.

Although some aspects of Trendelenburg's conception of philosophy were new and modern, others were older and more traditional.

8 *Logische Untersuchungen* (1862), I, 1–129.
9 Ibid., I, 130–31.

Trendelenburg was far from reducing philosophy down to episte-mology, as the neo-Kantians later did. The influence of the classical tradition upon him was such that he continued to stress the abid-ing importance of metaphysics, i.e., a knowledge of the universe as a whole.[10] It was the task of philosophy to provide such knowledge, he insisted, by attempting to construct a general system of the sci-ences. In a striking Platonic formulation, Trendelenburg states that philosophy is "the science of the idea" (*Wissenschaft der Idee*), where "the idea" determines the whole in its parts, the universal in the particular. The highest idea, the foremost goal of philosophy, is the universe as a whole. Yet Trendelenburg was careful to place regula-tive constraints upon such metaphysics. He insisted that the idea is only an ideal, a goal we should strive to approach even if we cannot attain it. He also stressed that this idea should not be the starting point but the result of system-building. Metaphysics had to follow an analytic method, proceeding from the parts to the whole rather than from the whole to the parts; and rather than leading the em-pirical sciences, which provided all its materials, metaphysics had to follow them.[11]

It was by this more cautious analytic approach, Trendelenburg believed, that he could rehabilitate the metaphysics of Plato and Aristotle. Their "organic worldview," he wagered, could be justified by all the results of the latest physiology and physics. While it could not be demonstrated by an a priori methodology like that of specu-lative idealism, it could find a basis in the a posteriori methods of observation and experiment. Hence the modern sciences would not antiquate but vindicate the *philosophia perennis*.

Yet this proved to be a risky strategy. When Trendelenburg first wrote the *Logische Untersuchungen* in 1840, the prevailing view in physiology still favored the retention of teleological and organic concepts. The so-called "vital materialist" or "teleomechanical" tradition of Friedrich Blumenbach (1752–1840), Carl Friedrich Kielmeyer (1765–1844), and Johann Christian Reill (1759–1813) had argued for the importance of understanding growth in teleological

---

10   Ibid., I, 5.
11   Ibid., II, 454.

and holistic terms.[12] This tradition continued well into the 1830s in the embryological research of Johannes Müller (1801–58) and Karl Ernst von Baer (1792–1876). Yet in the late 1840s a new "physicalist program" arose in physiology, led by Carl Ludwig (1816–95) and Ernst Brücke (1819–92) and later endorsed by some of Müller's rebellious students, Robert Remak (1815–65), Rudolf Virchow (1821–1902), Emil Du Bois-Reymond (1818–98), Hermann von Helmholtz (1821–94), and Ernst Haeckel (1834–1919).[13] All these thinkers pursued successfully, with rigor and vigor, a program of mechanical explanation in biology and physiology, making Trendelenburg's defense of an organic worldview seem obsolete. The challenges for Trendelenburg grew even greater in the 1860s with the rise of Darwinism, which was vigorously advocated by Haeckel and the physicalists. It was a sign of the revolutionary tumult of the age that the *philosophia perennis* no longer seemed so perennial after all.

3. PHILOSOPHY AS CRITIQUE

In the early 1840s, shortly after the publication of Trendelenburg's *Logische Untersuchungen*, another very different conception of philosophy was being forged by a group of young intellectuals in Halle and Berlin, the so-called "young" or "left-wing Hegelians." The chief players in this group were Ludwig Feuerbach (1804–72), David Friedrich Strauss (1808–74), Max Stirner (1806–56), Arnold Ruge (1802–80), Friedrich Vischer (1807–87), Bruno Bauer (1808–82), and Karl Marx (1818–83). What held this diverse group of young philosophers together, besides their radical political agenda and Hegelian origins, was their conception of philosophy. For the young Hegelians, philosophy was first and foremost *"critique,"* i.e., the scrutiny of all beliefs, be they metaphysical, religious, or political, to determine their origins and to assess their claims to validity.

12 On this tradition, see Timothy Lenoir, *The Strategy of Life, Teleology and Mechanics in Nineteenth Century German Biology* (Chicago: University of Chicago Press, 1989).

13 On Müller's students, see Laura Otis, *Müller's Lab* (Oxford: Oxford University Press, 2007).

This critique was meant to be radical, i.e., a belief was to be accepted or rejected strictly according to the degree of evidence for it, regardless of the consequences for religion, morality, or the state. The young Hegelians thus stood for, as the young Marx put it, "the ruthless criticism of everything existing."[14]

Such a program was, at least as it was initially conceived, the young Hegelian solution to the identity crisis. Critique seemed all that was left to philosophy after the collapse of the foundationalist program and the end of the speculative idealist tradition. The critical philosopher not only banished speculative metaphysics but also made no attempt to provide a foundation for the sciences. Yet criticism was a task that only the philosopher could perform, so that philosophy stood in danger of obsolescence from the empirical sciences. Although the young Hegelians were severe critics of traditional philosophy, they still held that, as critique, it had a valuable role to perform. It was only through "the purifying fire of criticism," they believed, that humanity could free itself from the deep illusions that enthralled it. There was a noble tradition behind this definition of philosophy. Since the early eighteenth century, criticism had been vital to philosophy, indeed the hallmark of the Enlightenment itself. In advocating critique, then, the young Hegelians were waving the banner of Enlightenment and following a hallowed tradition of their own.

The left Hegelian program of critique began in theology, more specifically with the criticism of the Bible. Strauss's *Das Leben Jesu*, which first appeared in 1835,[15] and Bauer's *Kritik der evangelischen Geschichte der Synoptiker*, which was published in 1841,[16] sparked a firestorm of controversy. Sons of Spinoza, Strauss, and Bauer treated the Bible not as the inspired word of God but like any historical document, so that it is the product of human beings in a specific time and place. They doubted that there is any credible evidence for the claims of miracles, and they interpreted

---

14   Karl Marx to Arnold Ruge, September 1843, in "Ein Briefwechsel von 1843," *Deutsch-Französische Jahrbücher* I (1844), 37.

15   David Friedrich Strauss, *Das Leben Jesu, kritisch bearbeitet* (Tübingen: C. F. Osiander, 1835), 2 vols.

16   Bruno Bauer, *Kritik der evangelischen Geschichte der Synoptiker* (Leipzig: Wigand, 1841), 3 vols.

the gospel stories as either myths (Strauss) or poetry (Bauer). The culmination of this critique of religion came in 1841 with Ludwig Feuerbach's *Das Wesen des Christentums*,[17] which also aroused an enormous outcry. Feuerbach analyzed religious consciousness in terms of the reification or hypostasization of human powers. The gods and spirits that appeared to rule over human beings, Feuerbach argued, are really only their own subconscious creations, the projection of their powers onto the world outside them. For this process, by which human beings enslave themselves to their own creations, Feuerbach took a redolent word from the pages of Hegel: "alienation" (*Entfremdung*).

Though it began in theology, neo-Hegelian criticism soon extended to other spheres. It was the task of critique to expose alienation in all its lairs, whether in society, economy, state, or church. Besides faith in God, self-enslavement assumed many forms: the belief in a divinely ordained prince; the doctrine of absolute spirit; the belief in natural economic laws; the ethic of absolute commands. The neo-Hegelians made it their business to expose alienation wherever it took place, so that people would cease to enslave themselves to their own creations and begin to take control over their lives. Law, state, and economy should be the self-conscious creations of human beings rather than imagined forces ruling over them. Nothing more suited the powers-that-be than alienation, which seemed to give a metaphysical sanction for church, state, and economy. Reveal the self-delusion behind that alienation, the neo-Hegelians believed, and these powers would crumble.

The origins of the left Hegelian program shed much light on its purpose and meaning. One source was the so-called "Tübingen school" or "critical school of theology," which originated in the Tübinger Stift in the 1830s. This school was the nursery for several young Hegelians, among them Strauss and Vischer. One of the best accounts of the school was provided by another young Hegelian educated there, Eduard Zeller (1814–1908).[18] What was fundamental to and characteristic of that school, Zeller explained,

17 Ludwig Feuerbach, *Das Wesen des Christentums* (Leipzig: Wigand, 1841).
18 Eduard Zeller, "Die Tübinger historische Schule," *Historische Zeitschrift* IV (1860), 90–173.

was its critical method, its manner of treating sacred texts strictly as historical documents, i.e., as writings produced by human beings under particular social and historical circumstances. This meant laying aside the traditional orthodox assumption that the Bible is the product of supernatural inspiration. The method of the historical school, as Zeller described it, was that of historical criticism, pure and simple. Such criticism consists in the rigorous examination of the evidence behind historical texts to determine their authorship and accuracy, so that we accept or reject what a text states about the past strictly according to the degree of evidence for or against it. The origins of this methodology, Zeller said, lay with the new critical history formed in the early 1800s by Barthold Niebuhr (1776–1831) and Leopold Ranke (1795–1886). Niebuhr had applied the method to Roman history in his *Römische Geschichte*,[19] and Ranke had done the same to early modern history in his *Geschichte der germanischen und romanischen Völker*.[20] The program of the Tübingen school—so we are told—was simply to extend Ranke's and Niebuhr's method to sacred history. Hence Zeller wrote: "Its ruling principles are only the same as those that have governed all German historical writing outside theology since Niebuhr and Ranke."[21]

The origin of the neo-Hegelian program did not lie in historical criticism alone. Another source lay with Kant's critical philosophy. The left Hegelians were very much indebted to Kant's conception of the goal of criticism: self-consciousness of freedom, self-awareness of human autonomy, i.e., the power to create and live according to one's own laws. They were also very much influenced by Kant's analysis of the chief obstacle lying in the path of such self-consciousness: hypostasis, the reification of our own ideas into forces governing over us. Their program of dehypostasization or demystification began in the Transcendental Dialectic of Kant's

---

19   Barthold Georg Niebuhr, *Römische Geschichte* (Berlin: Realschulbuchhandlung, 1811–12).

20   Leopold Ranke, *Geschichte der germanischen und romanischen Völker von 1494 bis 1535* (Leipzig: Reimer, 1824). The crucial writing for Ranke's methodology is his appendix to this work, *Zur Kritik neuerer Geschichtsschreiber. Eine Beylage zu desselben romanischen und germanischen Geschichten* (Leipzig: Reimer, 1824).

21   Zeller, "Die Tübinger historische Schule," p. 173.

Kritik der reinen Vernunft, where Kant had taught that hypostasis of the ideas of pure reason is the main source of the fallacies of traditional metaphysics. What Kant saw as a fallacy in metaphysics, though, the young Hegelians deemed the original sin of humanity, the source of its self-enslavement. Hypostasis was indeed their solution to Rousseau's famous paradox: "Man is born free; everywhere he is in chains."[22] Self-enslavement arose because people reified their own creations, believing them to be objective laws and entities governing themselves. Expose this illusion through criticism, the left Hegelians were convinced, and human beings would become self-conscious of their own powers and begin to take control over their lives. The riches they had once squandered on heaven they would now use to build a better home on earth.

Another source of the neo-Hegelian program was, not surprisingly, Hegel himself. Although the young Hegelians were critical of Hegel's dialectical method, especially the metaphysics he drew out of it, they still adopted aspects of it, especially its so-called "immanent critique." Hegel's method in the *Phänomenologie des Geistes* was for the philosopher to bracket his standards and ideals, for him to criticize a form of consciousness strictly according to *its* own standards and ideals. The task of the philosopher was to point out internal contradictions within a form of consciousness, to show the discrepancies between its ideal and reality. New principles or ideals could emerge only by showing the consequences of old ones, by showing how the new ones alone resolved the tensions or contradictions in the old. The young Hegelians strived to practice such internal criticism. As Marx wrote: "We develop new principles for the world from the principles of the world itself."[23] And as Bauer more graphically put it: "Is a principle not overthrown when we show its consequences? ... Must something be overcome only by something alien to it, by throwing a block against its head? By thunder and lightning?"[24] Motivating this demand for internal

---

22 J. J. Rousseau, *Du contract social* in *Œuvres complètes*, ed. Bernard Gagnebin and Marcel Raymond (Paris: Gallimard, 1964), III, 351.

23 "Ein Briefwechsel von 1843," p. 39.

24 Bruno Bauer, *Die gute Sache der Freiheit und meine eigene Angelegenheit* (Zurich: Verlag des literarischen Comptoirs, 1842), p. 119.

critique was historicist skepticism about the philosopher's claims to be in possession of eternal and universal standards of criticism. Since it was the task of critique to reveal the historical origins and contexts of beliefs, it would show how their meaning and validity are determined by these origins and contexts. Hence the claim to eternal and universal standards is suspect, the result of universalizing beliefs and practices beyond one's own age.

Despite its rich heritage and historical accomplishments, there were still serious questions hanging over the neo-Hegelian program. One such question concerned the future of philosophy. If the task of critique is only negative, if its aim is simply to demolish the illusions behind alienation, what happens to philosophy when this task is complete? Should it not just wither away like church and state, as some neo-Hegelians believed? It was not surprising that Feuerbach, Bauer, and Marx eventually ceased to believe in the future of philosophy and that they held it should eventually disappear into anthropology (Feuerbach), history (Bauer), or political economy (Marx). Another question concerned the neo-Hegelians' theory of history. Although they were highly critical of Hegel's metaphysics, which to them seemed only another form of alienation, they never ceased to believe in the Hegelian doctrine of reason in history, according to which old forms of historical consciousness are doomed to disappear of necessity with historical progress. But was this belief in progress, in historical laws, not simply another form of hypostasis? Did not human beings make their history, just as they made their own governments and religions? Finally, what were the career prospects for a critical philosopher? The left-Hegelian conception of philosophy, because it was so devoted to criticism of church and state, was not likely to win anyone a respectable place in a university. It was an utterly Bohemian conception of philosophy. Its practitioners doomed themselves to an outsider status, and it is not surprising that Feuerbach, Strauss, Marx, Bauer, Ruge, and Zeller were victims of government persecution. Radical uncompromising criticism was both glorious and miserable: glorious, because it stood steadfast for the ideal despite persecution; and miserable, because it could never last long in any society or state. The neo-Hegelian conception of philosophy was the child of its time, an expression of the political hopes and ambitions behind the Revolution of 1848. When that Revolution failed, radical criticism disappeared with it, only to resurface in Frankfurt in the 1920s.[25]

4. SCHOPENHAUER'S REVIVAL OF METAPHYSICS

Sometime in the early 1840s, the very years when the young Hegelians were organizing themselves, another philosopher was busy clarifying his thoughts about the purpose and nature of philosophy. He, too, was addressing the identity crisis, attempting to give philosophy a purpose and identity distinct from the empirical sciences while still avoiding the errors of speculative idealism. His views could not have been more antithetical to the aims and assumptions of the young Hegelians, whose political agenda he did not share and whose attachment to Hegel he deplored. This philosopher was none other than that old scrooge of Frankfurt, Arthur Schopenhauer (1788–1860). In the early 1840s Schopenhauer was living a solitary and secluded existence in Frankfurt, far from public attention. He was nursing his wounds, holding a grudge against the academic and literary establishment for their neglect of his masterpiece, *Die Welt als Wille und Vorstellung*, which had appeared more than two decades earlier, in December 1818.[26] Schopenhauer had put all his wisdom, all his heart and soul, into that book, only to find that, because of a lack of sales, half of the original print run had to be pulped. Still, he did not abandon hope. Convinced that recognition could still come his way, he embarked upon a very risky and dubious project: an enlarged second edition of his masterpiece. Could the public really want even more of what they already did not want? But Schopenhauer persisted, writing another whole volume to complement his first. The enlarged two-volume edition appeared in March 1844.[27] Remarkably,

25 On its resurrection, see Martin Jay, *The Dialectical Imagination* (London: Heinemann, 1973), pp. 40–85.

26 Arthur Schopenhauer, *Die Welt als Wille und Vorstellung* (Leipzig: Brockhaus, 1819).

27 Arthur Schopenhauer, *Die Welt als Wille und Vorstellung, Um den granzen zweiten Teil vermehrte und durchweg ergänzte Auflage* (Leipzig: Brockhaus, 1844). All references to Schopenhauer's works will be to *Sämtliche Werke*, ed. Wolfgang

Schopenhauer's gamble paid off: *Die Welt als Wille und Vorstellung* became one of the most widely read philosophical works in the second half of the nineteenth century.[28] And out of this apparently foredoomed project also came some very interesting and important philosophy. Among the riches of that second volume were some essays outlining Schopenhauer'sconception of philosophy,[29] which eventually proved to be one of the most influential in the second half of the century.

Going directly against the current of his age, Schopenhauer's conception of philosophy was expressly metaphysical. Schopenhauer did not believe, as Trendelenburg had, in a *philosophia perennis*, a single perennial philosophy since the Greeks; but he did think that philosophy should go back to its traditional vocation, which was metaphysics, i.e., the study of the first principles of being. About his allegiance to metaphysics he left no doubt: "One can declare as the necessary *credo* of all the just and good: 'I believe in a metaphysics'" (II, 227; P 175). True to this *credo*, Schopenhauer firmly believed that philosophy should go back to the most fundamental question of metaphysics, to what he called "the puzzle of existence" (*das Rätsel des Daseins*). Schopenhauer means by this puzzle the classical conundrum why there is something rather than nothing. He thinks that existence is contingent, that it is logically possible for the universe to be as well as not be, which raises the question why something exists at all. But it is important to see that he meant something more with this question: namely, why should we human beings exist at all? What is the value of life? Is life worth living at all? So, ultimately, Schopenhauer's question was as ethical

---

Freiherr von Löhneeysen (Stuttgart: Insel, 1968). References to *Die Welt als Wille und Vorstellung* will be abbreviated as WWV, where "I" and "II" refer to the first and second volumes. "P" will refer to the English translation of this work by E.F.J. Payne, *The World as Will and Representation* (New York: Dover, 1969).

28   There were at least five editions of Schopenhauer's writings between 1877 to 1911. In 1938 the Schopenhauer scholar Hans Zint asked Reclam Verlag how many copies they had sold of their popular edition, which first appeared in 1892. The answer: an astounding 750,000–800,000 copies! See his *Schopenhauer als Erlebnis* (Munich: Ernst Reinhardt Verlag, 1954), pp. 188–89.

29   See especially Kapitel 17, "Über das metaphysische Bedürfnis," WWV II, 206–43; and Capitel 18, "Von der Erkennbarkeit des Dinges an sich," WWV II, 247–58 (P II, 196–200).

as it was metaphysical. His puzzle of existence is what we might call "the Hamlet question": "To be or not to be?"

This question arises naturally and necessarily, Schopenhauer thinks, whenever we reflect on two fundamental facts of human life: the existence of evil and the omnipresence of suffering. There is so much evil, and so much suffering, that it sometimes just seems better that we did not exist. Sometimes, nothingness appears better than existence. Which raises the question: Why exist at all?

Although it is a classical problem as old as the Greeks, Schopenhauer's problem differs in an important respect from a very similar one that had bothered philosophers for millennia: namely, What is the meaning or purpose of life? Or, to give the question its more modern Protestant formulation: What is the vocation of man? This question had been posed anew in the eighteenth century by J. J. Spalding in his famous book *Die Bestimmung des Menschen*, which was first published in 1748 and went through no fewer than thirteen editions.[30] Spalding's question had sparked much discussion, and there had been in the 1760s a famous controversy surrounding it in which Thomas Abbt, Moses Mendelssohn, and Johann Gottfried Herder were all participants.[31] Spalding's question was not new at all, however, but simply a fresh statement of a perennial problem of the Judeo-Christian tradition. It assumes that there is a God who creates nature and humanity according to a plan or design and that each individual is assigned his or her proper role or place in it. The meaning of life, the purpose of existence, the vocation of man, is to fulfill one's role in this plan, to play one's allotted part, and so to satisfy the purpose of God in creating us.

Compared to this older and traditional question, Schopenhauer's is new and very modern, chiefly because it denies the teleological and theological presuppositions of the Christian one.

30 Johann Joachim Spalding, *Betrachtung über die Bestimmung des Menschen* (Greifswald: Struck, 1748). See the modern edition *Die Bestimmung des Menschen*, ed. Wolfgang Müller (Waltrop: Harmut Spenner, 1997). This edition contains the first of 1748 and the last of 1794.

31 On this controversy, see my article "Mendelssohn versus Herder on the Vocation of Man," and George di Giovanni, "The Year 1786 and *Die Bestimmung des Menschen*, or *Popularphilosophie* in Crisis," in *Moses Mendelssohn's Metaphysics and Aesthetics*, ed. Reinier Munk (Dordrecht: Springer, 2011), pp. 217–45.

Schopenhauer was, as Nietzsche later said, "our first officially athe-istic philosopher." He not only denies theism, but he also disputes the teleology behind eighteenth-century metaphysics. The very existence of evil and suffering was telling evidence against the ex-istence of God and his providential order—unless, of course, one assumes that it is God's purpose to torment us. So when Schopen-hauer poses the question of the value of life, he does so from the new secular framework characteristic of the nineteenth century. If there is no God to redeem suffering, and if there is no God who designs the universe, the problem of existence poses itself anew. Why is life worth living if it contains more suffering than joy, more evil than good, and if it promises no reward or redemption, either now or in some life to come?

It was Schopenhauer's great merit to have returned philosophy to this age-old question and to have revived it in a more secular age. He clearly saw that the problem would not go away if we reject the theology and teleology behind its traditional formula-tion. It is indeed striking how Schopenhauer restates the problem of evil even when he rejects the old theist assumptions behind it. For Schopenhauer, no less than theologians of the Judeo-Christian tradition, the problem of evil is central to philosophy, and he even goes so far as to say that the origin of philosophy lies in the con-templation of the existence of evil. It is a problem for him, how-ever, not because it impugns the existence of God but because it impugns existence itself. Evil and suffering are for Schopenhauer the great stains upon existence itself—even if that existence is not created by God.

So much for the basic problem of metaphysics. But it was one thing to revive that problem, quite another to believe that there was a way to solve it. After all, Kant had declared that it is the sad fate of human reason to raise questions that it cannot answer.[32] It was just here, it seemed, that Schopenhauer's conception of philos-ophy ran into an obsolescence crisis all its own. For that conception rests upon its attempt to rehabilitate metaphysics. And had not Kant shown that metaphysics is impossible? Schopenhauer's meta-physics seems to violate, blatantly, the most basic Kantian teach-

32 Kant, KrV, A vii.

ings about the limits of knowledge. Schopenhauer assumes that we can know the thing-in-itself, the inner essence of nature and the self, and even Platonic ideas. Could a metaphysics be more bold and pretentious? To the neo-Kantians, Schopenhauer's call for a revival of metaphysics was a step backward, a call for a return to the recently defunct and disgraced metaphysics of Fichte, Schelling, and Hegel. In their view, it was anything but a viable option for the future of philosophy.

No one was more aware of the Kantian challenges than Schopenhauer himself. In the second edition of *Die Welt als Wille und Vorstellung* he went to great pains to respond to them. Schopenhauer was convinced that he had a new reliable method for metaphysics, a method that could steer "a *via media* between the omniscience of the earlier dogmatism and the despair of Kantian critique" (WWV I, 578; P 428). What, exactly, is this method? It does not consist in a priori demonstration, in chains of syllogistic reasoning, as in Wolff's metaphysics. Still less does it involve intellectual intuitions, the favored organon of Fichte, Schelling, and the young Hegel. And least of all does it consist in the "*Hokus-Pokus*" of the dialectic of the mature Hegel. All these methods are specious, Schopenhauer charges, because they attempt to derive content from thinking alone. Content, Schopenhauer insists, has to be given to us in sense experience, and it cannot be created by any form of pure thinking. All abstract thought has a meaning and cognitive value, he emphasizes, only if it gets its content from experience. Philosophy must begin, therefore, from the intuition of what is given, and it must limit itself to the interpretation and understanding of that alone (WWV I, 609–10; P 452–53). Its task is to interpret the meaning of what lies in experience, and never should it stray beyond that to speculate about its ultimate causes. The business of metaphysics, therefore, is "the correct understanding of experience," and its method consists in "the interpretation of its meaning and content" (WWV II, 238; P 184). On these grounds Schopenhauer would stress that his philosophy is strictly *immanent*, that it stays within the limits of possible experience (WWV I, 375–79; P 271–74). It was this immanent conception of metaphysics as an interpretative discipline that was his *via media* between Kantian skepticism and dogmatic rationalism.

In stressing that metaphysics must be immanent, Schopenhauer was, of course, simply trying to justify it by the Kantian standard of knowledge: possible experience. Tirelessly, Kant had insisted in the first *Kritik* that the limits of knowledge are those of ordinary experience; but for this reason he went on to deny the possibility of metaphysics, because, in the quest to know the unconditioned, it of necessity goes beyond the limits of experience. While Schopenhauer agrees with Kant that such a transcendent metaphysics is impossible, he does not think that metaphysics needs to be transcendent in the first place. Metaphysics is for him not the quest for the unconditioned beyond experience but simply the attempt to interpret what is given or present in experience.

Kant also went astray, Schopenhauer argues, in assuming that the method of metaphysics must be a priori, that it must be based on the analysis of concepts and abstract reasoning alone (WWV I, 577; P 427). That made it seem impossible for metaphysics to follow empirical guidelines. But in making this assumption, Schopenhauer argues, Kant revealed just how much he was still stuck in the paradigm of eighteenth-century rationalism. Although Schopenhauer agrees wholeheartedly with Kant that such a method is useless in metaphysics, he insists that there is no reason why metaphysics must follow it.

So far, however, Schopenhauer's restatement of the problem and method of metaphysics seems to beg a basic question. If metaphysics is only the interpretation of what is given in experience, then how does it know anything more than appearances? How does it give us knowledge of reality in itself? How do we know the thing-in-itself if we must remain within experience? On Kantian premises this would seem to be a squaring of the circle. To understand Schopenhauer's solution to this problem, we need to consider his account of one very troublesome and notorious Kantian concept: the thing-in-itself.

Schopenhauer's attempt to justify metaphysics lies crucially with his reinterpretation of this concept. The thing-in-itself, he maintains, is not a transcendent entity lying behind appearances, an *ens extra mundanum*; in that sense Schopenhauer is happy to dismiss the thing-in-itself as a mere abstraction or nonentity. An object that is neither representation nor will, he writes in the first section of *Die Welt als Wille und Vorstellung*, is "a dreamed nothing," "an illusion in philosophy" (I, 33; P 4). The thing-in-itself is not something that lies beyond appearances, Schopenhauer explains, but it is "that which appears in appearances" (*das in ihr [die Erscheinung] Erscheinende*).[33] Or, to use another of his formulations, it is the *what* that appears as opposed to the *how*, *when*, and *where*.[34] Hence the thing-in-itself, properly seen, is simply the *content* or *essence* of appearances. It is not a supernatural object lying beyond appearances but the inner essence or intrinsic nature of appearances themselves.[35]

Following this proposal, Schopenhauer recommends that the distinction between thing-in-itself and appearance be redrawn in terms of that between the form and content of experience.[36] The appearance is the form, the content is the thing-in-itself. The form of experience consists in the *relations* between things, all of which are expressible in mathematical or causal terms. The content of experience, however, consists in the *inner nature*, *quality*, or *essence* of appearances, that which stands in the relations between things. We cannot grasp this content or inner nature through its relations alone, Schopenhauer insists. No matter how far knowledge of relations extends, there will always be some remainder, something which resists analysis into mere relations, namely, that which stands in these relations.[37]

It is in just this context that we must understand another aspect of Schopenhauer's metaphysics: his appropriation of the Platonic distinction between archetype and ectype. No part of his philosophy seems more wantonly and brazenly metaphysical, more recklessly and daringly speculative, than his reintroduction of this Platonic doctrine in Book III of *Die Welt als Wille und Vorstellung*. Schopenhauer argues, however, that the Platonic distinction between archetype and ectype mirrors Kant's distinction between

---

33 Cf. WWV I, 379, §53 (P 274) and WWV II, 237, Kap. 17 (P 183).

34 See WWV I, 185, 187, 24 (P 121–22); 257, §34 (P 178); and 379, §53 (P 274).

35 Schopenhauer made this interpretation especially clear in his August 1852 letter to Julius Frauenstädt, August 1852, *Gesammelte Briefe*, ed. Arthur Hübscher (Bonn: Bouvier, 1978), p. 291.

36 See WWV I, 184, 185, 187, §24 (P 121–22, 123).

37 Ibid., I, 188, §24 (P 124).

thing-in-itself and appearance (WWV I, 246–47; P 170–71). Whatever one makes of that conflation on scholarly grounds, it shows how Schopenhauer construed the Platonic doctrine. For just as he understood the distinction between thing-in-itself and appearance in terms of the content and form of experience, so he understood the distinction between archetype and ectype in similar terms. The archetype is the content of experience, the "whatness," essence, or intrinsic nature of things, while the ectype is the form of experience, how one thing stands in relation to others.[38] Understood as a distinction between form and content, the distinction seems less wildly metaphysical, less a distinction between two worlds than two aspects of experience itself. Like the thing-in-itself, the archetype for Schopenhauer is not a transcendent supernatural entity but the intrinsic nature of the object of experience itself.

How, though, do we *know* the inner essence of things? That is the crucial question of method for Schopenhauer's metaphysics. Unfortunately, however, it is precisely here that Schopenhauer leaves us with little more than hints and suggestions. The crux of his defense of metaphysics rests with his claim, scarcely explored or explained, that the task of the philosopher lies in the "*interpretation*" (*Deutung*) and "*explication*" (*Auslegung*) of appearances (WWV II, 237; P 183). The metaphysician does not engage in dogmatic demonstration, in trains of syllogistic reasoning, and still less in causal explanations of things according to general laws. Rather, his task is, as Schopenhauer puts it, "*to decipher* appearances," as if they were texts, or as if they were someone speaking to us.[39] After all, the aim of the metaphysician is to know "the meaning" (*die Bedeutung*) of appearances, not the laws that govern them (WWV I, 151, 156; P 95, 98–99). What Schopenhauer needed, then, was a hermeneutics, an account of the logic of interpretation, a theory about how interpretation differs from demonstration and causal explanation. Nowhere, however, does he provide such an account. It was a remarkable shortcoming for an old student of Boeckh and Schleiermacher, two fathers of modern hermeneutics.

---

38   See ibid., I, 257, §34 (P 178); and I, 270, §36 (P 189).

39   See Schopenhauer, "Über Philosophie und ihre Methode," in *Parlipomena, Werke* V, 25.

5. RISE AND FALL OF THE NEO-KANTIAN IDEAL

In the early 1860s, some twenty years after Trendelenburg, Schopenhauer and the neo-Hegelians had developed their conceptions of philosophy, a new philosophical movement appeared on the horizon that put forward yet another conception, one that would have a lasting impact on German philosophy for the rest of the century. This movement was neo-Kantianism. We can trace its origins back to the late eighteenth century, to the criticisms of speculative idealism by Jakob Friedrich Fries (1773–1843), Johann Friedrich Herbart (1776–1841), and Friedrich Beneke (1798–1841), the three thinkers who formed the "lost tradition." There were neo-Kantian spokesmen throughout the 1840s—Ernst Mirbt (1799–1847), Christian Weiße (1801–66), and Carl Fortlage (1806–81)—and in the 1850s Kant's philosophy found a major advocate in the physicist and physiologist Hermann Helmholtz (1821–94). But the movement became self-conscious and widespread only in the 1860s, in the writings of Kuno Fischer (1824–1906), Eduard Zeller (1814–1908), Otto Liebmann (1840–1912), Friedrich Lange (1828–75), and Jürgen Bona Meyer (1829–97). What gave this movement its rationale, focus, and energy was its conception of philosophy, which was explicitly conceived as an answer to the identity crisis.

The defining documents of the neo-Kantian conception of philosophy are two lectures delivered in the early 1860s, one by Kuno Fischer and the other by Eduard Zeller. Fischer's lecture, "Das Problem der menschlichen Erkenntniß als die erste Frage der Philosophie," was delivered in April 1860; and Zeller's lecture, "Ueber Bedeutung und Aufgabe der Erkenntnistheorie," was given in October 1862.[40] Though Fischer and Zeller did not collaborate, and did not even know one another at the time, their lectures revealed a strikingly similar conception of philosophy. Both saw their conception as the only way forward, as the only means to ensure a future for philosophy. Their conception alone, they argued, would give philosophy a unique vocation apart from the empirical sci-

---

40 Fischer's lecture was the second part of his *Kant's Leben und die Grundlagen seiner Lehre* (Mannheim: Bassermann, 1860), pp. 89–115. Zeller's lecture was first published in his *Vorträge und Abhandlungen* (Leipzig: Fues, 1877), II, 479–96.

ences and ensure that it did not relapse into the bad old ways of speculative idealism.

Fischer and Zeller saw the fundamental task of philosophy as, in a word, *epistemology* (*Erkenntnistheorie*), second-order reflection on the basic concepts, methods, and presuppositions of the empirical sciences. Since epistemology is a "transcendental" enterprise, they explained along Kantian lines, its concern is with the conditions and limits of knowledge rather than with its objects. The special interest of the natural scientist, however, is with just these objects, not with the methods and presuppositions by which he acquires knowledge of them. Hence reflection on such methods and presuppositions remains, Fischer and Zeller reasoned, the distinctive task of the philosopher. There is no danger of obsolescence at the hands of the empirical sciences, then, since they always deal with some aspect of the world, whereas the philosopher analyzes discourse about that world. He explains what all scientists presuppose but can never explain themselves: the possibility of empirical science.

It is no accident that Fischer and Zeller were, in their earlier days, neo-Hegelians. Both wrote articles for neo-Hegelian journals in the 1840s, and both were friends of David Friedrich Strauss, the biblical critic who inspired much neo-Hegelianism. Initially, they shared the neo-Hegelian conception of philosophy as critique. Their new conception of philosophy as epistemology was an organic development of that earlier one. When the critical conception of philosophy becomes mainstream, examining the logic of the sciences rather than religion, morality, and the state, it becomes epistemology. For both Fischer and Zeller, epistemology was a retreat away from their political engagement in the 1840s and 1850s. Both had suffered political persecution for their earlier critique of orthodox religion. Fischer's *venia legendi*, his right to teach, was withdrawn in 1853; and during the 1850s Zeller was hounded by religious authorities in Tübingen and Berne. Now, however, that they transformed critique into epistemology, the path had been cleared for an academic career and bourgeois respectability.

Whatever its precise origins, we must be careful how we interpret neo-Kantian epistemology. It has been understood as a species of foundationalism, as if the neo-Kantians, in determining the possibility of scientific knowledge from their transcendental standpoint, somehow wanted to provide a new foundation for it.[41] It is important to note, however, that the neo-Kantians, one and all, utterly repudiated the foundationalism of the speculative idealist tradition. They very much accepted the autonomy of the empirical sciences, and they firmly believed the sciences stood in no need of a foundation from philosophy. The purpose of philosophy was not to ground the empirical sciences but to explain their logic. Thus the neo-Kantians very much followed in the footsteps of Trendelenburg: they, too, rejected the foundationalism of the speculative idealist tradition; they, too, fully recognized "the fact of science"; and they, too, wanted philosophy to examine "the logic of the sciences." They departed from Trendelenburg only in their greater skepticism toward metaphysics and in their greater emphasis on the epistemological mission of philosophy.

For several reasons, the neo-Kantian conception of philosophy proved strategic and successful. First, it ensured philosophy against obsolescence at the hands of the sciences, given that scientists have little or no interest in the logic of their own discipline. Their task is to investigate nature according to certain methods and principles, not to investigate these methods and principles themselves. Second, it made philosophy into something approximating a science, into a rigorous discipline of its own, given that reflection on the logic of the sciences demands rigor and technical expertise. Third, it allied philosophy with the sciences, aiding and abetting them by clarifying their logic; hence philosophy could borrow some of their luster and prestige. Although some might balk that this strategy made philosophy into a mere handmaiden of the sciences, partnership with them seemed a virtue and necessity in a scientific age.

For nearly two decades this definition of philosophy served the neo-Kantians well. It was adopted by many of them in the 1860s and 1870s: by Otto Liebmann (1840–1912), Friedrich Lange (1828–75), Wilhelm Windelband (1848–1915), Friedrich Paulsen (1846–1908), Hermann Cohen (1842–1918), Hans Vaihinger (1852–1933), and Alois Riehl (1844–1924). Such was the success of this

---

41 See Richard Rorty, *Philosophy and the Mirror of Nature* (Oxford: Blackwell, 1980), pp. 4, 131–32.

definition that, in the late 1870s, neo-Kantianism had come remarkably close in spirit to the budding positivist movement in
Germany. Several prominent neo-Kantians formed an alliance
with the positivists in the production of a new journal, *Vierteljahrschrift für wissenschaftliche Philosophie*,[42] which was devoted to
the epistemology of the new sciences. Paulsen, Liebmann, Windelband, Zeller, and Vaihinger wrote articles for the journal, while
Riehl helped with the editing.

Despite its virtues and successes, there were serious problems
with the neo-Kantian conception of philosophy. For one thing,
there was a deep ambiguity about the discourse and subject matter
of transcendental philosophy. Some neo-Kantians—Helmholtz,
Bona Meyer, Zeller, and Lange—understood transcendental
philosophy in *psychological* terms, so that the investigation into
knowledge determines its causes. However, other neo-Kantians—
Windelband, Cohen, and Riehl—saw transcendental philosophy
in *logical* terms, so that the investigation into knowledge determines the truth conditions of judgments. Still others—Fischer and
Liebmann—swithered on the issue, sometimes conceiving transcendental discourse in psychological terms, sometimes in logical
ones. The ambiguity was finally settled in the early 1870s in favor
of the logical reading. One argument in behalf of this reading, put
forward forcefully by Cohen and Windelband, was essentially exe-
getical: Kant was clear that his transcendental philosophy is more
about the *quid juris?*—What is the justification of knowledge?—
than the *quid facti?*—What are the causes and sources of knowledge? Another argument, however, claimed that only this reading
could solve the identity crisis. If transcendental philosophy is essentially psychology, what distinguishes it from the growing empirical
science of psychology? A psychological reading of transcendental
philosophy allows it to be too readily subsumed under the empirical sciences, so that philosophy loses its unique vocation and status.
Psychology, Windelband, Fischer, and Liebmann realized, is really

42 *Vierteljahrschrift für wissenschaftliche Philosophie*, ed. R. Avenarius (Leipzig:
Fues, 1877–1901), 24 vols. In 1902 the journal appeared under the new title *Viertel-
jahrschrift für wissenschaftliche Philosophie und Soziologie*, ed. Paul Barth (Leipzig:
Riesland, 1902–16), 15 vols.

only another empirical science, so that its possibility and methods should fall under transcendental philosophy.

The major problem with the neo-Kantian conception, however, was its narrowness. It was fine in defining *theoretical* philosophy; but it ignored entirely *practical* philosophy. In other words, it gave no place to the realm of value. What is the highest good? What is the criterion of morality? And what is the value and purpose of life? Since classical times these questions had been the heart and soul of philosophy; yet they fell outside the neo-Kantian paradigm, which was devoted entirely to the logic of the empirical sciences. Of course, Kant himself had given the greatest importance to these questions; but, because of the prestige and power of the empirical sciences in the second half of the nineteenth century, the neo-Kantians failed to imitate their master's example.

Not for long, however, could the neo-Kantians rest in their dogmatic slumbers. Their narrow definition of philosophy proved to be unpopular with students, who abandoned their lectures in alarming numbers. The neo-Kantians now realized that if they were to have an audience, they would have to make room for ethics, for the classical questions about the value and meaning of life. This new more practical direction of neo-Kantianism is apparent from several developments in the late 1870s and early 1880s. First, several eminent neo-Kantians, viz., Windelband, Liebmann, and Paulsen, abandoned the positivist *Vierteljahrschrift* and became highly critical of positivism.[43] Second, in 1877 Carl Schaarschmidt, an ambitious young neo-Kantian, restarted the *Philosophische Monatshefte* by giving it an ethical agenda to counteract the influence of the *Vierteljahrschrift*.[44] Third, starting in the late 1870s, there was a great increase in the number of lectures given by neo-Kantians on the

43 See Wilhelm Windelband, "Immanuel Kant. Zur Säkularfeier seine Philosophie" (1881), in *Präludien*, Neunte Auflage (Tübingen: Mohr, 1924), I, 112–45, esp. 123; Friedrich Paulsen, "Idealismus und Positivismus," *Im neuen Reich* 10 (1880), 735–42; and Otto Liebmann, *Die Klimax der Theorieen. Eine Untersuchungen aus dem Bereich der allgemeinen Wissenschaftslehre* (Straßburg: Trübner, 1884).

44 See Carl Schaarschmidt, "Vom rechten und falschen Kriticismus," *Philosophische Monatshefte* 14 (1878), 1–12. Also see the review of the new editorial policies by Johannes Volkelt, "Philosophsiche Monatshefte," *Jenaer Literaturzeitung* 5 (1878), 95–96.

topics of practical philosophy and the nature of philosophy in general.[45] This shift in direction is no less apparent from the writings of some prominent neo-Kantians in the early 1880s. Thus, in 1882 Johannes Volkelt wrote an article calling for a renewal of interest in ethics in the neo-Kantian movement.[46] And in 1883, Alois Riehl gave a lecture on philosophy that divided the discipline into two distinct halves: there was theoretical or scientific philosophy, which concerned the logic of the sciences; but there was also practical or nonscientific philosophy, which deals with ethics and aesthetics.[47] While dubbing practical philosophy "nonscientific" seems to give it less value and importance than theoretical philosophy, Riehl did not see things that way; for, as if to repent for his earlier positivist ways, he went on to devote the rest of his life to practical philosophy.

How do we explain this neo-Kantian shift toward the practical? It has been attributed to political events, to the hysterical reaction to the two assassination attempts on Kaiser Wilhelm I in 1878.[48] But a more likely explanation lies in the neo-Kantians' competition with the ghost of Arthur Schopenhauer, who had haunted their movement since the 1860s. The very decade in which neo-Kantianism became self-conscious and organized was the same decade in which Schopenhauer became the most famous philosopher in Germany. For the neo-Kantians, Schopenhauer's renown could only come as a thorn in their side. Although Schopenhauer died in September 1860, well before the neo-Kantians became established professors in German universities, no one could have been deluded about what his attitude would have been toward their success. University philosophers were Schopenhauer's *bête noire*. He already had made well-known his dislike of some early neo-Kantians, viz., Beneke, Fortlage, Fries, and Herbart; and so it would be an

---

45 These developments have been fully documented by Klaus Christian Köhnke, *Entstehung und Aufstieg des Neukantianismus* (Frankfurt: Suhrkamp, 1986), pp. 398–99, 404–5, 407, 601–9.

46 Johannes Volkelt, "Wiedererweckung der kantischen Ethik," *Zeitschrift für Philosophie und philosophische Kritik* 81 (1882), 37–48.

47 Alois Riehl, *Ueber wissenschaftliche und Nichtwissenschaftliche Philosophie. Eine akademische Antrittsrede* (Tübingen: Mohr, 1883).

48 See Köhnke, *Entstehung und Aufstieg*, pp. 421–27.

easy inference what he thought about their progeny. Not the least annoying aspect of Schopenhauer's fame for the neo-Kantians was his claim to be the sole true heir of Kant. For a movement that legitimated itself by appealing to Kant's name, that pretension was nothing short of provocation. And so Schopenhauer became for the neo-Kantians "the great pretender."

Because of his great fame, because of his antipathy to the early neo-Kantians, and because of his claim to be Kant's sole heir, the neo-Kantians became virtually obsessed with "the philosopher king of Frankfurt." Their preoccupation with him is apparent from their many writings about him. From the mid-1860s until the early 1900s, virtually every neo-Kantian wrote about Schopenhauer. Such, indeed, was their interest that Haym, Bona Meyer, Fischer, and Volkelt wrote some of the first monographs on him.[49]

The chief challenge of Schopenhauer to the neo-Kantians, however, came from his opposing conception of philosophy.[50] While the neo-Kantian conception was at first limited to the theoretical or epistemology, Schopenhauer's conception of philosophy put the ethical and existential interests of philosophy front and center. Ultimately, for the general public, and eventually for the neo-Kantians themselves, Schopenhauer's conception of philosophy proved a more attractive solution to the identity crisis. Schopenhauer's conception not only ensured philosophy against obsolescence—because the empirical sciences could not answer questions about the value and meaning of life—but it was also more true to the traditional vocation of philosophy. Furthermore, Schopenhauer's conception gave philosophy an immediate relevance and importance, given that the value of life is of direct interest to every human being. While the neo-Kantian conception made philosophy a specialized and esoteric academic discipline,

49   Rudolf Haym, *Arthur Schopenhauer* (Berlin: Reimer, 1864); Jürgen Bona Meyer, *Arthur Schopenhauer als Mensch und Denker* (Berlin: Carl Habel, 1872); Kuno Fischer, *Schopenhauers Leben, Werke und Lehre*, Zweite Auflage, Band IX of *Geschichte der neueren Philosophie* (Heidelberg: Carl Winter, 1898); and Johannes Volkelt, *Arthur Schopenhauer, Seine Persönlichkeit, seine Lehre, sein Glaube* (Stuttgart: Frommann, 1900).

50   We shall see in chapter 5 that the challenge of Schopenhauer also came from his pessimism.

Schopenhauer's conception made philosophy a public and exoteric concern. No wonder, then, that the neo-Kantian conception remained confined to the universities, while Schopenhauer's found favor among the general educated public.

Given the popularity and challenge of Schopenhauer's philosophy, then, the neo-Kantians shifted course and broadened the agenda of their program. There was no great compromise or concession involved in doing so. After all, the great Kant himself had always given great importance to ethics and aesthetics. And so, in expanding their program, the neo-Kantians could claim that they were only going back to their roots. The alliance with the positivists now seemed an embarrassing episode, which was abruptly terminated and quickly forgotten.

The culmination of the neo-Kantian efforts to define philosophy came very much in the wake of Schopenhauer's influence on their movement. This last great effort appears in two lectures given by Wilhelm Windelband in the early 1880s: his 1881 "Immanuel Kant," which was given on the centenary of the publication of the *Kritik der reinen Vernunft*, and his 1882 "Was ist Philosophie?"[51] In these lectures Windelband reflects on the crisis of philosophy as it had played out some four decades before him. With the benefit of hindsight, he pointed out the weaknesses of the earlier neo-Kantian definitions. They are defective, he argued, because they fail to determine the precise logical stature and object of epistemology. Windelband agreed with his neo-Kantian predecessors that philosophy is essentially epistemology; but he insisted that the crucial question remains *what kind* of epistemology it should be. Some neo-Kantians, viz., Helmholtz and Zeller, had defined epistemology in psychological terms, failing to see that psychology is just another first-order discipline whose methods and presuppositions stand in need of investigation. In any case, Windelband insisted, their definitions are too narrow because they are limited to theoretical rather than practical philosophy.

---

51 Windelband, "Immanuel Kant. Zur Säkularfeier seiner Philosophie," *Präludien* I, 112–46; "Was ist Philosophie," *Präludien* I, 1–54. Also see his 1882 lecture "Normen und Naturgesetze," *Präludien* II, 59–98.

To avoid these kinds of problems, Windelband put forward his own influential definition of philosophy. Philosophy, Windelband declared, should be "a general science of norms." What, exactly, is a norm? That question would much trouble Windelband in coming years; but its basic meaning was clear enough. Windelband understood a norm as a rule or procedure for guiding inquiry. He did not invent the concept of "norm" or "normativity," for which there was ample precedent in the writings of Lotze and Herbart. What is original to, and characteristic of, Windelband's approach, however, is that he uses it to define philosophy itself. Philosophy is now the science of norms. Its task is to determine the basic norms that govern all human activity, whether that be thinking, feeling, or willing. There are basic norms not only in science, Windelband stressed, but also in morality and art. Accordingly, there are three parts of philosophy for each kind of norm: scientific, ethical, and aesthetic.

There are two strategic advantages to Windelband's definition. First, it makes it clear that transcendental philosophy is more a logical than a psychological enterprise, so that there is no danger of obsolescence by psychology. As a science of norms, Windelband explained, philosophy is essentially concerned with the justification of knowledge rather than with its origins, with the reasons for beliefs rather than their causes. Second, with a single concept—that of normativity—it unites all the concerns of philosophy, so that it deals as much with ethics and aesthetics as the sciences. By thus broadening the agenda of the critical philosophy, Windelband ensured that it could maintain its appeal to a wide audience and not only to philosophical specialists concerned with the logic of the sciences.

Windelband's definition of philosophy proved to be successful and influential. It was the basis for the so-called "theory of value" (*Werttheorie*) of the Southwest school of neo-Kantianism. The conception of normativity remains one of the vital links between neo-Kantianism and contemporary philosophy, which has inherited, unbeknownst to itself, some of Windelband's central concerns.[52]

52 See my article "Normativity in Neo-Kantianism: Its Rise and Fall," *International Journal of Philosophical Studies* 17 (2009), 9–27.

6. EDUARD VON HARTMANN'S
METAPHYSICS OF THE SCIENCES

There was a fateful unresolved ambiguity hidden in Trendelenburg's conception of philosophy as "the logic of the sciences." This phrase could mean the *second-order* examination of the basic concepts and presuppositions of the empirical sciences, so that philosophy was the *epistemology* of the sciences. But it could also mean a *first-order* system of the sciences, so that philosophy was more a *metaphysics* of the sciences based upon their general results. On the whole, the neo-Kantians took the former interpretation; the latter interpretation was adopted by an original and influential philosopher having nothing to do with neo-Kantianism: Eduard von Hartmann (1842–1906). In a short essay published in 1872, "Naturforschung und Philosophie,"[53] Hartmann put forward a conception of philosophy as the metaphysics of the natural sciences.

Hartmann's essay immediately takes up the question of the obsolescence of philosophy which had so challenged his generation. The essay is conceived as an epistolary exchange between a natural scientist and a philosopher, where the natural scientist presses the case for the retirement of philosophy, and where the philosopher defends the eternal relevance and importance of his discipline. The natural scientist expresses the disillusionment with philosophy so common after the collapse of speculative idealism. Philosophy is for him nothing but arid abstraction and sterile a priori reasoning, and there is no point in pursuing it now that the methods of observation and experiment are leading to secure results. Furthermore, philosophy is fruitless because philosophers have never agreed about anything, and their methods have never led to reliable conclusions, still less to inventions of any utility for mankind. Responding to these criticisms, the philosopher agrees that the a priori methods of speculative idealism have been barren and sterile. But he disagrees with the natural scientist's conflation of philosophy with speculative

---

53 Eduard von Hartmann, "Naturforschung und Philosophie. Eine Unterhaltung in zwei Briefen," *Philosophische Monatshefte* 8 (1871), 49–58, 97–105, reprinted in *Gesammelte Philosophische Abhandlungen zur Philosophie des Unbewussten* (Berlin: Duncker, 1872), pp. 1–24.

idealism. Philosophy in general is not obsolete because there is no necessity that the philosopher should follow the method of speculative construction. Instead, it is possible for the philosopher to follow the same analytic or inductive method as the natural scientist. The philosopher, too, Hartmann insists, should base all his doctrines upon experience. He should know all the results of the most recent scientific research; and he should never draw broader conclusions than the evidence warrants. If a philosophical theory contradicts any results of the empirical sciences, it has to be rejected.

What distinguishes the philosopher from the natural scientist, Hartmann explains, is not his method, still less his subject matter, but his goals or interests. The goal of the philosopher is to create the general system of the sciences, which is no concern of the sciences themselves, which are all devoted to a particular aspect of reality. The interest of the philosopher is not in the *object* of knowledge but in its *form*, which consists in the *interconnections* between different disciplines. The empirical sciences on their own are simply too specialized, failing to see beyond their own particular patch. It is the task of the philosopher to see as a whole what the particular sciences see only in scattered and separate parts. Philosophy should be first and foremost metaphysics, Hartmann believes, but a metaphysics that is only the system of the sciences. We should not expect such a metaphysics to serve the material needs of mankind. The empirical sciences have been fruitful in terms of their power to serve these needs; but philosophy has to address other less material needs. Applying an idea of Schopenhauer, Hartmann insists that there is "a need for metaphysics" in all human beings, which it is the special task of philosophy to address.

No one could accuse Hartmann of having a purely programmatic conception of philosophy. He had already attempted to realize his conception, which took shape in his massive *Philosophie des Unbewussten*, which first appeared in 1869.[54] The aim of this

---

54 Eduard von Hartmann, *Philosophie des Unbewussten* (Berlin: Duncker, 1869). All references here are to the slightly expanded second edition of 1870. There were altogether eleven editions of this work from 1869 to 1904. By the seventh edition of 1875 it had expanded into two volumes; and by the tenth edition of 1890 it had become three volumes.

tome was to formulate a new metaphysics based on the latest results of the empirical sciences. Hartmann's mantra was "Speculative results according to the inductive-naturalscientific method!" His metaphysics was very much akin to "the organic view of the world" formulated by Trendelenburg, though it had none of its classical flavor. It was a paradoxical synthesis of Schopenhauer's voluntarism with Hegel's absolute idealism. Hartmann's unconscious was like Schopenhauer's will, though it was no blind striving or primitive urge, but more like Hegel's spirit because it acted purposively, striving to become self-conscious and rational. It was Hartmann's goal to rehabilitate the organic and teleological conception of nature as found in Schelling and Hegel. As much as he appreciated this classical doctrine, he insisted on founding it on the inductive methods of the empirical sciences rather than the deductive methods of his idealist forebears.

Hartmann's tome is impressive for its extraordinary depth and breadth of knowledge about the new sciences. Yet despite all the learning behind it, Hartmann's program faced stubborn obstacles. There was first of all the question whether the empirical sciences warranted the heavy metaphysical superstructure that Hartmann placed on them. He had already conceded in the introduction to his work that the inductive method did not lead to final principles or a unified system (10). Even worse, Hartmann faced the same challenge as Trendelenburg: how to defend the organic worldview in the face of Darwinism. The teleology of the organic worldview seemed undermined by Darwinism, which could apparently explain the origin of species as a mechanical process. Hartmann rose to the challenge in several chapters of *Philosophie des Unbewussten*,[55] and later in several books,[56] but it is clear that he is fighting a rearguard

---

55 *Philosophie des Unbewussten* (1870), B.V, pp. 235–37; and C.VIII, pp. 489–536.

56 Hartmann published anonymously a self-critique in *Das Unbewußte vom Standpunkt der Physiologie und Descendenztheorie. Eine kritische Beleuchtung des naturphilosophischen Teils der Philosophie des Unbewußten aus naturwissenschaftlichen Gesichtspunkten* (Berlin: Dunker, 1872). The book was celebrated as a refutation of Hartmann's position until its authorship was discovered. Hartmann later published *Wahrheit und Irrtum im Darwinismus* (Berlin: Dunker, 1875). This appeared later as volume 3 of the tenth and eleventh editions of *Philosophie des Unbewussten* (Leipzig: Hermann Haacke, 1890).

action. Following a line of criticism developed by the biologist Carl Nägeli,[57] Hartmann held that the theory of natural selection works in explaining the origins of varieties and changes within species but that it cannot explain the origin of higher species from lower ones, which is a process created by the cosmic unconscious alone (528, 533). But Hartmann's argument is unconvincing in the face of his concession that new species can indeed arise from the accumulation of changes in varieties (531). Although nothing Darwin said refuted Hartmann's theory of the unconscious, it also did not confirm it either; even worse, it made it superfluous. Why appeal to a cosmic unconscious force to explain the origin of species when the theory of natural selection is sufficient?

7. DILTHEY AND WORLDVIEWS

The last conception of philosophy to emerge out of the identity crisis is so familiar to us today that it has entered into ordinary English. According to this conception, philosophy is a "worldview" or, in the original German, which usually appears even in English dictionaries, a "*Weltanschauung.*" All of us have a rough idea of what a worldview means: "A particular philosophy or view of life; a concept of the world held by an individual or a group."[58] We have a much less clear idea, though, how this conception arose and what it originally meant.

Its chief source was Wilhelm Dilthey, who formulated it in direct response to the identity crisis. His main account of this conception appears in his late work *Das Wesen der Philosophie*,[59] which was first published in 1908, though its formulation goes back decades earlier. Some of Dilthey's early manuscripts from the 1870s

57 Carl Nägeli, *Entstehen und Begriff der naturhistorischen Art* (Munich: Akademie der Wissenschaften, 1865). On Nägeli's role in the debates about Darwin, see Robert Richards, *The Tragic Sense of Life: Ernst Haeckel and the Struggle over Evolutionary Thought* (Chicago: University of Chicago Press, 2008), pp. 315–18.

58 *Oxford English Dictionary*, 2nd ed. (Oxford: Clarendon Press, 1989), p. 2295.

59 See Wilhelm Dilthey, *Das Wesen der Philosophie*, in vol. 5 of *Gesammelte Schriften*, ed. Georg Misch (Göttingen: Vandenhoeck & Ruprecht, 1964), V, 339–412. All references in parentheses are to this edition. Subsequent references in the notes will be abbreviated "GS."

show his great concern with the vocation of philosophy in the new scientific age.[60]

Dilthey's conception of a worldview, as he finally formulated it in *Das Wesen der Philosophie*, shows a large debt to Schopenhauer. Like his great forebear, Dilthey believed that philosophy had first and foremost an ethical function, that its main purpose was to address "the puzzle of the world."[61] It was the task of the philosopher to determine ultimate values, to ascertain what makes life worth living. A worldview was first and foremost a statement of these ultimate values, of the reasons that make life worth living and the chief goals we should pursue in life. It was also, of course, a metaphysics, an attempt to formulate a general view of the world, and more specifically the reasons why there is something rather than nothing. But the metaphysics is subordinate to the ethics, because its purpose is to formulate the ontological or cosmic basis for these ultimate values, to rationalize why, given the nature of things, they alone should matter.

It was this ethical view of philosophy, Dilthey believed, that could ensure it against obsolescence in the modern scientific age. However much the sciences progressed, and however many disciplines they took over, they were still not concerned with the question of value, which remained the exclusive preserve and prerogative of philosophy. Dilthey then went on to stress that, in articulating these values, philosophy performed an important social and cultural function (371–72, 375–76). It determined the ultimate values not only for the individual but an entire culture and age. Now that religion was disappearing, philosophy was becoming more important.

It was thus Schopenhauer who had provided Dilthey with his solution to the obsolescence crisis of philosophy. But though he closely follows Schopenhauer's view of the purpose and problem of

60   See the 1875 essay "Über das Studium der Geschichte der Wissenschaften vom Menschen, der Gesellschaft und dem Staat," GS V, 31–73, esp. 48; and "Frühe Entwürfe zur Erkenntnistheorie und Logik der Geisteswissenschaften," GS XIX, 1–57.

61   The debt to Schopenhauer is especially apparent from Dilthey's language. He constantly states that the aim of philosophy is to address the "*Welt- und Lebensrätsel.*" See V, 345, 365, 370, 375, 404.

philosophy, Dilthey's conception of philosophy still differs markedly from that of his grouchy predecessor. Dilthey did not share Schopenhauer's confidence in the possibility of metaphysics, still less his presupposition that there could be some theoretical means to determine which is the true or ultimate worldview. The conflict between worldviews is for him theoretically undecidable, so that the choice between them ultimately depends more on the will than reason. Writing at the close of the century, Dilthey had lost all faith in the power of metaphysics to resolve its problems through strictly rational means. There was no magical method that would put metaphysics on the sure path to a science. He rejects not only the synthetic method of the speculative idealists but also the analytic method of Trendelenburg and Hartmann (355–56).

It is above all the historical dimension of Dilthey's conception of philosophy that distinguishes it from that of the Frankfurt sage. Schopenhauer had famously rejected the historical view of the world, insisting that human nature and reason stand above the historical flux. But here, too, Dilthey could not share Schopenhauer's confidence in a realm of eternal and universal values. The historical standpoint, Dilthey writes in *Das Wesen der Philosophie*, sets it above all particular philosophical standpoints (364). These standpoints claim a universal validity, as if they were true for all cultures and epochs; but the historical standpoint shows us how each philosophy arises from, and gets its meaning within, its own historical context. It therefore shows us how all philosophies are relative and historical. So it was not simply skepticism about metaphysics that made Dilthey doubt the rational decidability of worldviews; it was also his deep-seated historicism, his recognition of how each philosophy depends upon its specific historical context.

In stressing the historical dimension and theoretical undecidability of worldviews, Dilthey appeared to forfeit the traditional claim of philosophy to universal validity. Yet it was a claim that Dilthey still saw as integral to philosophy and that he did not lightly relinquish. To his critics, Dilthey seemed to be abandoning the claim that philosophy could be a science. "*Weltanschauung statt Wissenschaft*" was the slogan used to express a *reductio ad absurdum* of his position. Dilthey, however, bristled at the suggestion that he was a relativist and stressed how important it was for philosophy to retain its quest for universal values. He eventually admitted, however, that he could not resolve "the antimony" between philosophy's claim to universality and its historical roots. The task of resolving this irresolvable problem he passed down to a future generation.[62]

Such, in sum, were the most prominent definitions of philosophy from 1840 to 1900. None of them definitively resolved the crisis of philosophy, because all had their disadvantages. They were either too narrow (neo-Kantianism), too subject to obsolescence (Trendelenburg, Hartmann), too self-destructive (neo-Hegelianism), too vague in their methodology (Schopenhauer), or too prone to relativism (Dilthey). Not surprisingly, none of them survived long in the twentieth century. Neo-Kantianism seems closest to our contemporary analytic conception of philosophy; but the similarities are only vague, and little of the original neo-Kantian meaning remains. A neo-Kantian from the 1860s was a very different animal from our contemporary analytic philosopher.

The many failed attempts to define philosophy in the second half of the nineteenth century seem to show that the whole enterprise was doomed to failure. The diagnosis for the failure is clear: we cannot define philosophy for the simple reason that philosophy is indefinable. We philosophize whenever we attempt to define philosophy, and we can define it in all these different ways. But for just that reason philosophy is greater than all its definitions, and it eludes the very efforts to define it.

Yet, on second thought, the search for the true definition of philosophy was not all in vain. For if we consider this quest as a whole—the entire discussion over the decades about the meaning of philosophy—we find that it did resolve the anxiety that fueled the crisis. That anxiety rested on the fear that philosophy would somehow disappear, that it would never survive beyond the first half of the century. But the very indefinability of philosophy shows

62   See his "Rede zum 70 Geburtstag," GS V, 9.

that it is also inextinguishable and inexhaustible. Philosophy is protean; no sooner does one shape disappear than another appears. Thus philosophy will always survive its grave diggers. They will try to bury her; but, transformed like a phoenix, she will rise again from her ashes.

2

THE MATERIALISM
CONTROVERSY

1. CONTEXT AND CAUSES

Although largely forgotten today, the so-called "materialism controversy" was one of the most important intellectual disputes of the second half of the nineteenth century. The dispute began in the 1850s, and its shock waves reverberated until the end of the century. We understand little of German philosophy in the second half of the nineteenth century unless we know the chief issues posed by this controversy and the major responses to them.

The main question posed by the materialism controversy was whether modern natural science, whose authority and prestige were now beyond question, necessarily leads to materialism. Materialism was generally understood to be the doctrine that only matter exists and that everything in nature obeys only mechanical laws. If such a doctrine were true, it seemed there could be no God, no free will, no soul, and hence no immortality. These beliefs, however, seemed vital to morality and religion. So the controversy posed a drastic dilemma: either a scientific materialism or a moral and religious "leap of faith." It was the latest version of the old conflict between reason and faith, where now the role of reason was played by natural science.

The materialism controversy was not a little reminiscent of the "pantheism controversy" which had taken place some seventy years earlier.[1] In the late 1780s Friedrich Heinrich Jacobi had posed a very similar dilemma for his own generation. It had to choose, he

---

1 On the pantheism controversy, see my *The Fate of Reason: German Philosophy between Kant and Fichte* (Cambridge, MA: Harvard University Press, 1987), pp. 44–126.

contended, between Spinoza's pantheism or a *"salto mortale"* in theism, immortality and free will. Since Spinoza's pantheism represented for Jacobi a complete naturalism, whose consequences were
fatalism and atheism, the choice he posed was very much like that
of the materialism controversy. Just as the pantheism controversy
dominated the intellectual landscape of late eighteenth century, so
the materialism controversy did the same for the second half of the
nineteenth century.

The recurrence of the old conflict between reason and faith in
the mid-nineteenth century was another result of the collapse of
Hegelianism. It was the chief aim of Hegel's philosophy to resolve
the dilemma of the pantheism controversy, to show how the content, if not the form, of religious belief could be justified through
philosophy. The key to that reconciliation lay with Hegel's famous
dialectic, which was for him the paradigm of rationality. The dialectic would first reveal how finite forms of thought contradict
themselves and then show how their contradictions are resolved
only in the idea of the absolute, i.e., the infinite cosmic whole of
which all finite forms are only parts. The absolute was the philosophical concept for the religious belief in God. By the 1840s,
however, the dialectic had lost its magic, its power to bewitch the
young. Trendelenburg's painstaking criticisms of Hegel's logical
transitions were one blow to Hegelian confidence.[2] Another came
with Strauss's and Bauer's critique of positive religion, which cast
suspicion on the religious beliefs to be rationalized by the dialectic; these beliefs, which were supposed to be based on revelation,
proved to be upon critical examination not simple historical facts
but myths or poetry.[3] The *coup de grâce* for the dialectic came with
the critique of Feuerbach, Weiße, and Lotze,[4] who insisted that it

2 See his critique of Hegel in *Logische Untersuchungen*, Zweite Ergänzte Auflage (Leipzig: Hirzel, 1862), I, 36–129.

3 David Friedrich Strauss, *Das Leben Jesu, kritisch bearbeitet* (Tübingen: C. F.
Osiander, 1835); and Bruno Bauer, *Kritik der evangelischen Geschichte der Synoptiker*
(Leipzig: Wigand, 1841).

4 See Ludwig Feuerbach, *Grundsätze der Philosophie der Zukunft* (Winterthur:
Fröbel, 1843); Hermann Christian Weiße, *Ueber den gegenwärtigen Standpunct der
philosophischen Wissenschaft. In besondere Beziehung auf das System Hegel* (Leipzig:
Barth, 1829); and Hermann Lotze, *Metaphysik* (Leipzig: Hirzel, 1841).

could overcome the contradictions of finite experience only by abstracting from all its particularities and contingencies, a procedure that left a dualism between thought and experience. The net effect of these criticisms was that Hegel's dialectic could not bridge Lessing's "broad and ugly ditch," i.e., the insurmountable gap between the universal forms of thought and the particular facts of history.

The collapse of the Hegelian dialectic was only one condition for the recurrence of the conflict between reason and faith. Another necessary condition was the advance of science itself. The methods of observation and experiment, which had replaced Hegel's dialectic as the ruling paradigm of rationality, were now being pushed further than ever before, and they were leading to results that undermined the old religious and moral worldview. The growth of biology, psychology, and physiology in the first half of the century had extended the mechanical paradigm of explanation to life and the mind, which now seemed as much a phenomenon of nature as the fall of an apple from a tree. By the 1850s, the physicalist program of Müller's rebellious students was well under way, and it had achieved spectacular results in explaining living phenomena according to mechanical principles. The cell theory of Schleiden and Schwann, the theory of animal electricity of Du Bois-Reymond, the principle of the conservation of energy of Helmholtz, and the theory of disease of Virchow had all replaced the concept of a vital power or *Lebenskraft* in explaining organic growth and development. The old teleological view of the world, which was essential to the Christian idea of creation and providence, was rapidly becoming obsolete; and the concept of a soul, which was crucial to the dogma of immortality, was proving less tenable as physiology revealed the dependence of the mind on chemistry, nerves, and brain. By the 1860s the rapid rise of Darwinism in Germany gave added weight and momentum to the materialist cause by providing a natural explanation for the origin of species.

Roughly speaking, there were two phases to the materialism controversy. The first or classical phase, from 1854 to 1863, was mainly philosophical, characterized by the battle between idealists and materialists. The second or Darwinian phase, from 1863 until the end of the century, revolved around discussion of Darwin's theory of natural selection. The dividing line between these phases was drawn by Ernst Häckel's famous lecture "Über die Entwicklung-slehre Darwins,"[5] which was given to the *Versammlung deutscher Naturforscher und Ärtze* in Stettin in September 1863. Although Darwin's *Origin of Species* was translated as early as 1860,[6] it took a few years for German intellectuals to assimilate and appreciate it. Häckel's lecture marks the breakthrough for the public reception of Darwinism, which soon dominated discussion about materialism. Because we cannot do full justice to the entire dispute, we shall focus here upon the classical phase alone.

2. THE CONTROVERSY BEGINS: WAGNER VERSUS VOGT

We can assign a definite time and place for the beginning of the materialism controversy. It began September 18, 1854, in Göttingen. It was then and there that Rudolph Wagner (1805–64), the head of the Physiological Institute at Göttingen, gave his opening address to the thirty-first *Versammlung deutscher Naturforscher und Ärzte*. Wagner's address, entitled *Menschenschöpfung und Seelensubstanz*,[7] was an ad hoc piece that he had hurriedly and reluctantly thrown together just days before the conference at the request of some of its leading participants. It was only fitting and proper, they believed, for the host to hold the opening address. They soon got far more than they had bargained for.

For his address, Wagner chose a topic from anthropology that he hoped would interest everyone: the origin of man and his fate after death. He wanted to pose the question whether the latest

5 See Ernst Häckel, "Über die Entwicklungslehre Darwins," in *Gemeinver-ständliche Vorträge und Abhandlungen aus dem Gebiet der Entwicklungslehre*, Zweite Auflage (Bonn: Emil Strauß, 1902), I, 1–34. On the importance of Häckel's speech, see Robert Richards, *The Tragic Sense of Life: Ernst Haeckel and the Struggle over Evolutionary Thought* (Chicago: University of Chicago Press, 2008), pp. 93–104.

6 Darwin's book appeared first in England in 1859. See Charles Darwin, *On the Origin of Species* (London: John Murray, 1859). It was translated by Heinrich Georg Bronn as *Über die Entstehung der Arten im Tier- und Pflanzenreich durch natürlich Züchtung* (Stuttgart: Schweizerbart, 1860).

7 Rudolph Wagner, *Menschenschöpfung und Seelensubstanz. Ein anthropolo-gischer Vortrag, gehalten in der ersten öffentlichen Sitzung der 31 Versammlung deutscher Naturforscher und Ärtze zu Göttingen am 18. Sept. 1854* (Göttingen: Wigand, 1854).

scientific research had been able to shed any light on these ancient questions. Regarding the origin of man, it was his personal view, he openly confessed, that the latest research had not been able to demonstrate or refute the biblical doctrine that all human beings came from an original single pair. There were some anthropologists who held that, given the variety of human races, there must have been different original pairs, an Adam and Eve for each race; but they could not find convincing evidence for their views. All the latest research was still consistent with biblical doctrine, which therefore should remain inviolate. Regarding the fate of man after death, Wagner asked what recent scientific research had to say about the human soul and its possible immortality. He deplored how the mind had ceased to be sacred and how it had become instead the object of growing research in physiology and psychology. And here he believed he had to issue a warning about the direction of that research. Some physiologists were inclined toward materialism, so that they not only doubted but denied the immortality of the soul and free will. The problem with this new materialism, Wagner intoned, is that it undermines the beliefs necessary for moral and political order. The Christian doctrine of providence, according to which the virtuous are rewarded and the vicious punished, rests on the beliefs in immortality and free will. Whoever wants to uphold morality and religion among the masses should strive to protect these beliefs at all costs. Wagner then closed his address with a passionate plea: consider, natural scientists, where your research is heading! Refrain, at all costs, from spreading doctrines damaging to morals, religion, and the state!

Wagner's address aroused intense interest and heated debate. Within weeks, it had sold more than three thousand copies, brisk sales for an academic address. But this was only Wagner's first salvo in his long-planned holy war against materialism. Only a few weeks after the conference, he published another pamphlet, *Ueber Wissen und Glauben*,[8] which stated his general position regarding the basic issue of reason versus faith. Wagner reaffirmed his thesis that the latest results of scientific research give no evidence against belief in

8 Rudolph Wagner, *Ueber Wissen und Glauben. Fortsetzung der Betrachtungen über Menschenschöpfung und Seelensubstanz* (Göttingen: Wigand, 1854).

immorality. While there is no proof for this belief, there is also no proof against it, so that the believer is free to keep his faith with no fear that science contradicts him. Wagner then put forward his main rationale for this point: the double-truth doctrine of Protestantism. According to that doctrine, faith and reason operate in separate spheres; no conflict occurs as long as each stays within its boundaries. Faith should not pronounce on matters of science, which we can determine only through observation and experiment; but nor should science presume on matters of faith, which we know only through the Bible, the record of divine revelation. Like a true Protestant, Wagner held that faith is not simply a matter of belief, of assent to an abstract proposition, but, as Luther and Calvin taught, an immediate experience. Faith gives us knowledge of supernatural things just as reason does for natural things; and just as a blind man should not presume to judge what he cannot see, so the nonbelieving natural scientist should not dare to doubt what the Christian sees through "the eyes of faith." Although Wagner stressed the importance of keeping science and faith in their respective spheres, he admitted that there were "points of contact" between them and that in some cases conflict was inevitable. These cases concerned issues about the origins of things or matters of historical revelation. For example, the Bible states that the Earth was only thousands of years old; but geological and historical evidence indicates that it is much older. Who, in such cases, are we to believe? Science or faith? Wagner advised "double bookkeeping," i.e., assigning apparently contradictory views to different ledgers.

From afar, the proceedings of the Göttingen conference were watched closely by a young journalist in exile in Italy, Carl Vogt (1817–95). A corpulent and angry young man with a savage wit, Vogt was one of the most brilliant scientists of his generation. Having studied chemistry with Justus Liebig in Gießen in the 1830s, Vogt had received a doctorate in medicine and then gradually moved into journalism. He had acquired a reputation for himself in the 1840s by publishing some popular books on geology and physiology.[9] These works had revealed a growing sympathy for

---

9 Carl Vogt, *Ocean und Mittelmeer. Reisebriefe* (Frankfurt am Main: Literarische Anstalt, 1848), 2 vols.; *Bilder aus dem Thierleben* (Frankfurt: Literarische Anstalt,

materialism in their affirmation of a complete naturalism and their denial of creation *ex nihilo*.[10] A man of decidedly left-wing political views, Vogt had hung out with Bakunin and Proudhon in Paris in the early 1840s and engaged in revolutionary activity in Berne in 1846. In 1848 he was elected as a member to the Frankfurt Parliament, where he stood on the extreme left of the Assembly. Predictably, Vogt's radical views got him into trouble, and after the collapse of the Revolution he found himself dismissed from his post in Gießen. From his exile in Italy, he would rage against the German establishment, especially its universities. No one represented the worst side of that establishment, in Vogt's bilious view, than one professor in Göttingen: Rudolph Wagner. In his *Bilder aus dem Thierleben* Vogt singled out Wagner as the worst German science had to offer, a superstitious theist whose beliefs set limits to his research.[11] Vogt's remarks were not unprovoked but a response to an article of Wagner's published in the *Allgemeine Zeitung*, where he took Vogt to task for his "crass materialism."[12] In his opening address, Wagner cited passages from Vogt's *Physiologische Briefe* to the effect that there is no free will, that the mind is nothing more than brain activity, and that there is no such thing as the immortality of the soul.[13] He especially took exception to a provocative analogy of Vogt: that thought is to the brain as urine is to the kidneys.[14]

After hearing about Wagner's address, Vogt became enraged. Wagner had the nerve to use a public podium to attack him when he was not there to defend himself! Although Wagner promised

---

1852); and *Physiologische Briefe für Gebildete aller Stände. Zweite vermehrte und verbesserte Auflage* (Gießen: Ricker, 1853).

10   See Vogt, *Ocean und Mittelmeer*, pp. 9–26.

11   See Vogt, *Bilder aus dem Thierleben*, p. 367.

12   Rudolph Wagner, "Physiologie, Psychologie und christliche Weltanschauung," *Allgemeine Zeitung*, Nr. 20, Dienstag, 20. Januar 1852 Beilage, pp. 313–15.

13   Ibid., p. 314; Wagner, *Menschenschöpfung und Seelensubstanz*, pp. 20–21. In neither piece does Wagner mention Vogt or his work by name. The passages he cites are in Vogt, *Physiologische Briefe* (2nd edition), pp. 322–23, 626–27.

14   Vogt, *Physiologische Briefe* (2nd ed.), p. 323. Vogt's dictum goes back to the French materialist Pierre Cabanis, with whom Vogt studied in Paris. See Cabanis, *Rapports du Physique et du Moral de l'Homme*, in *Œuvres complètes* (Paris: Bossange, 1823), III, 19.

in a later session to discuss the materiality of the soul, he abruptly canceled it, claiming that he was suffering from "a sudden cold." To Vogt, that was the excuse of a coward. He resolved that Wagner would not escape so easily. Now that Wagner had thrown down the gauntlet, Vogt would pick it up and pursue him relentlessly. And so, in a few heated and inspired weeks in the autumn of 1854, Vogt wrote a blistering and brilliant polemic against Wagner, his *Köhlerglaube und Wissenschaft*, which first appeared in 1855.[15]

The first part of Vogt's tract is a vicious personal attack on Wagner's moral and intellectual integrity. It indicts Wagner for his sloppiness as a scientist, for allowing his personal beliefs to interfere with his research, and for his temerity in taking credit for publications for which he had done little or nothing. The second part addresses the major intellectual issues raised by Wagner. Vogt found Wagner's distinction between the realms of science and faith utterly artificial and arbitrary. There is overwhelming empirical evidence *against* the two beliefs Wagner was so eager to protect: that all humanity originated from a single original couple and that there is an immaterial soul. Regarding the first belief, all the evidence from geography and anatomy reveals such differences between the human races, Vogt contended, that each must have had its own original pair; it is also evident from geology that the age of the Earth is much older than anything said in the Bible and that human beings originated much earlier than four thousand years ago. So, rather than standing inviolate above empirical falsification, as Wagner declared, the biblical doctrines are flatly contrary to the facts, in which case it is clear that one has to side with science against them. Regarding the belief in an immaterial soul, the latest physiological research gives no evidence whatsoever for the existence of a soul separate from the brain, Vogt argued. On the contrary, it shows how closely mental activity is tied to brain functions. If the brain were severely injured, mental activity would cease; and it is even possible to identify specific parts of the brain that are used for specific mental functions. While Vogt admitted that it is difficult to explain how brain processes give rise to consciousness

15 See Carl Vogt, *Köhlerglaube und Wissenschaft: Eine Streitschrift gegen Hofrath Wagner in Göttingen* (Gießen: Ricker, 1855).

and mental events, he insisted that all the evidence indicates the utter dependence of consciousness upon brain processes. Given such a fact, it is not likely that human beings possess an immortal soul that somehow survives the death of the body. Against all Wagner's warnings, Vogt declared that he had no fear in drawing the appropriate conclusions from all these facts: that these religious beliefs are nothing but superstitions. To uphold such beliefs, when they are contrary to all the plain evidence of science, is to take a desperate leap into the irrational.

Lying just underneath the surface of Vogt's dispute with Wagner was their clashing politics. While Vogt was a radical who had fought for democracy in Bern and Frankfurt, Wagner was a reactionary whose fondest hope was to maintain monarchic rule. It was indeed telling that, at the close of his speech, Wagner cited, and vowed to uphold, the political testament of a leading conservative statesman and publicist: Joseph Maria von Radowitz (1793–1853). The politics of Vogt and Wagner were decisive for their philosophical positions. Wagner wanted *to uphold* the beliefs in providence and immortality to legitimate the monarchy and to control "the dechristianized masses." Vogt intended *to undermine* these beliefs because they were an ideological weapon to control the people, a veil of deception to prevent them from taking control over their lives in a new democratic order. Thus the dispute between Vogt and Wagner was not only philosophical but also political. It was indeed a battle between two complete worldviews, a life-and-death struggle of the materialism of the left against the theism of the right.

Given its explosive beginning, it should not be surprising that the materialism controversy spread rapidly. Vogt's personal spat with Wagner was only the beginning of a much longer and more complex controversy, one which would eventually pull every major thinker in Germany into its vortex. As it happened, Wagner's warning backfired. Rather than frightening the materialists, it provoked them. Out of their closets they came, now marching headstrong, banners waving, in a thick phalanx to challenge the establishment. 1855, the very year Vogt published *Köhlerglaube und Wissenschaft*, also witnessed the appearance of two mighty materialist tomes: Heinrich Czolbe's *Neue Darstellung des Sensualismus* and Ludwig Büchner's *Kraft und Stoff.* What Vogt had announced in a polemical context—that the natural sciences are heading inevitably toward materialism—Czolbe and Büchner would now defend in a more general and systematic manner. These works laid out the basic principles for a materialist worldview, which claimed that it is based on nothing less than the latest scientific research. Thus Wagner's worst nightmare had become reality. The sons of Lucretius were now dancing on the streets of Germany!

3. PHILOSOPHICAL STRUWWELPETER

Sitting in the audience of the 31st Assembly that September day was a shy and taciturn man who listened to Wagner's speech with growing apprehension. The more Wagner spoke, the more he shrank into his seat. The last thing he wanted was to get involved in controversy. That would deprive him of the privacy and tranquility he needed to work! But there was Wagner on the podium attempting to enlist him in his crusade against materialism. In his speech Wagner cited a long passage from his latest work,[16] as if its content should frighten off any materialist. The man to whom Wagner referred, this reluctant recruit to his antimaterialist campaign, was an up-and-coming professor of philosophy in Göttingen: Hermann Lotze (1817–81). Though then little known, he would eventually make his mark in German intellectual history, becoming one of the most famous philosophers of the nineteenth century. The crucible for his mature philosophy came from the materialism controversy.

Lotze had good reason to stand back from Wagner's crusade. He did not share Wagner's worldview, viz., its Christian fundamentalism, its belief in the divisibility of the soul, its doctrine of "double bookkeeping." To be sure, Lotze had been a critic of materialism; but he was never a champion of Wagner's brand of vitalist physiology. In a famous early article,[17] much celebrated by mate-

---

16 Wagner cites verbatim from Lotze's *Medicinische Psychologie* (Leipzig: Weidmann, 1852), sec. 18, p. 30. See Wagner's *Menschenschöpfung und Seelensubstanz*, pp. 19–20.

17 Hermann Lotze, "Leben, Lebenskraft," in Rudolph Wagner, ed., *Handwörterbuch der Physiologie* (Braunschweig: Vieweg, 1842), pp. ix–lvii.

rialists, he attacked the vitalist doctrine of *Lebenskraft*, according to which organic growth is directed by a nonmaterial agency. A force is not a special quality inherent in objects, Lotze argued, but it is only the hypostasis of the general name we give for the lawful interactions between things. Yet Wagner, in his desperate bid for allies in his forthcoming struggle against materialism, had chosen to ignore Lotze's earlier position. It was a shrewd strategy, for, as it happened, his appeal to Lotze on the podium that day proved successful. For the materialists now saw Lotze as their most formidable foe, as indeed Wagner's henchman. In a metaphor that he would never live down, Vogt branded Lotze "a speculative Struwwelpeter,"[18] i.e., that naughty boy with wildly overgrown fingernails and absurdly long red hair used to scare German children into good grooming habits.

So, willy-nilly, Lotze had been dragged into the materialism controversy. Not wanting to be stereotyped by Wagner or the materialists, he had no choice but to enter the fray and make his own position clear. And so, for much of the next decade of his career, Lotze would spend most of his time and energy formulating his own position, which he conceived as a middle path between the extremes of vitalism and materialism. The culmination of his efforts was his *Mikrokosmus*, a massive three-volume work, which appeared from 1856 to 1864.[19] *Mikrokosmus* became one of the most widely read philosophical works in the second half of the nineteenth century. It went through six editions, and it was translated into as many languages.

Mikrokosmus was Lotze's grand attempt to resolve the conflict between science and faith made apparent during the materialism controversy.[20] Lotze regarded that conflict as "an unnecessary tor-

---

18 Vogt, *Köhlerglaube und Wissenschaft* (4th ed.), p. 91, note.

19 Hermann Lotze, *Mikrokosmus. Ideen zur Naturgeschichte und Geschichte der Menschheit. Versuch einer Anthropologie* (Leipzig: Hirzel, 1856–64), 3 vols. All references in parentheses in the text will be to the fourth edition, which appeared from 1884 to 1888. Volume numbers are designated by Roman numerals. For a fuller account of Lotze's intentions and arguments in *Mikrokosmus*, see my *Late German Idealism* (Oxford: Oxford University Press, 2013), pp. 239–83.

20 See Lotze's self-advertisement for the work, *Göttingische gelehrte Anzeigen*, Stück 199 (1856), 1977–92.

ment" because he believed it resolvable in principle. A profound optimist, he was confident that there could be a middle path between a scientific materialism and an irrational leap of faith. This *via media* would be a new metaphysics, one that would fully recognize the claims of science to investigate all of nature but also one that would provide a foundation for our moral, religious, and aesthetic beliefs, so that they are free from the mythology and anthropomorphism of the past, and so that they are consistent with the methods of the new sciences. The task of *Mikrokosmus* was to expound and defend this new metaphysics.

It is essential to the solution of this conflict, Lotze insisted, that one recognize the powers as well as the limits of science. Science has the power to explain, at least in principle, all the phenomena of the natural world according to laws of cause and effect. These powers hold as much for the organic as inorganic realm. We should strive for mechanical explanations in physiology and psychology, and we should never impose artificial limits on inquiry for moral or religious reasons. Nevertheless, Lotze also emphasized the *limits* of science, claiming that its mechanical methods ultimately play only a small role in understanding the universe as a whole. As he summed up his position on mechanism at the very end of *Mikrokosmus*: "the validity of mechanism is limitless but its meaning everywhere only subordinate" (III, 618). Mechanism is *limitless* because it can explain everything in the natural world, but it is valid only in that world; it cannot understand everything in the universe because there is also a realm of value, without which we would never grasp the purpose and meaning of things. Mechanism has only a *subordinate* meaning, because the entire realm of cause and effect is subject to the realm of values, which comprise the purposes for which all of nature exists.

The solution to the conflict also involved, Lotze stressed, recognizing the validity and limits of faith. There could be no return to the old anthropocentric metaphysics of the past, no retreat to the old mythological conceptions of traditional theism. The old religion and metaphysics cannot stand up to the progress of scientific inquiry, and it is therefore necessary that we abandon it, no matter how hard this might be. It is as important to rethink our morality and religion, Lotze taught, so that it is at least consistent with the scientific view of the world. Still, for all its weakness, the old moral and religious conception of the world was profoundly correct in one important respect: it saw the significance of values for our understanding of the world. Without value, all of existence would have neither purpose nor meaning.

Lotze's requirements for a solution to the conflict between reason and faith were of a tall order, and indeed apparently contradictory. On the one hand, it was an essential part of his strategy that there be a clear distinction between the realms of nature and value. While science could explain everything within nature, it still could not account for the dimension of value, which is necessary to understand the meaning and purpose of existence. On the other hand, however, Lotze insisted that a complete resolution of the conflict should not leave us with dualism, a schism between utterly separate realms. He rejected Wagner's doctrine of double bookkeeping on the grounds that it would leave us with "an intellectual schizophrenia." Instead, Lotze stood first and foremost for a monistic vision of the world, a single unifying conception according to which the realms of nature and value are integrally united and form a single whole. Somehow, then, the solution to the conflict would have to perform the apparently impossible: it would have to distinguish yet unify the realms of nature and value.

Lotze was confident that his new metaphysics could perform these apparently conflicting tasks. His metaphysics was a form of teleological monism, which he at first called "teleological idealism" but later "spiritualism." According to this metaphysics, the entire realm of nature forms a single indivisible whole which is governed by ends, so that everything exists for a purpose. While everything in nature happens according to mechanical laws, so that mechanism holds complete sway over it, these laws are only means for the realization of ends, which are the realization of goodness and beauty. There is no conflict between the mechanical and teleological order of things, because ends never interrupt or interfere with the working of mechanism; these ends indeed *require* mechanism, which is the necessary means for their realization. Lotze rejected, therefore, the old religious conception of teleology, according to which purposes stand outside nature and can suspend or interfere with its operations. His own teleological idealism, he was convinced, could both unite yet separate the spheres of nature and value: unite them, because mechanism is the tool of cosmic purposes; and separate them, because value, in the form of purposes or ends, is not reducible to mechanism.

In advocating such an idealism, Lotze was self-consciously attempting to preserve the metaphysics of the romantic and idealist traditions. He wanted to defend the view of the universe as an organic living whole, as a beautiful work of art, the monistic vitalism or vitalistic monism that appears in the works of Schelling, Hegel, and the romantics. Lotze was first and foremost a neo-romantic or late idealist. Although he knew all too well that Romanticism and idealism were fading into history, he saw it as his goal to preserve and protect their legacy against the advent of materialism. Still, like a true post-Hegelian, Lotze did not share the methodological precepts of his romantic and idealist predecessors. He rejected intellectual intuitions, a priori constructions, or dialectical reasoning as a method of knowing the world. In a new scientific age, the romantic and idealist visions of the world would have to be placed on a new foundation: the latest scientific research, the strictest conformity to the logic of the sciences.

The metaphysics that Lotze defends in *Mikrokosmus* is different from its romantic and idealist forebears in several respects, primarily in the broader place it assigns to mechanism in the cosmos. Lotze's earlier critical stance toward vitalist physiology continues in *Mikrokosmus*. He regards mechanism as the chief form of scientific explanation, and he maintains that it is sufficient to explain all living as well as nonliving phenomena. Life does not distinguish itself from nonlife by conforming to a distinct kind of law, still less by the possession of a unique kind of power, but only by a specific form of organization; yet its unique form of organization is just as explicable according to mechanical laws as all other events in nature (I, 58). We can account for growth and reproduction, Lotze contends, simply by the interaction of the parts of an organism, so that there is no reason to assume that there is some force or idea acting within it (I, 69, 72–74, 75, 78–79, 83). The first volume of *Mikrokosmus* closes with an adamant affirmation of mechanism, with what Lotze calls its "first commandment": just as we are to have no gods before us but one, so we are to have no other form of explanation of finite being before us but mechanism (I, 451).

Although Lotze was eager to defend the rule of mechanism over the natural world, he never ceased to maintain that mechanism also has its limits. There are two fundamental problems with a strictly mechanical conception of the universe as a whole. First, it could not explain why things existed in the first place. Even if the scientist could explain organic reproduction and growth on the basis of mechanical laws, he could not explain why there is life in the first place. Second, though mechanism held entirely for the realm of nature, it could not explain the dimension of value, which alone accounts for the meaning and purpose of things.

Lotze also never saw his affirmation of mechanism as an endorsement of materialism. On no account did he accept the thesis that all scientific explanation leads to materialism. To explain something mechanically, he argued, does not mean that it has to be a material thing, i.e., something whose essence consists in inertia or extension. Lotze saw mechanism chiefly as a thesis about a form of explanation, not as a thesis about the nature of things. The mechanist's central thesis is that we can explain all phenomena through causal laws, where the laws are formulable in some hypothetical-deductive form and where the cause consists in prior events in time. But the mechanist, he insisted, sticks to the data of experience, and he is completely neutral about the inner identity of things, about what they might be in themselves (II, 36, 37–38). It is therefore perfectly consistent with mechanism, Lotze contends, for the mechanist to hold that the ultimate elements of things consist in immaterial forces or points (I, 37–41; II, 33).

Lotze's response to the threat of materialism is to deprive matter of its basic reality (I, 397–405). Rigorous reflection on the logic of the sciences shows us, he contends, not that matter is fundamental but that it is the product of the more basic realities. Lotze maintains that there are two sides to matter: its outer and inner side. Its outer side consists in its spatial properties, its extension in space as it appears to our senses; but its inner side consists in forces, which are not themselves spatial. Matter is for Lotze, as it was for Leibniz, to whom he alludes at one point (I, 406), simply a secondary or derived reality, a *phenomenon bene fundata*.

Following Leibniz, Lotze maintains that space is essentially divisible and that a specific space arises from the aggregation of more simple units, which are themselves forces; when a series of such units is added together and laid alongside one another, the result is a specific space or place. Space is not a primitive or basic property of matter, for the simple reason that it is necessary to ask why a body fills a space or occupies a place; and the reason lies in the body possessing a force of resistance, a power to repel any other body from taking its place (I, 402–3). Space as a whole then arises from a system of bodies resisting and attracting one another; it is the product of the interaction of their inner forces of attraction and repulsion (I, 403). The net effect of Lotze's argument, then, is that space is epiphenomenal, the product of particular things interacting with one another. But if space is epiphenomenal, so is the entire world of material objects whose essential properties are spatial.

For all his loyalty to the romantic and idealist traditions, Lotze began to distinguish his own metaphysics from them in *Mikrokosmus*. He disapproved of the idealist's homogeneous or undifferentiated monism, which did not attribute enough reality to individual things within the single universal substance. The monism of Spinoza, which Schelling and Hegel adopted, had to be supplemented, Lotze believed, with the principle of individuality of Leibniz, according to which each individual has its own unique idea or substantial form. He also disliked the idealist's impersonal conception of the absolute, which made the universe an impersonal and indifferent thing, operating according to cold and bloodless laws. Finally, he insisted that idealism alone cannot be sufficient to explain the universe, because ideas on their own are simply inert and static structures, lacking the force or energy for their realization. To avoid these difficulties, Lotze argued, we need a conception of the single universal substance that is personal, active, and pluralistic, allowing for the wealth of universal forms. He called such a metaphysics "spiritualism," because it stressed the personal, active, and individual qualities of spirit. Toward the end of *Mikrokosmus* Lotze revealed his own personal credo, his belief that the single spiritual force behind the cosmos was nothing less than love. It was a remarkably romantic confession—Schiller had made it some fifty years earlier[21]—but also a remarkably personal one not likely to convince a tough-minded materialist. But the vulnerability of Lotze's metaphysics did not really lie with the personal confession of its author. That credo was noble and sublime, even if it was indemonstrable. The weakness of Lotze's metaphysics lay more with his method, his claim to base his metaphysics on science. Like his late idealist counterparts, Trendelenburg and Hartmann, Lotze assumed that the latest scientific investigations would confirm rather than refute his organic vision of the world. That was a perfectly plausible strategy when Lotze began writing *Mikrokosmus* in the early 1850s; but by the 1860s he would have to reckon with Darwinism, which was a great challenge to Lotze's teleological worldview. Upon the urging of Wagner, Lotze began to reckon with Darwin in later editions of his book; but, claiming that he had already refuted such naturalism, his efforts were only half-hearted. Lotze, it must be said, failed to appreciate the new challenges presented by Darwin.

Today Lotze's teleological and monistic metaphysics appears dated, no less obsolete than the idealist and romantic traditions it so bravely and so desperately attempted to preserve. Nevertheless, one important aspect of his philosophy lingers to this day. In the course of his struggle against materialism, Lotze made an important distinction between the sphere of existence and that of value, validity, or truth.[22] He sometimes formulated this distinction in terms of two kinds of questions: "What exists?" (*Was ist?*) and "What is valid or valuable?" (*Was gilt?*). We must distinguish, he wrote, between the existence and the validity of things. The relation between contents of representations is valid or true, even if these contents refer to nothing that exists, and even if no one ever thought of them. This point applies especially well to mathematical truths, but it extends no less, Lotze insisted, to all truths about

---

21 See Schiller's "Theosophie des jungen Julius," in his *Philosophische Briefe*, in *Werke, Nationalausgabe*, ed. Benno von Wiese (Weimar: Böhlaus Nachfolger, 1962), XX, 107–29, esp. 119–22.

22 The locus classicus for this distinction is Book III, chapters 2–4, of Lotze's *Logik*. See *System der Philosophie: Erster Theil: Drei Bücher der Logik* (Leipzig: Hirzel, 1874), I, 465–97.

content, even empirical ones (e.g., "Red is different from black"). Such propositions are true, he observed, on whatever occasion we think of them, and indeed even if no one thinks of them. There is a realm of objective truth, then, independent of the existence of the external world, so that skepticism about that world proves to be an epistemic irrelevance. Lotze then went on to argue that this was the point Plato attempted to make with his world of forms. Plato did not really think that these forms have an existence of their own, and he was far from hypostasizing them; his only point was that their validity is independent of the changing realm of existence. It was this Platonic realm of validity—"the most wonderful fact in the world," as Lotze called it—that proved an intoxicating discovery for the new generation. This was the fount from which the young Brentano, Cohen, Husserl, Windelband, Rickert, Lask, and Frege would drink. In their revelry in the discovery of this new world they gratefully acknowledged themselves to be the heirs of old Lotze.

4. THE BIBLE OF MATERIALISM

If Lotze's *Mikrokosmus* was the chief statement of idealism during the materialism controversy, Ludwig Büchner's *Kraft und Stoff* was the main manifesto of materialism.[23] Büchner's work, which became known as "the Bible of materialism," proved even more popular than Lotze's. First published in 1855, at the beginning of the controversy, it went through no fewer than twenty-one editions, and it was translated into seventeen languages.

Kraft und Stoff was so successful not least because of its simple and plain exposition. Aiming at the general public, Büchner focused on basic principles and laid aside argumentative subtleties. Because of the lack of technicality, many critics dismissed him as a poor philosopher; but they failed to understand his intentions. Büchner had deliberately refrained from technicality, partly because of his audience and partly because he had no faith in abstract

23 Ludwig Büchner, *Kraft und Stoff oder Grundzüge der natürlichen Weltordnung*, 21st ed. (Leipzig: Theodore Thomas, 1904). The first edition appeared in 1855 with Meidiger Verlag, Frankfurt. All references in parentheses are to the 1904 edition.

reasoning. Philosophical argument was for Büchner a relic of scholasticism, an antiquated methodology that should be replaced with the observation and experiment of science.

For Büchner, like all materialists, the world consists in nothing more than matter in motion. But what is matter? Directly tackling that hoary question, Büchner immediately declares in his first chapter that matter has to be understood through two basic concepts: stuff (*Stoff*) and force (*Kraft*) (3–9). These concepts are interdependent, he insists. We cannot have stuff without force because stuff consists in, and manifests itself as, force, i.e., in attracting and repelling other pieces of stuff. If we were to separate stuff from its particular ways of moving and acting, we would reify a mere abstraction. But we also cannot have force without stuff, because force cannot exist on its own but must act in and through some thing. Force can no more exist without stuff, Büchner says, than seeing without an eye. Electricity, magnetism, and heat are paradigmatic forces; but they are just abstractions on their own because they have a determinate meaning only as the specific ways of acting of bodies. Because stuff and force are interdependent, Büchner makes his mantra: "*Keine Kraft ohne Stoff—kein Stoff ohne Kraft.*"

Büchner is eager to dispel the old Cartesian cloud hanging over materialism, which still cast a dark shadow in his day. According to the Cartesian tradition, matter consists in nothing more than extension; and it is inert, moving only if another body moves against it. Thus all motion is entirely mechanical, the product of one body acting upon another. The whole universe is then nothing more than a vast machine, void of life and energy. This was the common image of materialism shared by Goethe and the romantics, which made the doctrine seem so gloomy and unappealing. Büchner, however, insists that we get beyond such outdated and inaccurate stereotypes. His materialism was from not the Cartesian but the *vital* materialist tradition,[24] which had an underground existence for more than a century among free-thinkers and philosophes. According to this

---

24 On this tradition, see John Yolton, *Thinking Matter: Materialism in Eighteenth-Century Britian* (Minneapolis: University of Minnesota Press, 1983); and Margaret C. Jacob, *The Radical Enlightenment: Pantheists, Freemasons and Republicans* (London: George, Allen & Unwin, 1987).

tradition, force and motion are essential to matter, and extension and inertia only derivative, the result of the interaction of repulsive and expansive forces. Matter is indeed self-organizing, having the power to form diverse elements into a unified whole (75–80). Life, therefore, is not a force alien to matter but inherent in it.

Recognizing that form and motion are inherent in matter is a crucial step toward explaining the origin of life itself, Büchner argues. The dualism between life and matter arises only when we insist on retaining the old Cartesian conception of matter as inert extension. If, however, we reject that conception, if we see form and motion as implicit and potential within matter, that dualism breaks down, so that we can restore the *lex continui* between the material and living worlds. Life does not consist in an immaterial power, nor does it have sui generis laws, Büchner argues, but it is the result of the combination of chemical and physical powers (366). The basic materials of organic things are the same as the inorganic, because they have the same chemical components. If organic beings have properties different from inorganic, that is only because of the special characteristics of their chemical constitution (368). In stressing the material basis of life, Büchner points out how the French chemist Pierre Bertholet (1827–1907) managed to concoct hydrocarbons, the basic building blocks of life, by combining carbon and hydrogen (374). The net result of Bertholet's work, Büchner believes, is that there is no fundamental difference between the organic and inorganic. Any difference between them is one of complexity or degree but not of substance or kind.

In advancing his materialism, Büchner took careful aim at the teleological conception of nature, which had been so central to the idealist worldview. Teleology he rejects as a completely anthropomorphic conception of the universe. The only reason that the idealists postulate a realm of ends, he argues, is because they remain stuck in the Cartesian concept of matter. They artificially separate matter from its form because they ignore the historical process by which form and order evolve from the forces inherent in matter (181). The idealist's classic objection against materialism is that it attributes too great a role to chance, which alone cannot produce the order of things. But that objection fails to see, Büchner argues, that what we now call accident or chance is really the product of necessity working its way through history, the result of a long chain of events and circumstances which we have not fully understood (187). Because he ignores natural history, the teleologist poses a false dilemma: either design or chance. But, Büchner insists, there is something in between: the gradual development of order in the natural causes of things through natural selection and the struggle for existence.

While it seemed plausible to explain life on Büchner's materialist principles, consciousness and self-consciousness created much greater difficulties. Like Vogt, Büchner stressed the dependence of mental activity on the brain. The soul is only a collective term, he maintained, for all the different activities of the brain and the nervous system (250). That said, Büchner admitted that Vogt went too far in equating thought with urine (252). The comparison was inappropriate, he conceded, because there is no analogy between urine and thought. Urine is waste, a palpable and weighable substance; but thought is not waste; nor is it palpable and weighable. Having laid that embarrassing metaphor aside, Büchner then felt confident enough to put forward his own rather speculative theory about the relationship between thought and the brain. The secret of thought lies not in the brain material as such, he explained, but in the special manner of its organization and its function in achieving goals (253). Thinking must be seen as a special form of natural motion, more specifically as the motion of the central nervous system, which consists in a form of electricity (257). Psychic activity in general, Büchner theorized, is really nothing more than "the emission of a movement between the cells of the cerebral cortex stimulated by external impressions" (254). Following this line of thought, Büchner then put forward definitions of consciousness and self-consciousness. Consciousness is "the execution, performance or expression of activity of certain parts or structures of the brain" (267), while self-consciousness is nothing more than "the total sum of our sensations or their aggregation, the serialization of images stored in memory" (259).

It was a central objective of *Kraft und Stoff* to bury once and for all the worldview of Christianity. Accordingly, many passages are devoted to a critique of the existence of God, miracles, free will, and personal immortality. The critique comes not from an examination of the traditional arguments in behalf of these dogmas but in showing how they are incompatible with natural science. In the great battle between reason and faith, Büchner does not attempt to reconcile faith with reason; rather, faith, at least in its chief historical forms, is deliberately demolished in the name of reason. There are passages where Büchner seems to make some concessions to the tender consciences of believers, where he allows for something of a distinction between faith and reason (94); but these concessions are more apparent than real, for Büchner insists that reason is constantly encroaching on and diminishing the domain of faith. Belief is for those who cannot accept the truth; but in science only truth is the guide. *Kraft und Stoff* was meant to be an instruction manual for the tough-minded.

The materialist concept of matter, Büchner argues, forbids the theist's belief in a creation *ex nihilo*. Such a creation presupposes that there could be a superforce independent of matter that creates it out of nothing. But since force cannot exist without matter, no force can create matter (9). Matter is indeed eternal and indestructible (15). Modern chemistry teaches us, Büchner maintains, that the birth and death of organic forms do not come from the creation and annihilation of new material; instead, there is a constant recycling of the same basic matter, whose quantity and constitution remain forever the same (16). Birth and death involve a reorganization of the same elements, which do not themselves change. Atoms are in constant motion, and they change constantly in their combinations with other atoms; but they change only in their combinations and each retains its basic nature (17–18). Appealing to recent work on the conservation of energy,[25] Büchner argues that force is no less eternal than matter itself. Force or energy can assume many different forms, but it cannot be increased or diminished and only its individual forms can change.

The eternity of matter and force means, Büchner explains, that there cannot be any such thing as personal immortality. Rather than speaking of the mortal body and the immortal soul, we should say just the opposite (19). The soul or mind, which consists

---

25 Büchner, *Kraft und Stoff*, pp. 23–24. Büchner refers to the work of Friedrich Mohr, Robert Mayer, and James Joule.

in nothing more than an organization of material parts, ceases to exist when that organization disappears; the parts, however, remain forever. Since the mind cannot exist without the brain, and since the brain dies and decays like any other part of the body, we have no reason to think that the mind survives physical death (342–43). It is pointless trying to defend personal immortality on the basis of the conservation of matter and energy, Büchner contends, because, though the whole cycle of nature is stable and constant, the same is not so for the particular phenomena in it (344). While force itself cannot be destroyed, the soul, as the product of a definite combination of matter and force, eventually disappears (344–45). Büchner also thinks that it is pointless, as Kant had once done, to defend personal immortality on ethical grounds alone. True to his Epicurean roots, he insists that the idea of annihilation is more comforting than that of immortality; only annihilation gives the prospect of eternal peace (349–50).

Büchner's materialism is a thoroughgoing naturalism, according to which everything that exists falls within nature alone. This naturalism therefore prohibits the existence of any realm above and beyond nature, whether that realm consists in Platonic forms or pure spirits (93). The realm of nature is governed strictly by laws, which determine everything that happens in it (84). A law of nature does not stand outside or above nature, as if it were prescribed by some creator, but it is only an expression for the patterns of activity of material things (82). Since form and organization are inherent in matter, it obeys only its own laws, not those some creator imposed upon it. Since nothing takes place in nature except according to these laws of matter, everything happens of necessity and cannot be otherwise (84). This means, Büchner argues, that we must abandon two old religious dogmas: miracles and free will. Büchner is willing to allow a limited form of free will when it is understood only as acting on our own wants; but he prohibits any form that implies either spontaneity, the power to begin a series of events uncaused, or the power to do otherwise (399–400). After we have finally abandoned the belief in such freedom, Büchner concludes, we will look upon criminal proceedings as people now look upon witchcraft trials (402). Madame de Staël was right: to understand an action is to pardon it.

Büchner discusses the idea of God only toward the close of *Kraft und Stoff*, where it receives a brief and brutal treatment. It is a great mistake to think, Büchner contends, that the idea of God is innate or natural. The anthropological evidence is overwhelming that many peoples of the world have created great civilizations and moral ways of life without belief in God (324–25). Buddhism and Confucianism, two of the major religions of the world, contain no such belief but demand of their followers only the strictest moral conduct (406). While Büchner rejects theism as little more than superstition, it is noteworthy that he also has no time for pantheism (340). If we should not place God above the world, he says, neither should we place him within it. The problem with pantheism is that it cannot overcome the problem of evil any more than theism can. Indeed, pantheism makes evil part of the very nature of God, which is even worse than making God the cause of evil (341).

Although Büchner rejects the ideas of God, freedom, and immortality, on which so much traditional Christian ethics rests, he declines to be the crusader for a new morals. His task, as he sees it, is only a critical one: to free mankind from superstition and illusion. He cites Voltaire: "Now that I freed you from a Tiger, you want me to put something in its place?" Not the least reason for Büchner's hesitation to legislate morals is that he is skeptical about general or absolute moral laws. In his chapter on innate ideas he attacks the thesis that there are natural moral principles and espouses instead a complete moral relativism. A society adopts moral principles only in order to preserve itself; and since how it preserves itself depends on constantly changing historical and natural circumstances, its principles change accordingly (313). There are no universal standards of justice and morality that hold for all peoples, Büchner insists, and it is impossible to decide between the different conceptions of them that have held throughout history. Büchner simply dismisses Kant's categorical imperative, the attempt to find universal maxims of conduct through reason alone, as mere wishful thinking that should be placed in "the land of fairytales" (314n).

Such, in crude summary, are the main ideas of Büchner's *Kraft und Stoff*. To be sure, many of his criticisms of religion are crude and hasty, directed against a straw man, and many of his explanations of mental life are highly speculative. But Büchner's great merit was to have presented, in a consistent and lively manner, the materialist worldview to a broad public. Any careful reader could learn from it the materialist stance on a wide array of issues. Whatever the ultimate defects of materialism, we can be grateful to Büchner for presenting its standpoint so clearly and simply. We have good reason to bestow upon him a title he would have loved: the German Lucretius.

5. SCHOPENHAUER ENTERS THE FRAY

Schopenhauer was still alive and well when the materialism controversy broke out in 1854. At first he looked upon the strife with Olympian contempt and detachment. After all, it was just more evidence that the world had wrongly ignored him. If people had only read his work, they would have seen long ago that materialism is really no threat at all. Materialism, he argued in *Die Welt als Wille und Vorstellung*,[26] simply presupposes what it attempts to explain: it tries to derive the subject from the laws holding for the object; but it fails to see that these laws have their source in the subject itself. But such was Schopenhauer's hunger for fame that he eventually began to see the controversy as an opportunity.[27] If people could be convinced that his philosophy held the solution to the problem behind the controversy, they would finally begin to appreciate its importance and merits.

Schopenhauer would probably never had seen the materialism controversy in such a light if it were not for his loyal disciple, Julius Frauenstädt (1813–79). Before his association with Schopenhauer, Frauenstädt was a philosopher in his own right, having written three books on problems in Hegelian thought.[28] He had first read

26 *Die Welt als Wille und Vorstellung*, §7, *Werke* I, 62–3 (P 27–28).

27 See Schopenhauer to Julius Frauenstädt, May 2, 1855, in *Gesammelte Briefe*, ed. Arthur Hübscher (Bonn: Bouvier, 1978), p. 362.

28 See J. Frauenstädt, *Die Freiheit des Menschen und die Persönlichkeit Gottes* (Berlin: Hirschwald, 1838); *Die Menschwerdung Gottes nach ihrer Möglichkeit, Wirklichkeit und Nothwendigkeit* (Berlin: Voß, 1839); and *Studien und Kritiken zur Theologie und Philosophie* (Berlin: Voß, 1840). These works are highly critical of Hegel though they also attempt to defend some essentials of his philosophy against materialist criticism.

Schopenhauer in 1836 and was very impressed with him;[29] but he became a convert only in 1848 when he began to see Schopenhauer's philosophy as the only tenable system to solve the conflict between reason and faith.[30] It was the great merit of Schopenhauer's philosophy, Frauenstädt argued, that it avoids a superstitious theism and a soulless materialism. It saves the essentials of religion—the doctrines of sin, redemption, and salvation—without having to accept the problematic beliefs in the existence of God and personal immortality. It endorses the main principles of scientific naturalism without accepting the doctrine that matter alone exists.

A tireless crusader for Schopenhauer's philosophy, Frauenstädt was convinced that he could prove its enduring value by explaining its contribution to the materialism controversy. What Reinhold had done for Kant's philosophy in the 1790s, Frauenstädt believed he could do for Schopenhauer's in the 1850s.[31] Reinhold had shown Kant's philosophy to be the solution to the conflict between reason and faith in the pantheism controversy; Frauenstädt would now show Schopenhauer's philosophy to be the solution to the same conflict in the materialism controversy.

And so Frauenstädt set to work. In the mid-1850s he wrote two books discussing the materialism controversy and championing Schopenhauer's role in it. His first book is his *Die Naturwissenschaft in ihren Einfluß auf Poesie, Religion, Moral und Philosophie*,[32] which appeared in 1855. This work is essentially a critique of Rudolph Wagner's views on reason and faith. The second book, *Der Materialismus*,[33] which appeared in 1856, is a critique of Büchner's *Kraft und Stoff*. Though largely forgotten, these writings should not

29 See Julius Frauenstädt, *Arthur Schopenhauer.Von ihm. Ueber ihn* (Berlin: Hayn, 1863), pp. 133–34.

30 See J. Frauenstädt, *Ueber das wahre Verhältniß der Vernunft zur Offenbarung* (Darmstadt: Carl Wilhelm Leske, 1848). See pp. 89–90 for Frauenstädt's explanation for his turn toward Schopenhauer's philosophy in the later 1840s.

31 Schopenhauer himself noted the Reinholdian precedent. See Schopenhauer to Frauenstädt, September 19, 1853, *Briefe*, p. 321.

32 Julius Frauenstädt, *Die Naturwissenschaft in ihrem Einfluß auf Poesie, Religion, Moral und Philosophie* (Leipzig: Brockhaus, 1855).

33 Julius Frauenstädt, *Der Materialismus. Seine Wahrheit und sein Irrthum. Eine Erwiderung auf Dr. Louis Büchner's "Kraft und Stoff"* (Leipzig: Brockhaus, 1856).

be ignored in any account of the materialism controversy. They are not only a notable contribution to that controversy but also historically important because of their role in the reception of Schopenhauer's philosophy. Along with another work of Frauenstädt's, his *Briefe über die Schopenhauer'sche Philosophie*,[34] they were instrumental in making Schopenhauer the most popular philosopher of the second half of the nineteenth century.

In both works, Frauenstädt's essential concern is to address the conflict between reason and faith at the center of the materialism controversy. Like Lotze, Frauenstädt believes that there is ultimately no conflict between reason and faith, and that it is perfectly possible to reconcile them. It is possible to reconcile them, however, only under two conditions: first, that we do not equate science with materialism, as Büchner does; and second, that we do not identify faith with the old Christian orthodoxy, i.e., theism and the belief in personal immortality. It is a mistake to conflate science with materialism, Frauenstädt argues, because materialism is really only a philosophy claiming to be based upon science. We can investigate nature according to the methods of observation and experiment, and we can assume that everything in nature conforms to laws, without ever assuming the central tenets of materialism (that matter alone exists and that everything should be explained mechanically). It is a mistake to identity faith with theism and personal immortality because the essential concern in religion is with salvation, the elevation of the soul above all the evil and suffering of life, and for that we do not need the beliefs in God or immortality. Buddhism shows us that we can have all the essentials of religion without these beliefs.

In the struggle between Christianity and materialism Frauenstädt was willing to yield much ground to the materialists. He agreed with Vogt and Büchner that some of the old theistic beliefs—creation *ex nihilo*, the descent of mankind from a single original pair, the existence of an immortal soul that survives the death of the body—had been falsified by the latest physiological research. While he held that the belief in the existence of a

---

34   J. Frauenstädt, *Briefe über die Schopenhauer'sche Philosophie* (Leipzig: Brockhaus, 1854).

personal God is compatible with natural science, he still rejected it on the grounds that it could not solve the problem of evil. Other beliefs, however, Frauenstädt was not so ready to sacrifice to materialism. He still could not accept a complete mechanistic explanation of nature, human life, and action. Such mechanism is in his view incompatible with two indispensable moral and religious beliefs: the beliefs in freedom and the purposiveness of nature and history. We need the belief in freedom to take responsibility for our actions; and we need the belief in purposiveness for our actions to have value and meaning. If nothing we did made a difference in the world, we would lose the incentive to do good and create a better world. It was one of the major advantages of Schopenhauer's philosophy, Frauenstädt argued, that it still upheld the necessity of a teleological explanation of nature. In his *Über den Willen in der Natur* Schopenhauer had shown how the results of the latest scientific research vindicated his theory that the will is the ultimate cause of all organic phenomena in nature.[35]

The incompatibility of mechanism with these beliefs still does not imply, Frauenstädt insisted, that there is a conflict between science and faith. He readily agreed with the materialists that everything in nature is explicable according to mechanical causes and that we should set no limits to such explanation. He maintained, however, that mechanical explanation is valid only in the phenomenal or natural world and not beyond it. Following Schopenhauer, Frauenstädt upheld a dualism between phenomena and noumena, appearances and things-in-themselves, and used it to separate the realm of science from that of morality and religion. The beliefs in freedom and purposiveness hold for the realm of things-in-themselves, where they are inaccessible to scientific or naturalistic explanation.

For all his resistance to materialism, Frauenstädt still believes that this worldview has some fundamental strengths, which are both "formal" and "material." Its *formal* strengths concern its discourse, its method and way of doing philosophy. These are threefold:

---

35 Schopenhauer did not, however, extend teleology to history. See his famous essay "Über Geschichte," Kapitel 38 of WWV II, 563–73 (P 439–46). This is only one of many differences between Schopenhauer and Frauenstädt.

(1) its empiricism, its insistence on basing theories upon the evidence of sense experience; (2) its clear and distinct language, which makes it intelligible and accessible to the general public; and (3) its determination to know the truth, regardless of the consequences for our moral and religious beliefs. All these formal strengths, Frauenstädt insisted, give materialism a great advantage over the tradition of speculative idealism, the philosophy of Fichte, Schelling, and Hegel. The *material* strengths of materialism concern the content or general principles of its metaphysics. These are twofold: (1) its monism,[36] its insistence on explaining everything within the world according to a single principle; and (2) its naturalism, its demand that we explain everything in nature according to natural laws, avoiding all reference to the supernatural.

Despite these strengths, Frauenstädt insists that materialism suffers from some very basic shortcomings. The most serious of these, he argues in *Der Materialismus*, is its *realism* and *dogmatism*, i.e., its naïve acceptance of the reality of the external world (43–45). The materialists write as if Kant's critical philosophy never existed, as if there were no need to investigate the faculty of knowledge. Materialism is a species of naïve or (as Kant called it) "transcendental" realism, i.e., it assumes that the world that we perceive through our senses is the world as it exists in itself, apart from and prior to our perception of it. Its belief in the reality of matter is based on this naïve realism, because it assumes that the spatial and temporal objects of our ordinary experience are things-in-themselves, that they continue to exist when we do not perceive them. In making this assumption, however, it completely ignores Kant's critical teaching about the a priori conditions for knowledge: that the object we perceive in our sense experience is only an appearance, determined by the conditions under which we perceive it. If we take this teaching into account, it then becomes clear that matter is not a thing-in-itself, a reality that exists independent of our consciousness, but that it is really only an appearance for consciousness. Frauenstädt

36 This monism seems at odds with Schopenhauer's acceptance of Kant's dualism between thing-in-itself and appearance. In his later *Neue Briefe über die Schopenhauer'sche Philosophie* (Leipzig: Brockhaus, 1876), Frauenstädt attempted to correct Schopenhauer's system by making it more monistic.

then goes on to add that this critical teaching has been vindicated by the latest empirical research on sense perception, by the work of Hermann Helmholtz and Johannes Müller. Their work has shown that what we perceive very much depends on our nervous apparatus and intellectual activity, that the objects of perception do not just float unchanged into the mind.

Frauenstädt explains the materialist's basic error thus: they wrongly assume that matter is something given to us, as if its reality were complete in itself before we perceive it (64–70). All that we are given in sense perception, however, are mere sensations, viz., intensive magnitudes of different qualia. We make these sensations into an object by applying the intuition of space and the category of causality to them, i.e., by assuming that there is something external to us that is the cause of these sensations. But this apparent external object causing our sensations, Frauenstädt insists, is not an objective entity but simply the construction of the mind, the product of our a priori intuition of space and the category of causality. The materialist therefore hypostasizes the object of perception, treating a creation of the mind as if it were an entity.

The other serious mistake of materialism, Frauenstädt maintains, is its belief in the eternity and permanence of the laws of nature. It assumes that the combination and groupings of matter that we see now will be the same forever and that they have been always the same, because the laws operating upon matter are eternal and essentially one with matter itself (94). But Frauenstädt finds this assumption at odds with natural history, which shows that there are different laws and powers in operation in the early stages of earth (92). If we accept the materialist views about the eternity of matter, we then find ourselves incapable of explaining natural change and development. The materialists, Frauenstädt says, are like small town dwellers who assume that the entire world follows their own customs (82). We have no a priori reason to assume, however, that the laws governing matter now will forever be the same, or that the laws holding on Earth will also be the same on other planets. As Frauenstädt expounds his argument, however, it suffers from a grave ambiguity: whether the laws of nature themselves change or whether they operate differently under different conditions, where only the conditions change.

Most of the argument in *Der Materialismus* is a critique of mechanism, the materialist's program for accounting for all the phenomena of life on the basis of efficient causality and its material elements. Frauenstädt agrees with the materialists that life has to be explained according to mechanical and chemical powers, but he insists that it cannot be fully explained according to them alone (95, 98–99). While these powers are necessary, they are still not a sufficient condition for the explanation of life. It is also necessary to have recourse to final causes and some form-giving principle or *Bildungstrieb* (109, 115). The problem with materialism is that it does not see how and why all the elements of an organism come together and combine in the first place (111, 167–68). The materialist indeed reverses the proper order of explanation. He reasons: because there is matter combined in such and such a way, there is life; but the very opposite is the case: because there is the will to life, matter becomes combined in such and such a way (152). Without ears we cannot hear, and without eyes we cannot see; but it does not follow from this that we hear only because we have ears and that we see only because we have eyes. Ears and eyes presuppose a purpose, a will in nature itself (153). Without a will in nature, there would be no seeing and no hearing (153). Seeing and hearing will emerge on their own in nature no more than a house or a ship will appear without a builder and designer.

Such were the basic arguments of Frauenstädt's writings on the materialism controversy. Though they succeeded in making Schopenhauer a major voice in this controversy, they were also noteworthy for what they did *not* say about Schopenhauer. Never did Frauenstädt discuss the most problematic side of Schopenhauer's philosophy: his pessimism. Even his *Briefe*, his chief exposition of Schopenhauer's system, barely mentions Schopenhauer's pessimism. So dark and depressing was that doctrine, Frauenstädt realized, that it was unlikely to gain Schopenhauer many adherents. Sure enough, Frauenstädt himself eventually broke with this side of his philosophy.[37] We will see in chapter 6 how pessimism would consume the 1870s and 1880s.

---

37   See Frauenstädt, *Neue Briefe*, pp. 97–99, 265–70, 290–96.

6. CZOLBE'S SENSUALISM

In 1855, the very year Büchner published *Kraft und Stoff*, another controversial materialist work appeared, the discussion of which would mark another instructive episode in the materialist controversy. This book was entitled *Neue Darstellung des Sensualismus*,[38] and its author was a young military doctor, Heinrich Czolbe (1819–75). Czolbe's book was a self-conscious attempt to provide a systematic foundation for materialism, a foundation its author called "sensualism." In his preface Czolbe complains that the work of his fellow materialists—Feuerbach, Vogt, and Moleschott—had been much too fragmentary and vague, and that, as a result, the concept of matter itself had been left unclear. The main goal of his sensualism is "to exclude the supersensible," i.e., to purge the concept of matter of every trace of the supersensible, where the supersensible stands for the realm of spirit, or whatever cannot be perceived by the senses (1, 60). Toward that end, Czolbe rummages through all the disciplines—psychology, logic, physiology, and physics—in a campaign to rid them of any tincture of the supersensible. Materialism thus involves for Czolbe a form of radical empiricism, according to which all meaning and knowledge originate in, and are based upon, sense perception. The fundamental principle of his empiricism is what he calls "intuitiveness" (*Anschauulichkeit*), i.e., the power to give a precise empirical meaning to concepts (2, 3). Czolbe gives such importance to empiricism because the chief redoubt of the idealist lies in epistemology, and more specifically in the thesis that we have a priori concepts that originate entirely in intellectual activity. Having a purely intellectual origin, these a priori concepts seem to provide evidence for a purely supernatural or intelligible dimension of meaning. Hence in his treatment of logic Czolbe attempts to trace concepts, judgments, and inferences back to their origin in sense experience (52–65). Even the law of contradiction, he claims, owes its validity to the fact that we cannot unite in thought what we cannot perceive together in experience (60). After tracing all thinking back to sense percep-

---

38 Henrich Czolbe, *Neue Darstellung des Sensualismus* (Leipzig: Costenoble, 1855). This is the sole edition, references to which appear in parentheses.

tion, Czolbe then takes the next decisive step: he explains sense perception in terms of material processes. Perception consists in nothing more than vibrations in the nerves and brain (11–18). Even the more subtle and sophisticated processes of judging and reasoning arise from, and indeed consist in, physical processes (52). Self-consciousness, Czolbe maintains, consists in a circular activity in the brain whereby it turns in upon itself. All in all, Czolbe's work is a rather crude and naïve empiricist epistemology filled with fanciful materialist speculations about the origins of cognition. Its chief merit lies in its recognition that materialism stands in need of an epistemic foundation.

The *Neue Darstellung* would probably have faded into oblivion if it were not for some incidental remarks in its preface. There Czolbe stated that he regarded his book as "a kind of positive refutation" of Lotze's views. While paying tribute to Lotze as materialism's worthiest critic, he made a stunning personal confession: that it was Lotze's critique of vital powers that was the inspiration for his own materialism! Surely Lotze would not take it amiss then, Czolbe reasoned, if his critique were expanded into a whole worldview? If Lotze were only consistent, Czolbe implied, he, too, would be a materialist. After all, what was the soul but another hypostasized vital power?

These remarks were provocative enough, forcing Lotze to cast aside, once again, his misgivings about intellectual controversy. After reading them, he knew he would have to set the record straight. A review of Czolbe's book was inevitable, and it duly appeared the very same year in the *Göttingische gelehrte Anzeigen*.[39] Lotze's review is an interesting historical document, not only because it reveals many of the issues dividing materialism and idealism but also because it anticipates later themes of Frege.[40]

Lotze begins his review by stating that he finds it odd Czolbe virtually equates materialism with empiricism. After all, it is

39 *Göttingische gelehrte Anzeigen* no. 153–55 (1855), 1521–38, reprinted in Hermann Lotze, *Kleine Schriften* (Leipzig: Hirzel, 1891), III, 238–50. All references are to this later edition.

40 On the importance of this review for Frege, see Hans Sluga, *Frege* (London: Routledge, 1980), p. 32.

possible for a materialist, i.e., someone who believes in the sole reality of matter, to maintain the existence of innate principles and ideas (240). He also misses any proof on Czolbe's part that everything imperceptible and supersensible is obscurantist, given that the most lucid intellectual activity is not perceptible by the senses (241). Lotze focuses chiefly on Czolbe's empiricism, especially his attempt to eliminate the supersensible from all intellectual activity. All Czolbe's efforts are doomed to utter failure, Lotze contends, for all thinking consists in the addition of something supersensible to the material of intuition (240). All that the senses show consists in the succession and coexistence of sensations; but they reveal nothing about their inner connections, which are supplied by thinking alone. To some extent, we can derive the principle of causality from experience, from the constant conjunction of impressions, just as Hume and Czolbe insist; but, as Kant famously argued, such a derivation is not enough: causality also involves a necessary connection between sensations, and for that there is no corresponding sensation (241). Even the most simple concepts, viz., that of a thing, arise from the activity of the mind, from uniting a manifold of representations, and in no sense is that unity given in the material of sensation (241). So far, then, Lotze's argument is basically a restatement of Kant's famous reply to Hume, a timely reminder for materialists of a basic philosophical point: that the universal and necessary connections of our most fundamental concepts cannot be derived from experience.

Having taught Czolbe that lesson, Lotze then went on to teach him another: that empiricism cannot explain the unity of consciousness (242–43). Though Czolbe went to great lengths to explain thinking in material terms, attempting to reduce it down to processes of association, he failed to ask the crucial question: *For whom* do these processes exist? (243). He rightly recognized that self-consciousness has to be involved in each representation; but he had not considered that there needs to be a *single* self-consciousness throughout a series of representations. Hence the Kantian self or subject is not so easily eliminable. Lotze also took exception to Czolbe's materialist psychologism, his attempt to explain logical inference in terms of the cumulative result of brain processes. The meaning of the syllogism, Lotze explains, rests not in such processes but in the "thought of the law" that makes it necessary to infer conclusions from premises (246). Czolbe's chief sin, Lotze claims, is that he has a very crude conception of the supersensible, which he seems to conflate with mysterious powers like telekinesis, viz., the power to move objects at a distance by the mind. But if this is what Czolbe means by the supersensible, then it is hard to see what he has against it, Lotze claims, for such a power is easily explicable in sensible terms. We can measure that power by seeing how far and fast it moves objects a definite distance. After giving Czolbe such a drubbing, Lotze closes his review by making a last noble gesture: the hope that it will at least help Czolbe get clear about his own principles.

The gesture was not in vain. Czolbe answered it by writing an entire tract in response to Lotze's criticisms, his *Entstehung des Selbstbewußtseins*.[41] For the most part, Czolbe stuck to the position he laid out in his earlier work. He defended his peculiar theory that self-consciousness consists in the self-reverting activity of the brain. Lotze objected to that theory on the grounds that it cannot be a sufficient analysis of self-awareness, given that circular motion can be found in purely physical phenomena, such as the turning of a wheel. Czolbe insisted, however, that he never claimed to provide a sufficient analysis of self-consciousness, and that in any case its activity must have a chemical and physical base (7). Regarding the unity of consciousness, Czolbe accepted Lotze's point that it is necessary to admit a single self-awareness throughout a manifold of representations; but he denied that this self need be anything more than an abstraction and insisted that there is no need to assume that it is spiritual (18). Though Lotze, in a later review of the work,[42] complained that Czolbe made no significant concessions, on one important point Czolbe had made a very significant concession indeed. This concerned the analysis of sense perception.

41 Heinrich Czolbe, *Entstehung des Selbstbewußtseins: Eine Antwort an Herrn Professor Lotze* (Leipzig: Cosenoble, 1856). All references in parentheses are to this text. See also Czolbe's defense of his position, "Die Elemente der Psychologie vom Standpunkte des Materialismus," *Zeitschrift für Philosophie und philosophische Kritik* 26 (1855), 91–109.

42 Hermann Lotze, *Göttingische gelehrte Anzeigen* 32 (1857), 313–20, reprinted in *Kleine Schriften* III, 315–20.

In his introduction Czolbe scolded the materialist for not having done enough to examine sense perception, even though the whole case for materialism rested upon it (1). The problem was this: if Lotze were correct that there is a logical gap between the stimulus and content of sensation, then the idealist would be right after all! It would not be possible to infer any resemblance between our representations and the external world, so that the basis for the belief in the reality of matter would be undermined. It would then be necessary to admit something like a distinction between appearances and things-in-themselves—the starting point of Kant's transcendental idealism. Czolbe then went on to complain that the materialists had done nothing to overcome this gap.

Though Czolbe could now clearly see the danger to his position, he still clung to it all the same. He now stated very clearly a basic premise behind his analysis of perception in the *Neue Darstellung*: that sensible qualities reveal the nature of external objects, which are fully present and completely given to us (14). In other words, Czolbe's response to the problem was to affirm a kind of naïve realism! Though Lotze had already dismissed this as "an old error," because it failed to acknowledge the role of the subject's cognitive activity in constituting experience, Czolbe went on to affirm it all the more passionately. While he could not give compelling evidence on its behalf, he went on to emphasize one of its advantages: it allowed for an aesthetic dimension to nature, because it implies that nature really has the colors we perceive it to have (16). In saying this, however, Czolbe virtually admitted that he had no evidence for his materialism, which presupposes, but cannot justify, the assumption that we can know things as they are in themselves. All that lay between materialism and idealism, it seemed, was the thin and flimsy line marked by naïve realism.

How long could Czolbe uphold such naïve realism? The answer, of course, is not very long. Sure enough, in a later work, *Die Grenzen und der Ursprung der menschlichen Erkenntniß*,[43] Czolbe confessed the error of his materialist ways. He now realized that materialism could not explain the reality of consciousness and that there is

---

43   Heinrich Czolbe, *Die Grenzen und der Ursprung der menschlichen Erkenntniß im Gegensatze zu Kant und Hegel* (Leipzig: Costenoble, 1865), p. vi.

indeed a gap between the stimuli and content of perception. The idealists, it seemed, were right after all. Ironically, Czolbe's journey of intellectual discovery had proven to be vindication of the anti-materialist cause.

7. FRIEDRICH LANGE, NEO-KANTIAN AND MATERIALIST *MANQUÉ*

1866, the year after Czolbe's dispute with Lotze came to its pathetic close, is an important year in the history of the materialism controversy. This was the publication date of the first edition of Friedrich Lange's *Geschichte des Materialismus*,[44] one of the most important and influential works in German philosophy in the nineteenth century. Lange's work was not simply a history of materialism, as its title suggests, but a reckoning with materialism and the statement of an entire worldview. In its historical and philosophical importance Lange's *Geschichte* was the peer of Lotze's *Mikrokosmus* and Trendelenburg's *Logische Untersuchungen*. The book appeared to great critical acclaim, and among its admirers were Hans Vaihinger, Hermann Cohen, Paul Natorp, and Friedrich Nietzsche. Such was the success of the book that it appeared in ten editions, the last in 1974. Two editions appeared in Lange's lifetime, the first in 1866 and the second from 1873 to 1875.[45]

---

44 Friedrich Lange, *Geschichte des Materialismus und Kritik seiner Bedeutung in der Gegnwart* (Iserlohn: J. Baedeker, 1866).

45 Friedrich Lange, *Geschichte des Materialismus und Kritik seiner Bedeutung in der Gegenwart. Zweite, verbesserte und vermehrte Auflage* (Iserlohn: J. Baedeker, 1873–75). The reader should be aware that the two editions differ greatly. The first edition was a single volume of 557 pages; but the second edition came in two volumes, the first consisting in 428 pages and the second in 569 pages. Thus the book almost doubled in size! But the second edition did not simply expand the first; much of the material of the first edition, which is very interesting, was dropped or rewritten. There are important changes in opinion and outlook in the second edition. But there is also a significant shift in Lange's whole conception of the work. In the preface to the first edition he said he wrote for the enlightenment of his contemporaries and did not want to write an academic book; he therefore set aside the scholarly apparatus of footnotes. But the second edition eventually became just that academic book, adding very extensive notes after each chapter.

In the preface to the first edition of his book Lange stated that he wrote it in the hope of providing a solution to some issues raised by the materialism controversy (iii). He did not specify which issues, but the content of the book makes it clear that chief among them is the conflict between science and faith. In striving to resolve that conflict, Lange took his cue from a philosopher who was already undergoing a remarkable revival in the 1860s: Immanuel Kant. Though often very critical of Kant, Lange still held that his philosophy provides the right general strategy to overcome the dilemma between science and faith. Kant's philosophy, because of its distinction between the phenomenal realm of science and the noumenal realm of value, offers a middle path between a soulless materialism and an irrational leap of faith. While the principles of mechanism and naturalism hold without exception in the phenomenal realm, they do not impinge on the values of the noumenal realm, which are based upon reason rather than blind faith or revelation. It was the great advantage of Kant's philosophy that it could save the autonomy of moral and aesthetic ideals without metaphysics and that it could uphold the principles of mechanism and naturalism without sacrificing these ideals.

In seeing Kant's philosophy as the middle path between science and faith, Lange was following a great eighteenth-century precedent: Karl Leonhard Reinhold's *Briefe über die kantische Philosophie*.[46] Reinhold championed Kant's philosophy on the grounds that its doctrine of practical faith is the middle path in the conflict between Spinozistic naturalism and Protestant theism. Despite the clear analogy between Reinhold and Lange, it is important to see that there is still a great difference between them. Kant's doctrine of practical faith defends the beliefs in God, providence, and immortality not on *metaphysical* or *theoretical* grounds, i.e., through a priori demonstrations of their truth, but on *moral* or *practical* grounds, i.e., by showing them to be necessary means for moral action. While Lange approved the general strategy of defending

---

46 Karl Leonhard Reinhold, *Briefe über die kantische Philosophie* (Leipzig: Göschen, 1790–92), 2 vols. The first essays appeared in a series of articles in the *Der Teutsche Merkur* III (1786), 99–127, 127–41; I (1787), 3–39, 117–42; II (1787), 167–85; III (1787), 142–65, 247–78.

the realm of value on practical rather than theoretical grounds, he still disapproved of Kant's doctrine of practical faith, which he saw as a relic of eighteenth-century theism. He accepted the materialist's criticism that the beliefs in God, providence, and immortality are incompatible with a scientific view of the world. Nevertheless, though ready to sacrifice theism, Lange was not willing to surrender autonomy and integrity of the realm of value in general. On the contrary, he insisted on reinterpreting the Kantian distinction between noumena and phenomena, so that the noumenal world is no longer an ontological realm filled with supernatural objects but a strictly normative realm containing moral and aesthetic values. These values are not things that exist, but they are things that we create, which have a universal and necessary validity of their own. The realm of value represents for Lange, then, the sanctum of human creativity, which we must forever protect against materialism, which threatens to reduce man down to a machine. In stressing the need to reconceive Kant's distinction along these lines, Lange had worked out, following his own path, something like Lotze's distinction between the realms of existence and value.

Lange's debts to Kant go well beyond his general dualism between the realms of nature and value. The real significance of Kant's philosophy, Lange believed, lay not with his doctrine of practical faith but with his critique of theoretical reason and metaphysics. This critique had the utmost importance for materialism, and it indeed posed a crisis for materialism, which marked "the beginning of the end, the catastrophe of the tragedy" (241). To be sure, the materialists were thriving in the 1850s, well over a half century after Kant's death. But they were prospering, Lange held, only because they had forgotten some of the fundamental lessons of his philosophy. Like Lotze and Frauenstädt, Lange made it his business to remind the materialists of these lessons and to show that Kant's philosophy poses insurmountable challenges to materialism.

There are two basic challenges. First, Kant had exposed the naïve realism of materialism, i.e., its belief that material things are the immediate objects of perception. He had shown how all sense qualities depend upon our perceptive and cognitive organization, so that the world would appear differently had we a different organization. Lange then went on to argue that this Kantian doctrine was confirmed by the latest research in physiology and psychology. The experiments of Johannes Müller and Hermann Helmholtz, for example, had demonstrated the active role of our sense organs and nerves in forming our perception of the external world. Thus, Lange insisted, the materialist is slain by his own weapons: the appeal to scientific findings, the results of observation and experiment. Second, Kant had shown how the concept of causal necessity cannot be derived from experience but originates in the a priori forms of cognition. Hence the materialist's faith that everything happens of necessity, that all events conform to regular laws, has no ground in nature but only in our cognitive constitution.

Both these problems of classical materialism are instances of what Kant had called "dogmatism." That term means at least two things in Kant: first, accepting beliefs without subjecting them to critical scrutiny, holding them without examining whether they are based on solid reasons; and second, being unaware or unreflective about the subjective sources of one's belief, hypostasizing or reifying them, as if they refer to things in the world when they really arise subconsciously from our mental activities. Hypostasis, Kant teaches, is the characteristic fallacy of dogmatism, the common source of its antinomies, amphibolies, and paralogisms. The materialist is guilty of dogmatism in both senses, Lange insinuated. In assuming that our representations resemble the world as given to us, and in positing necessary connections in nature itself, the materialist had failed to engage in a sufficient critical scrutiny of the faculty of knowledge; and as a result he reified the subjective sources of knowledge. Both dogmatic strands of materialism show that it is irredeemably naïve. Thus Lange again turned the materialists' weapons against them. They loved to expose the hypostasis behind religious belief; but they were no less guilty of this fallacy by hypostasizing the content of their representations.

But Lange's book is not simply a *critique* of materialism, still less only a history of materialism. In an important respect it is also a *defense* of materialism, an attempt to vindicate its enduring ethical and intellectual values. Lange not only believed that materialism had been misunderstood and underappreciated by its critics, both ancient and modern, but he also nurtured a fondness for some of its main doctrines. He admired the basic ideal of materialism—a complete scientific explanation of the world—and he embraced some of its fundamental doctrines—empiricism, nominalism, and mechanism.

Not the least reason for Lange's attraction to materialism was its ethical agenda: emancipation, the liberation of the individual from arbitrary authority and religious superstition. Behind the materialist critique of religion from Epicurus to Feuerbach, Lange rightly saw, lay its ideal of human autonomy, the right and power of the individual to lead his life according to his own laws and aspirations. The great danger to this autonomy came with religion, the materialist taught, because it introduces fear of the gods, who would punish those who did not obey their laws. Such fear grew out of superstition, i.e., the belief that natural events have spiritual or supernatural causes. The materialist's antidote to such superstition is natural science, which shows that the true causes of things lie in nature rather supernatural spirits. Lange embraced this critique, not because it would undermine religion as such but because it could destroy superstition, which was the basis for what he saw as the greatest source of human oppression, viz., dogmatic theology and ecclesiastical authority.

The first book of the *Geschichte*, the entire first volume of the second edition, is a history of materialism from Democritus in the fifth century BC to La Mettrie and Holbach in the eighteenth century AD It is a narrative about how natural science originated in materialism and how its advance was hindered, in late antiquity and the Middle Ages, by the hegemony of the church and the Platonic-Aristotelian philosophy. The birth of the natural sciences in the early modern era, Lange argues, was due in great measure to the rediscovery of materialism, to the reaffirmation of its central doctrines by Bacon, Hobbes, Gassendi, and Descartes. Enlightenment and materialism are for Lange almost one and the same: the more enlightened the philosophy, the closer it stands to materialism.

Why write a whole history of materialism if one's goal is a critique of materialism, especially its contemporary relevance? This seems like a long way around the barn. For Lange, however, critique is first and foremost *historical*, involving an account of the origins and development of the philosophy, religion, or art under investigation (II, 170, 171). Such a critique is especially relevant to the materialism controversy, Lange believes, because both materialists and their critics show a complete lack of historical sense (II, 68, 71, 90, 170). The materialists think that their materialism is the result of modern science alone, completely unaware how their main ideas, goals, and problems go back to fifth-century Athens. The critics of materialism dismiss it as if it were the latest intellectual fad, as if it were not worthy of discussion and not even a form of philosophy. But if one tells the glorious history of materialism, then that will show not only that it is no fad but also that it is a noble philosophical tradition. Behind Lange's history there also lay a political agenda: rehabilitating a tradition of religious and political criticism.

There is no specific chapter or section of the first book of the *Geschichte* devoted to a defense of materialism. Lange's sympathy for it is often implicit and disparate, scattered in various places in the text. It becomes clear, however, that Lange greatly admires the father of materialism, Democritus, whom he regards as the greatest thinker of antiquity (I, 11). And it is no less plain that he advocates two basic materialist principles: first, the principle of mechanical explanation, according to which every event is explained by prior events; and second, nominalism, i.e., the thesis that universals are only abstractions in the human mind and do not exist in their own right, whether above the natural world (Plato) or in things within it (Aristotle). In both respects, Lange opposes materialism to the Platonic-Aristotelian tradition, which he regards as the main enemy of materialism. The Platonic-Aristotelian tradition retarded the development of modern science, Lange argues, partly because it attempted to reinstate teleological explanation, which is fundamentally anthropocentric, and partly because its theory of universals reified abstractions, which give purely verbal explanations. For Lange, the triumph of modern science is very much a tale about the victory of materialism over the Platonic-Aristotelian tradition, whose teleology and hypostases have been obstacles to true scientific explanation.

For all his sympathy with materialism, Lange does not hesitate to criticize it severely in the first book of his *Geschichte*. He makes two fundamental criticisms. First, it cannot explain the origins of sense qualities, viz., colors, sounds, taste, and the qualitative dimension of experience, which resists reduction to quantitative forms

94

of measurement (I, 15–16, 18, 110–11, 232, 390). Second, materialism evaluates ideas strictly according to their theoretical value, whether they are true or false, and it ignores their "poetic value," whether they address our feelings and aspirations as human beings (I, 374, 376). Lange suggests that we evaluate moral and aesthetic ideas according to very different standards from those of objective truth or cognitive worth, and that the materialist has missed their point in dismissing them for not meeting theoretical standards. When we say that a painting is ugly, that a person is evil, that a fallacy has been committed, we are not saying that they are false but that they do not conform to ideals or norms.

That, in sum, is the gist of Lange's *Geschichte des Materialismus*. We cannot do justice here to the richness of its historical narrative or the subtlety of its philosophical arguments. But it should be apparent enough how Lange's work succeeded in throwing the materialists back on the defensive and why it was so influential in the late nineteenth century. Lange's book appealed to everyone who wanted the materialist critique of religion and its scientific program but who also could not approve of its naïve metaphysics and its failure to account for basic human values. It was no wonder that the book was so important for Nietzsche and the neo-Kantians. It was to many the final word in reckoning with the materialist legacy.

The second edition of Lange's *Geschichte* marks a break in the materialism controversy, the beginning of its second phase, the end of its first phase. In some retrospective passages added to the second volume of the second edition, Lange notes that Darwinism was a novel theme when he discussed it in his first edition; his main concern then was to discuss the work of Büchner, Moleschott, Vogt, and Czolbe (II, 240). By the time of the second edition, however, Darwin dominated the field, overshadowing the old materialists. No one, Lange remarked, was interested anymore in the latest edition of Büchner's *Kraft und Stoff*. Because of the increasing interest in Darwinism, Lange felt it necessary to add a lengthy treatment of it in his second edition. Only in that way, he reckoned, would his book retain interest for those concerned with the materialism controversy.

It has been estimated that, by the middle of the 1870s, Darwinism had triumphed in Germany.[47] By then the chief spokesmen for Darwin—Ernst Häckel and Carl Gegenbauer—had become professors in Jena, and they had control over two major journals, *Ausland* and *Kosmos*. The ranks of the anti-Darwinians, who belonged to an older generation, were now dwindling in numbers and energy. Commenting on the rapid rise of Darwinism in 1875, Otto Liebmann, a neo-Kantian, reckoned that, apart from a few religious bigots and crackpots like himself, intelligent opinion in Germany was now on the side of Darwin.[48] "Sir Charles," as he now needed to be called, had so grown in prestige that he received institutional recognition in Germany: in 1867 he was made a knight of the Prussia order *Pour le Mérite*, and in 1878 he was elected to the Berlin Akademie der Wissenschaften.

Despite the rise of Darwin, it would be a mistake to infer that his triumph was a vindication of materialism itself. Although the Darwinians had succeeded in pushing the old advocates of teleology back on the defensive, they had stopped far short of a justification of materialism. To widen the boundaries of mechanical explanation, as Lotze rightly pointed out, it is not necessarily to prove materialism, which assumes that the entities explained are solely and strictly material objects. The chief critics of materialism— Lotze, Frauenstädt, and Lange—had succeeded in revealing its soft underbelly: its naïve epistemology, its failure to vindicate its most fundamental belief, the reality of matter. As long as materialism remained so vulnerable, it could not ride to victory on the back of "Sir Charles." Lotze's, Frauenstädt's, and Lange's critique was, as we have seen, inspired by Kant's critical philosophy. It should not be surprising, therefore, that neo-Kantianism, not materialism, proved to be the dominant philosophy in Germany in the second half of the nineteenth century.

---

47 Alfred Kelly, *The Descent of Darwin: The Popularization of Darwinism in Germany, 1860–1914* (Chapel Hill: University of North Carolina Press, 1981), p. 21.

48 Otto Liebmann, "Platonismus und Darwinismus," in *Analysis der Wirklichkeit*, 3rd ed. (Straßburg: Trübner, 1900), pp. 318–19.

3

THE *IGNORABIMUS*

CONTROVERSY

1. DU BOIS-REYMOND'S SPEECH:
CONTENT AND CONTEXT

On August 14, 1872, Emil Du Bois-Reymond, Rector of Berlin University and one of the most prominent physiologists of his age, gave a lecture to the forty-fifth *Versammlung deutscher Naturforscher und Ärtze* in Leipzig. It was an auspicious occasion for a lecture: before such an eminent body, the lecturer had the best audience for testing his views and the best opportunity for publicizing them. Du Bois-Reymond's lecture, entitled *Über die Grenzen des Naturerkennens*,[1] was an attempt to take stock of the achievements of natural science in his age: how far it had gone, how far it could go, and what obstacles there might be to its progress. Du Bois-Reymond compared the modern scientist to a world conquerer who was now taking account of his dominions before marching forward in a victory parade.

Given that flattering metaphor, the audience had every reason to expect an optimistic prediction about the future of science. And given Du Bois-Reymond's reputation, they also had good reason to assume that he would stress the powers rather than limits of science. Du Bois-Reymond was well-known for his leading role in the physicalist program in physiology, according to which all life could be explained on a strictly mechanical basis. Yet the audience that day was in for a shock. Rather than extolling the powers of natural science, Du Bois-Reymond stressed its limits. The audience

---

1 Emil Du Bois-Reymond, *Über die Grenzen des Naturerkennens. Ein Vortrag in der zweiten öffentlichen Sitzung der 45. Versammlung Deutscher Naturforscher und Ärtze zu Leipzig am 14. August 1872* (Leipzig: Veit & Co., 1872).

97

expected to hear a dogmatic mechanist preaching against the obscurities of *Lebenskraft* and *Naturphilosophie*; instead, they seemed to hear an old Pyrrhonnian skeptic intoning about the limits of knowledge. Du Bois-Reymond declared that there are two insurmountable limits to all scientific knowledge: the nature of matter; and the connection between consciousness and the brain. All scientific knowledge oscillated between these two limits—matter and mind—which served as impassable border posts. About these two topics, Du Bois-Reymond maintained, we would forever remain ignorant. To emphasize the point, he concluded his speech with the solemn and emphatic Latin word: "*Ignorabimus!*" We will be ignorant.

The reaction to Du Bois-Reymond's lecture was as tumultuous as its content was controversial. It was the starting point for an intense discussion about the limits of natural science that would last for decades. Participating in the discussion would be some of the greatest minds of the nineteenth century: Eduard von Hartmann, Wilhelm Dilthey, Friedrich Albert Lange, Ernst Häckel, David Friedrich Strauss, and Ludwig Büchner. Well into the twentieth century, Heinrich Rickert, Ludwig Wittgenstein, and Rudolf Carnap would take issue with Du Bois-Reymond's lecture.[2] The lecture proved divisive and provoked extreme reactions. Some descried Du Bois-Reymond's lecture as a betrayal of the cause of science, while others celebrated it as a timely reminder of its limits. To many theologians, the fact that one of the chief spokesmen for the physicalist program would frankly admit the limits of science was telling: here, from the mouth of the devil, came a *mea culpa*. To his old colleagues, however, Du Bois-Reymond's lecture seemed to be the work of a traitor who had now given aid and comfort to the enemy.

What, exactly, did Du Bois-Reymond say on that August day to arouse so much controversy? To understand its impact, we need a better idea of its contents.

---

2 See Heinrich Rickert, *Die Grenzen der naturwissenschaftlichen Begriffsbildung*, Fünfte Auflage (Tübingen: Mohr, 1929), pp. 207, 402, 461, 631; Ludwig Wittgenstein, *Tractatus logico-philosophicus* (London: Routledge & Kegan Paul, 1961), 4.11, 6.5 and "Vorwort des Verfassers"; and Rudolf Carnap, *Der logische Aufbau der Welt* (Berlin-Schlachtensee: Weltkreisverlag, 1928), §§164–65.

Du Bois-Reymond begins his lecture by specifying what he means by scientific explanation. Before we determine the limits of scientific knowledge, we first have to know in what such knowledge consists, he says reasonably enough. What is the model of scientific explanation? Du Bois-Reymond gives an admirably clear answer: it consists in the laws of classical mechanics, and more specifically in the reduction of all changes in the physical world down to the movements of atoms (2). To explain natural events is therefore to subsume them under "the mechanics of atoms." Since the laws of such mechanics are mathematically formulable, they have all the certainty of mathematics. Following this paradigm, the ideal of knowledge is a system of differential equations from which we can determine, with complete precision and accuracy, what happens in the universe at any given place and time (3). If we know these equations, and if we also know the position, velocity, and direction of all the atoms in one moment of the universe, we can determine with complete precision their position, velocity, and direction at every other moment, whether in the past or future. Ultimately, we could formulate for this system of equations a single mathematical formula to express the whole of these mechanical relations, so that the whole world becomes, as D'Alembert said in the introduction to the *Encyclopédie*,[3] "a single fact and one great truth" (5). This was the ideal of knowledge once formulated by the French physicist Pierre Laplace (1749–1827), who held that a mind who knew the laws of mechanics could determine from the movements of all planets and atoms at one moment all their movements at every other moment in the past and future (3–4).[4] Although Du Bois-Reymond admitted that natural scientists are still far from achieving this Laplacian ideal, he stressed that, at least in principle, there is no obstacle to it; the problems in achieving it are simply practical and concern the collection of the data to fit the equations (5, 7–8).

3 Du Bois-Reymond cites D'Alembert, *Discours préliminaire* from the first volume of the *Encyclopédie* (Paris: Briason, David l'aîné, Le Breton, Durand, 1751), I, p. ix.

4 Du Bois-Reymond cites Laplace's *Essai philosophique sur les probabilités*, 2nd ed. (Paris: Courcier, 1814), p. 3.

Given that Laplace's ideal represents "the highest conceivable stage of our knowledge of nature," it is then possible to determine, Du Bois-Reymond contends, the limits of our knowledge of nature (8). What we cannot know according to this ideal will mark the limits of our knowledge in general, as the mathematical-mechanical paradigm is the most perfect form of *all* knowledge.[5]

There are two places, Du Bois-Reymond argues, where the Laplacian mind has to stop dead in its tracks and beyond which it cannot go. One of these concerns the nature of matter itself. Rather than the self-evident basis of explanation, matter is for Du Bois-Reymond the great mystery. The atomistic hypothesis, the assumption that the world consists in small indivisible particles, ultimately does not provide a satisfactory account of matter. Explaining phenomena in terms of these particles works so far, because we explain wholes by their parts; we want to go further, however, and explain the parts themselves. But then, Du Bois-Reymond insists, we find ourselves caught in irresolvable difficulties. A *physical* atom is really just a fiction of mathematical physics; nowadays physicists have ceased to talk about atoms and refer instead to the smallest elements of a given volume (9).[6] A *philosophical* atom, i.e., an indivisible and inert particle of some inactive substrate, is really "a nonentity" because there is no reason why divisibility should stop at any point (10). The atomistic hypothesis is really just a fantasy for Du Bois-Reymond, because we project onto the atoms, about which we really know nothing, the empirical qualities that we have from our own sense experience (11). All that we are supposed to explain on the macrocosmical level—properties like mass, density,

5   The generalization of the mathematical-mechanical paradigm, which became a major source of controversy, is only implicit in Du Bois-Reymond's lecture. But it is more explicit in a later writing: "There is no other knowledge for us other than the mechanical . . . and consequently there is only one true scientific form of thought, the physical mathematical." See *Darwin versus Galiani* (Berlin: Hirschwald, 1876), p. 26.

6   Here (p. 8) Du Bois-Reymond refers to Hermann Helmholtz's lecture, "Gedächtnisrede auf Gustav Magnus." See Helmholtz, *Vorträge und Reden* (Braunschweig: Vieweg und Sohn, 1896), II, 33–51, esp. 45–46. In maintaining that the atom is a fiction, however, Du Bois-Reymond is more radical than Helmholtz, who is agnostic about the issue.

impenetrability—we then simply presuppose on the microcosmical level, so that we have not really explained anything at all.

The other ultimate limit of our knowledge concerns the relationship between consciousness and brain states. Du Bois-Reymond, true to his physicalist program, thinks that there is nothing mysterious about the origin of life. We should not think that there is something supernatural about the origin of life; it is nothing more than a difficult mechanical problem (15). Even if we could not observe the original creation, we could still retrodict from a Laplacian equation what happened (15).[7] Problems begin not at the level of life but at that of consciousness, which will always remain inexplicable (17). Why? Du Bois-Reymond rejects all dualistic presuppositions, any assumption that the soul is a different substance from the body. These presuppositions in the past made it impossible to explain the interaction between mind and body. But even if we discard these old preconceptions, Du Bois-Reymond argues, we find it impossible to explain the origins of consciousness. The problem lies with our original Laplacian paradigm of explanation, which determines from the position, direction, and velocity of particles at one moment their position, direction, and velocity at any other moment; it makes the explanans the position, direction, and velocity of particles; but we cannot attribute such physical characteristics to consciousness itself. The paradigm is therefore limited to explaining only matter (24–25). We could perhaps have a complete brain science where we might be able to determine from chemical elements active in nerves and tissues the basis of our sensations and thoughts; we might even be able to correlate certain chemical interactions with particular sensations and thoughts. But we still would not understand the *connection* of the chemistry with those sensations and thoughts. It is forever inconceivable to us just how a combination of carbon, hydrogen, and oxygen produces consciousness (26).

Such were, in essence, Du Bois-Reymond's chief arguments for the limits of natural science. At first thought, it is difficult to see

7   Du Bois-Reymond was not always as optimistic and simplistic as he appears in this lecture. In *Darwin versus Galiani*, pp. 13–15, he stresses that organic laws of development have at best a greater or lesser degree of probability.

why they created such a furor. These were old and worn arguments, having a history going back at least to Locke and the French materialists. It is noteworthy, though, that Du Bois-Reymond himself made no claim for their discovery or originality; indeed, he later confessed that he was almost ashamed to pass off such "stale beer" to his eminent audience.[8] Why, then, all the hubbub? The reason for the stormy reaction had as much to do with the context as the content of the lecture.[9] It was important that Du Bois-Reymond was such a prominent figure—the Rector of the University of Berlin—and that he spoke on such a prominent occasion: a public session of a prestigious conference. It was no less important that Du Bois-Reymond was neither a theologian nor a philosopher but a famous scientist. Most of the spokesmen for the limits of science during the materialism controversy had been philosophers with idealist commitments or theologians with theistic convictions. Now, with Du Bois-Reymond, the limits of science theme was coming from the mouth of a scientist, who presumably was less biased and who surely knew the inner workings of his discipline. Add to this the fact that Du Bois-Reymond had been a physicalist, his testimony had even more weight. As that old saying goes: Never is the sound of truth so sweet than when spoken from the mouth of the devil.

Another source of turmoil, although it is never made explicit, came from the political context of the *Ignorabimusstreit*. The beginning of the dispute in 1872 coincides, not accidentally, with the onset of the first major political conflict of the new German Reich: the *Kulturkampf.* This conflict concerned the rights of the Catholic Church in the new Reich, which was now under the control of traditionally Protestant Prussia. The main problem was how to control and integrate Catholics in the New Reich. The problem was especially acute, because the pope had declared his infallibility in 1870, giving himself, at least in theory, absolute power over laymen and even the state. Fearful of the power of the pope and its new Catholic

8 Emil Du Bois-Reymond, "Die Sieben Welträtsel. Nachtrag," *Monatsbericht der Königlich-Preussischen Akademie der Wissenschaften zu Berlin* (1880), 1045–72, esp. 1045.

9 As has been well argued by Kurt Bayertz, Myrian Gerhard, and Walter Jaeschke in their introduction to *Der Ignorabimus-Streit* (Hamburg: Meiner, 2012), pp. xxi–xxvi.

citizens, the Prussian state enacted measures against the Church: it banished Jesuits, closed Catholic schools, and abolished the Roman Catholic Office of the Prussian Cultural Ministry. With the *Maigesetze* of 1873, the Prussian state attempted to limit the powers of the Church even further, imposing restrictions on the disciplining of laymen, clerical appointments, and training. The Church pushed back, refusing obedience to the laws. It eventually became clear to Bismarck and others that these policies were not going to integrate the Roman Catholics into the new Reich and that they posed a major danger to its unity. Rather than clamping down harder on the Roman Catholics, it was necessary to be more conciliatory.

It was in this atmosphere that some scientists in Berlin became troubled by the prospects for freedom of the sciences. The Roman Catholic Church was utterly opposed to the physicalist program and Darwinianism, and it could demand placing restrictions on science as a condition for integration into the Reich. Resistance on the part of the Church, and a clampdown on scientific freedom, would be certain if scientists insisted on putting these doctrines into the school curriculum. These dangers were pointed out by Rudolf Virchow (1821–1902), the head of the Institute for Pathology in Berlin, in a remarkable lecture he gave in 1877 at the fiftieth *Versammlung deutscher Naturforscher und Ärtze* in Munich, "Die Freiheit der Wissenschaft im modernen Staat."[10] Virchow pleaded with the natural scientists to restrain themselves and not to introduce evolutionary and materialist theories into the school curriculum. They had to distinguish between fact and theory, and it was only facts that should be placed in the curriculum. If they insisted on teaching theory, he warned, they would encounter stiff reaction and the potential loss of their academic freedom.

In a strong counterattack on Virchow's speech,[11] Ernst Haeckel, the chief advocate of evolutionary theory in Germany, charged his old teacher with surrendering to the forces of darkness. There

10   Rudolf Virchow, *Die Freiheit der Wissenschaft im modernen Staat* (Berlin: Wiegandt, Hempel & Parey, 1877).
11   Ernst Haeckel, *Freie Wissenschaft und freie Lehre. Eine Entgegung auf Rudolf Virchow's Münchener Rede* (Stuttgart: Schweizerbart'sche Verlagsbuchhandlung, 1878).

was a veiled threat behind Virchow's speech: those who preach evolution and materialist doctrine would be dismissed from their posts by the government. Though the precise content of Haeckel's reply does not concern us here, it was striking that he connected Du Bois-Reymond's earlier speech with Virchow's.[12] He saw both lectures as episodes in one conservative campaign. Both were attempts to limit natural science to appease the conservative opposition. Both preached self-restraint as a necessary means to preserve academic freedom.

In many respects the *Ignorabimusstreit* was simply a continuation of the materialism controversy from a different perspective. Now the focus was more strictly epistemological: the limits of science. There was less emphasis on the directions of science, and its implications for religious and moral faith, though these issues were never far from view. Simply because Du Bois-Reymond's lecture raised so much controversy on its own, it is legitimate and useful to treat it separately.

It is impossible to do full justice here to the many contributions to the *Ignorabimusstreit*. We will examine only the highlights. Needless to say, the responses were very various; but we can permit one generalization about them. There were two kinds of opponents to Du Bois-Reymond's lecture: those who accepted his mathematical-mechanical paradigm but demanded that he not limit it (Büchner, Haeckel, Nägeli); and those who questioned his paradigm as an undue limitation upon other kinds of knowledge (Hartmann, Dilthey, Rathenau).

2. HARTMANN'S DEFENSE OF METAPHYSICS

It was with great consternation that the young Eduard von Hartmann read Du Bois-Reymond's lecture a few months after its publication in August 1872. This was a threat to everything that he had been struggling to accomplish for many years. The chief aim of his *Philosophie des Unbewussten*, which had appeared a few years earlier, was to rehabilitate metaphysics on the foundation of natural science. But in his lecture Du Bois-Reymond assumed that the limits

12   Ibid., pp. 78–93.

of natural scientific knowledge are the limits of knowledge, and he argued that any attempt to go beyond these limits ends in contradiction. A metaphysics that attempted to give a unified picture of the world beyond those limits is therefore impossible. Implicitly, Du Bois-Reymond ruled out the possibility of Hartmann's entire project.

Given such a threat, it was self-evident that Hartmann would want to defend his project and to examine Du Bois-Reymond's lecture. He did so in an article in the *Wiener Abendpost*, which appeared in February 1873.[13] The article is of interest not only for its defense of Hartmann's metaphysics but also for its critique of Du Bois-Reymond's arguments.

Hartmann begins his article by locating Du Bois-Reymond's lecture in its historical context, the state of philosophy, and the sciences in the 1870s. After decades of decline Hartmann sees signs for hope in the future of philosophy. The statistics about book sales in the previous three years, he writes with his own book in mind,[14] show a remarkable sign of interest in metaphysics among the general public (447–48). There is also a new spirit of self-reflection and self-criticism in the natural sciences, of which Du Bois-Reymond's lecture is a sterling example (448–49). Gone are the days when the materialists—Moleschott, Vogt, and Büchner—could claim that their philosophy represents the spirit of the natural sciences. Philosophers nowadays, thanks to the rise of neo-Kantianism, are aware of the difference between natural science and the metaphysics based upon it (448). Du Bois-Reymond has helped destroy the illusion that all the puzzles of life, and all the problems of existence, can be solved by natural

13 Eduard von Hartmann, "Anfänge naturwissenschaftlicher Selbsterkenntniss," *Wiener Abendpost*, Nr. 33 (10. Februar 1873), 260; Nr. 34 (11. Februar, 1873), 268–69; Nr. 35 (12. Februar 1873), 276, reprinted in *Gesammelte Studien und Aufsätze gemeinverständlichen Inhalts* (Berlin: Duncker, 1876), 445–59. All references in parentheses are to this later edition.

14 Hartmann does not explicitly mention his book, but he could justifiably point to a renewal of philosophical interest from its remarkable success. Published originally in 1869, *Die Philosophie des Unbewussten* went through eleven editions until 1903. For all the editions and copies printed, see Carl Heymons, *Eduard von Hartmann, Erinnerungen aus den Jahren 1868–1881* (Berlin: Duncker, 1882), p. 60.

science; in place of such naiveté and dogmatism he has advanced a modest and healthy sense of its limits (449).

As much as Hartmann praises Du Bois-Reymond for determining the limits of natural science, he criticizes him for thinking that it provides the paradigm of knowledge in general. By making the natural sciences such a model, he actually goes far beyond their limits and implicitly endorses a scientific dogmatism (449). The fatal error of his lecture is that there are no methods or kinds of knowledge other than those of the natural sciences (451). Du Bois-Reymond is perfectly correct in defining the methods of the natural sciences by the paradigm of classical mechanics; but that simply goes to show the limits of natural science itself: what cannot be determined in numbers and covering laws does not exist for it (450–51). Even within the domain of nature alone, leaving aside the human sciences, there is more than just classical mechanics, Hartmann argues (449–51). We should recognize that there are three stages of knowledge regarding nature. First, there is natural history (*Naturkunde*), which collects facts about natural objects and events, classifies them from a comparative standpoint, and orders them into a system. Second, there is natural science proper (*Naturwissenschaft*), which determines the causal connections between these facts and the general laws governing nature. Third, there is natural philosophy (*Naturphilosophie*), which investigates the principles with which natural science operates and which determines the nature of the cosmos as a whole. Du Bois-Reymond considers only the second stage and refuses to acknowledge the possibility of the third. That he denies the possibility of a natural philosophy is clear: he maintains, in a passage reminiscent of Kant's Antinomies, that any attempt to go beyond the limits of classical mechanics will result in "unresolvable contradictions" (452).

Hartmann thinks that it is a grave blindness on Du Bois-Reymond's part not to acknowledge the possibility of a natural philosophy. What he fails to see is that the natural sciences themselves presuppose principles that cannot be based on any experience, e.g., the principle of causality (452). These principles are residues of earlier natural philosophy, which have been incorporated into the sciences themselves. They are simply presupposed by them, and they are used as long as they are useful; but they are not examined by the natural sciences themselves. All of natural science, Hartmann declares, is possible only on the foundation of an already presupposed natural philosophy. It is self-evident that the progress of the sciences sometimes shows the deficiencies of these presuppositions; but it does not follow from this that the philosophical foundation of natural science is superfluous (453). Furthermore, Kant's antinomies are no threat to a future natural philosophy, Hartmann claims, because the progress of the sciences shows the need for a convergence of the dynamic and atomistic theories of matter, a synthesis that shows their compatibility and interdependence (453).[15]

The indefensible narrowness of Du Bois-Reymond's conception of knowledge is especially apparent, Hartmann argues, when it comes to the sciences of the mind or the *Geisteswissenschaften* (452, 456–57). By insisting that all knowledge is the natural scientific knowledge of classical mechanics and by teaching that knowledge of consciousness stands beyond its reach, Du Bois-Reymond relegates the entire realm of consciousness to the realm of the unknowable. But there is something deeply paradoxical to this, Hartmann finds. Rather than unknowable, the realm of consciousness is more knowable than the natural world that exists outside us. While our self-consciousness is clear and immediate, knowledge of nature is obscure and mediate, based upon inferences from our consciousness (452). So if all consciousness is unknowable, how can we claim to have knowledge of nature itself? So limited is Du Bois-Reymond's vision that he does not recognize the increasing progress and stature of the science of history, whose methods and standards of knowledge are no less scientific than the natural sciences (447).

In the confines of a short article Hartmann could not do much to establish the possibility of metaphysics. The most he could do is show the hole in Du Bois-Reymond's argument in excluding its possibility. Hartmann contented himself simply with pointing out the necessity for a metaphysics. Its great value consisted partly in its critical examination of the principles and concepts presupposed

---

15 Here Hartmann refers us to the discussion in *Philosophie des Unbewussten*, chapter C.V, and his article "Dynamismus und Atomismus," in *Gesammelte Philosophische Abhandlungen zur Philosophie des Unbewussten* (Berlin: Duncker, 1872), pp. 113–32.

by the natural sciences and partly in its attempt to provide a unified picture of the world, one which would lay bare the unity of physical and mental phenomena. There is an irrepressible need for a unifying and enclosed worldview, he insists, and it is a great loss to philosophy, and the human spirit itself, to declare its impossibility. It is in declaring its impossibility that we go beyond the limits of science.

Whatever its merits, Hartmann's plea for a new metaphysics did not go unheeded; we will soon see how it was taken up by another unhappy spirit in the 1890s.[16]

3. THE MATERIALIST POSITION

The materialist reaction to Du Bois-Reymond's lecture appears in its greatest clarity and force in the writings of Ludwig Büchner, which are the loci classici of the materialist response. These writings include later editions of *Kraft und Stoff*,[17] passages from the third edition of his *Physiologische Bilder*,[18] and two later articles reprinted in his collection *Im Dienst der Wahrheit*.[19]

In *Kraft und Stoff* Büchner is almost incredulous that Du Bois-Reymond, whom he once regarded as an ally in the battle against spiritualism and obscurantism, could have delivered such a lecture. Could he not see that he had given aid and comfort to "spiritualist fools" and "men of darkness"? Büchner takes exception especially to Du Bois-Reymond's declaration that the realm of consciousness is inexplicable by the methods of natural science (268). Was this really the same Du Bois-Reymond who had banished the idea of a *Lebenskraft* from physiology, and who had maintained that the origins of life could be explained on a mechanical basis? Büchner had duly cited Du Bois-Reymond's lines to the effect that

16 See section 7.
17 Ludwig Büchner, *Kraft und Stoff*, Einundzwanzigste durchgesehene Auflage (Leipzig: Theodore Thomas, 1904), pp. 2, 151, 267–69, 421–22.
18 Ludwig Büchner, *Physiologische Bilder*, Dritte Auflage (Leipzig: Theodore Thomas, 1886), I, 430ff and Band II, 179ff.
19 Ludwig Büchner, "Über den Begriff der Materie und über Materialismus" and "Das Unerkennbare," in *Im Dienste der Wahrheit* (Gießen: Emil Roth, 1900), pp. 16–22, 266–74.

original creation could be produced in a laboratory under the right conditions (151). If life could be explained on the basis of material conditions, why not consciousness, too? Büchner thought that Du Bois-Reymond was drawing an artificial line between life and consciousness. This was all the more inappropriate given that we still knew too little about matter to make such a dogmatic pronouncement as we would *never* be able to explain consciousness. With a dogmatic confidence of his own, Büchner declares that consciousness and thinking are "an organization, performance, or expression of activity of certain parts or structures of the brain" (267). It is still unknown exactly *how* consciousness arises from matter, Büchner concedes, whether it is from a mind implicit in molecules or from an organization of molecules under specific conditions. But that does not matter, Büchner insists. The general point remains: there is no immaterial substance present in consciousness, some spiritual thing that prevents an explanation according to mechanical laws (267). We have no reason to depart from the "monistic standpoint," Büchner reassures us, according to which consciousness and thinking are parts of nature and explicable according to the laws of mechanical causality (268). The final paragraph of *Kraft und Stoff* closes with a parting shot at Du Bois-Reymond and all the agnostics of modern science who believe in a realm of the unknowable (422). That realm, Büchner declares, is an *Asylum ignorantiae*, "nothing more than the old dear God of the theologians."

In a later article, "Das Unerkennbare,"[20] Büchner states with greater clarity and generality the philosophical issues dividing him from Du Bois-Reymond. Here he takes issue with all those philosophers and scientists who express an "agnosticism" about the ultimate causes of the universe. Among these protagonists of the unknowable he includes Spencer, Huxley, and Darwin, though he advises the English to take note that their views had already been formulated years earlier by Du Bois-Reymond. Büchner finds the belief in the unknowable objectionable chiefly because it is "dualistic as well as supernaturalistic" (270). It divides the world into two distinct realms, one natural and knowable and another super-

---

20 Ludwig Büchner, "Das Unerkennbare," in *Im Dienste der Wahrheit*, pp. 266–74.

natural and mystical. But we have no reason to postulate such a supernatural and mystical realm, Büchner argues, because we cannot presume that what is unknown now will be unknowable in the future (270). The whole idea of the unknowable arises from making an absolute limit and final stopping point out of the present state of science. We cannot foresee now, however, where science will lead us, so that it is unwise to infer that there is a limit beyond which we cannot go. The more science progresses, the more it shrinks the realm of the unknown, so that we have reason to think that the unknown will eventually, or at least in principle, disappear. There are many problems that we have not solved, and there are many things of which we still know nothing; but there are no phenomena in the world that are in principle inexplicable (271). Against the dualistic view of the agnostics, Büchner declares his own monism, according to which everything that exists falls within the realm of nature, so that it is in principle explicable according to mechanical laws: "Nature is a whole for itself, and all of its appearances are connected with one another according to the law of causality" (271). Because nature is a single whole, and because everything within it falls under the principle of causality, which is the principle for the explanation of things, it follows that nature is a completely comprehensible realm: "The problems that nature gives us to solve are innumerable, the field of research is unlimited. But all problems are resolvable, as far as the causes of natural phenomena are concerned; nature knows no unknowable" (274).

Büchner's point about a premature drawing of limits is made all the more forcefully and clearly in another later article, "Über den Begriff der Materie und über Materialismus."[21] Here Büchner reminds his readers of how much the concept of matter has changed in the last decades and how far removed it has become from our commonsense idea of matter as an inert mass. We now know that matter possesses chemical and electromagnetic properties that were formerly regarded as separate from it (18). Scientists formerly regarded electricity, heat, and light as phenomena distinct from matter; but they are now seen as intrinsic to it. When authors

21 Ludwig Büchner, "Über den Begriff der Materie und über Materialismus," in *Im Dienste der Wahrheit*, pp. 16–22.

like Du Bois-Reymond hold that consciousness is inexplicable on a material basis they have in mind the old commonsense idea of matter, which has been antiquated by science. To be sure, inert masses by themselves cannot explain the rise of consciousness; but the prospects of a material-mechanical explanation are very different once we recognize that matter includes properties like electromagnetism and chemical interactions (19). If we declare that matter cannot bring forth consciousness, we are simply abstracting from these properties and lapsing into the old commonsense notion (20, 21). Using the old concept of matter, who could have understood a flash of lightning? Or the sending of messages through a telegraph wire? These phenomena are bound to appear as supernatural for a primitive or savage mind. But is not Du Bois-Reymond, Büchner suggests, indulging in the same primitive habits in assuming that the mind is something supernatural?

Although Büchner is confident that there can be, eventually and not only in principle, a materialist explanation of consciousness, he is careful to say that such an explanation does not mean that consciousness and thought are material themselves (20). Consciousness and thought are not material things but they are products or manifestations of the activity of matter. Just as electricity, magnetism, and heat are forms of the activity of matter, so are consciousness and thought. They are not properties of what matter *is* but what it *does* (21). There is a great difference between what one normally calls matter and the phenomena that it is capable of producing, so that we cannot say that life, consciousness, and mind are only matter or the movement of matter; all that we can say is that the phenomena are appearances or manifestations of the powers inherent in matter when its particles combine in certain ways under certain conditions (21–22).

So Büchner's universe is ultimately a very comprehensible, rational place. No mysteries or puzzles dwell within it. We comprehend things when we subsume them under the law of causality; and everything in nature conforms to that principle. Hence there are no limits, at least in principle, to what we can know. Never did Büchner take exception to Du Bois-Reymond's paradigm of scientific explanation; still less did he invoke another or additional paradigms, as Dilthey would, to extend the realm of science. He indeed noted that he shared with Du Bois-Reymond the same mechanical account of scientific explanation.[22] The only difference between the two mechanists ultimately concerned their explanans: the nature of matter itself. Büchner thought matter a much richer concept than did Du Bois-Reymond, who, he rightly complained, remained stuck in the old Cartesian paradigm.[23]

Yet for all Büchner's contempt for the incomprehensible and mysterious he did not entirely avoid it himself. In "Das Unerkennbare" he stated that everything we know exists within the realm of nature but that we cannot know the ultimate cause of nature itself (273). The final puzzle of existence, about which people would never cease to trouble themselves, is the eternal question "Why?" i.e., what is the purpose of existence or why is there something rather than nothing (274). We could designate this question with the name "unknowable," so long as we did not misuse the word for theological ends. But Büchner had simply moved the goalposts back another step. If the unknowable is nowhere in nature—not in matter or consciousness—it still lies beyond nature. But that gives the theologians, spiritualists, and obscurantists all the play room they could have ever desired.

4. LANGE'S DEFENSE OF DU BOIS-REYMOND

Of all the participants to the *Ignorabimusstreit*, none came closer to Du Bois-Reymond's position than Friedrich Albert Lange. In the second edition of his *Geschichte des Materialismus*, which appeared in 1875, he introduced two new chapters discussing Du Bois-Reymond's lecture.[24] The first of these chapters is a defense

---

22 Büchner, *Kraft und Stoff*, p. 268.

23 Du Bois-Reymond wrote in his *Die sieben Weltraetsel*, p. 1054, fully in accord with the Cartesian paradigm, that motion is something accidental for matter. It was for this reason that the origin of motion was one of the seven mysteries of the universe.

24 Friedrich Albert Lange, *Geschichte des Materialismus und Kritik seiner Bedeutung in der Gegenwart*, Zweite, Verbesserte und Vermehrte Auflage (Iserlohn: Baedeker, 1875), II, 139–81, Buch II, Zweiter Abschnitt, "Die Naturwissenschaften": Kap. I, "Der Materialismus und die exacte Forschung," 139–81, and Kap. II, "Kraft und Stoff," 181–220.

of Du Bois-Reymond against his many critics. Incorporating Du Bois-Reymond's arguments into his critique of materialism, Lange gave them a Kantian twist: they demonstrated that we cannot have knowledge of things-in-themselves, that all knowledge is limited to appearances. But this twist Du Bois-Reymond disliked. He found Kant's philosophy esoteric and scholastic, qualities that ran counter to the spirit of modern science.[25]

Lange could not but see Du Bois-Reymond's lecture as a vindication of his own account of the methods and limits of knowledge as it appeared in the first edition of *Geschichte des Materialismus*,[26] which was published in 1866. Lange had endorsed the same mechanical-atomistic paradigm of knowledge as Du Bois-Reymond. The first volume of his *Geschichte* is a critique of the organic and teleological worldview of the Platonic-Aristotelian tradition, and a defense of the mechanical and atomistic worldview of Democritus and Lucretius. No less than Du Bois-Reymond, Lange argued that it is a mistake to think that the application of the mechanical-atomistic method results in materialism. Although it claims to be based strictly on the natural sciences, materialism is a dogmatic metaphysics that goes beyond the evidence of the senses and makes inferences about the nature of ultimate reality. Lange's account of the limits of the mechanical-atomistic paradigm also anticipated Du Bois-Reymond. Lange had stressed that it had been one of the classical problems of materialism that it could not explain the qualities of sensation from the movements of matter.[27] There seemed to be a gap between the world as we experience it in consciousness and the world as it is formulated in mathematics. He had also found some of the same problems with the ultimate comprehensibility of matter.[28]

---

25 See his comments in "Die sieben Weltraetsel," p. 1046. It is unclear whether Du Bois-Reymond is commenting on Lange. Hartmann had made similar remarks about the similarity between Du Bois-Reymond's and Kant's theories about the limits of knowledge.

26 Friedrich Albert Lange, *Geschichte des Materialismus und Kritik seiner Bedeutung in der Gegenwart* (Iserlohn: Baedeker, 1866).

27 Ibid., pp. 216, 228.

28 Ibid., pp. 371–81.

Given the confirmation Lange found for his views, it stood to reason that he would want to discuss and defend Du Bois-Reymond in the second edition of his *Geschichte*. Chapter I of Section II examines Du Bois-Reymond's first limit on knowledge, while chapter II goes on to consider his second limit. Lange contends that both the materialists, who have opposed Du Bois-Reymond, and the spiritualists, who have approved and celebrated him, have misunderstood him. Both think that Du Bois-Reymond has made the mental realm into something supernatural and inaccessible to scientific explanation. But Du Bois-Reymond never took that position. From the very beginning he assumed that there could be, at least in principle, a science of the human mind, that the Laplacian genius could predict with complete accuracy human feelings, thoughts, desires, and actions from the movement of atoms in their brain and nerve states (156–57). Where Du Bois-Reymond drew a line in the explanation of mental life was regarding the causal relation between mental and brain states. Although they could be correlated in a system of laws so that one covaries with the other, it is impossible to understand, because they are so heterogeneous, how one can be the cause or effect of the other (160). The best way to understand Du Bois-Reymond's theory of the limits of science, Lange suggested, is to assume that there are two worlds which are ultimately identical, where one consists in the movements of machines, in which nothing is thought, sensed, or felt, and where the other consists in inner experience; the formula for the two worlds would be the same even if their characteristics are heterogeneous (156). That interpretation sounds distinctly Leibnizan, like Leibniz's preestablished harmony. But Lange later proposes a more Spinozist interpretation: that we conceive of the two worlds as the attributes of a single substance, as if they were one and the same thing conceived in different ways or perspectives (163).

Lange thinks that Du Bois-Reymond's account of the limits of scientific knowledge concerning matter is no less correct than that concerning consciousness. He shows the same skepticism and reservations about the atomic theory as Du Bois-Reymond. One can say that atomism has been demonstrated, Lange argues, but only if by that one means natural explanation presupposes that there are discrete particles that move in space; but this formulation does not resolve but only begs questions about the ultimate constitution of matter (208). The sole virtue of atomism is that it is intuitive—we imagine little balls moving around in space—but the progress of physics is making this picture useless. The concept of matter as a small solid body occupying space is now being replaced with the idea of matter as a locus of force, where force is something supersensible (192). Like Du Bois-Reymond, Lange thinks that the concept of the atom is really a fiction that we read into nature, and that it arises from projecting our ordinary intuitions from the macrocosm onto the microcosm. Not surprisingly, then, he takes issue with Büchner's claim that the reality of the atom is now a confirmed fact (181). The atom, understood as a solid body in which forces are located, is really only an hypostasis, a reification arising from the assumption that there must be some substrate in which forces inhere (205). Lange finds that even the idea of force, if we imagine it as a strange power pushing things around, is no less an hypostasis (205–6). Force is not the cause of motion, and matter is not the cause of force; there is only movement and force has to be understood as a function of movement (206). Lange anticipates the later philosophy of science of the Marburg school when he claims that scientific knowledge consists in the analysis of things into relations where the thing itself, the subject of relations, increasingly disappears (207).

For all the affinities between Lange and Du Bois-Reymond, there remained important differences between them. Though both objected to materialism, they did not agree about what is wrong with it. Lange objected to materialism first and foremost because of its transcendental realism, its naïve belief in the independent existence of matter, and its assumption that the primary qualities of our experience exist independent of our perception of them. But Du Bois-Reymond never took Lange's step toward transcendental idealism. His arguments against materialism are still compatible with a transcendental realism; and even though he argues that the notion of an atom is a fiction, this does not mean for him that the objects of our ordinary experience are dependent on our consciousness. Whatever his beliefs about the status of consciousness, Du Bois-Reymond seemed to believe perfectly happily in the existence of matter itself. He seemed to have little interest or inclination to investigate the claims of transcendental idealism about its ultimate reality.

Though Du Bois-Reymond disapproved of Lange's Kantian rendition of his arguments, he was especially grateful for Lange's sympathetic and sophisticated interpretation of his arguments. He paid kind tribute to Lange, who had died in 1875, the very year the second edition of *Die Geschichte des Materialismus* appeared. Lange, he wrote, was one of the few to understand that it was never his purpose to reestablish dualism. He taught all his critics a valuable lesson: "Whoever has not understood me should to learn to read better."[29]

5. NÄGELI'S METHODOLOGICAL MATERIALISM

In June 1876 the Swiss botanist Carl von Nägeli (1817–1981) was preparing for a trip to the Alps to collect specimens of plants and flowers. He was surprised by a request from the *Versammlung deutscher Naturforscher und Ärtze* to hold a plenary lecture for the forthcoming assembly in September. The planned speaker could not come to Munich, so a replacement was urgently needed. Despite the short notice and great inconvenience, Nägeli graciously accepted the request and hastily threw together a lecture. He later apologized for its lack of polish on the plausible grounds that it is hard to collect one's thoughts and philosophize while on an Alpine expedition. Yet Nägeli's inconvenience has been our gain. Despite the challenging conditions of its composition, his lecture was one of the best contributions to the *Ignorabimusstreit*.[30] Its often incisive reasoning reveals the author's philosophical inclinations and training.[31]

---

29 See Du Bois-Reymond, "Die sieben Weltraetsel," p. 1048.

30 Carl von Nägeli, "Ueber die Schranken der naturwissenschaftlichen Erkenntniss," in *Amtlicher Bericht ueber die Versammlung deutscher Natuforscher und Ärtze* Bd. 50 (1877), 25–41. All references in parentheses are to this edition. The article has been reprinted in *Der Ignorabimus-Streit*, pp. 109–52.

31 Nägeli's first inclination was to study philosophy. He studied *Naturphilosophie* under Lorenz Oken and logic under Hegel. His later thinking moved away from their metaphysics, however.

Nägeli started his lecture by reminding his listeners of Du Bois-Reymond's lecture to the *Versammlung* five years earlier, and by informing them that he would approach the question of the limits of knowledge from a very different and much broader perspective. The broader perspective is immediately apparent in Nägeli's attempt to answer the general question of how we know nature. Part of Nägeli's answer is a straightforward empiricism: it is through sense perception that we first acquire knowledge of nature. Although the senses have to be refined and strengthened through instruments and strict methods of observation and experiment, they still provide the basic evidence on which all knowledge of nature rests (28). We must recognize, however, that our human senses provide us with only a very limited knowledge of nature. The senses we have are only those that our organism needs; other creatures sometimes have sharper senses for their different needs (28–29). We probably lack senses that are necessary to perceive many parts of nature; and the senses that we do have inform us about only a small part of time (the present) and about only a small part of space (our immediate surroundings). We can extend our knowledge beyond our immediate present and place by careful reasoning and inferences; but we cannot expect to conquer all of nature through our understanding alone (29). Just as the effect of a natural cause decreases with distance in time and space, so our knowledge decreases as time and space increase.

Following these empiricist guidelines, Nägeli was led to question Du Bois-Reymond's Laplacian ideal of knowledge. According to that ideal, a scientific genius who knew the general laws of mechanics, and who also knew the speed, direction, and position of all the particles of the universe at any one moment, would be able to determine the speed, direction, and position of all the particles at all other moments. But, Nägeli notes, there is a false premise behind this ideal: that the world is finite in space and time (30). Space, however, is infinitely divisible, and time is infinitely extendable, having no beginning or end (30–31). Du Bois-Reymond himself admits as much. But if space and time are infinite, the Laplacian genius could not make reliable inferences about the universe as a whole from any particular time and place; he would lack sufficient data, because the analysis of what is present in that time and place would never come to an end. For any given place in space and time, we will never have a complete analysis of the speed, velocity, and direction of all the particles (31).

Nothing better illustrates the limits of scientific knowledge, and the finitude of human knowledge in general, Nägeli holds, than our need to measure things. We know one thing only relative to another by comparing its size, shape, and weight to other things: "We know a phenomenon, we grasp its value with respect to other things, when we *measure, count* and *weigh* it" (33). Given the importance of measurement, it follows, Nägeli reasons, that our knowledge of nature is fundamentally mathematical. He accepts Kant's famous dictum: there is only as much science in a discipline as there is mathematics in it (35). But the need for mathematical knowledge means that our understanding of nature is limited to quantities (35). Qualities transcend our knowledge because we have no means of measuring them.

In stressing a mathematical paradigm of natural knowledge, Nägeli was in fundamental accord with Du Bois-Reymond. It is striking, however, that he disagrees with him about the ideal application or limitation of this paradigm. Du Bois-Reymond puts this paradigm under too much stress, Nägeli argues, when he demands that its ideal formulation, its standard application, be mechanical atomism (35). Knowledge of nature does not require that we penetrate to the ultimate atomic level of all phenomena. If we make atomistic reductivism a requirement of scientific explanation, we make many disciplines unscientific—even those that can still use the mathematical paradigm. To declare Du Bois-Reymond's mechanical-atomistic paradigm a necessary condition of all scientific knowledge would be to limit natural science down to one aspect or part of nature alone. There is in fact no need for a science to begin with atomic particles; we can start our explanation at any level or degree of organization (35). Nägeli warns us against measuring one form of scientific discourse by the standards of another. He makes it his general principle: "Each natural scientific discipline finds its justification essentially within itself" (35).

Regarding the question of the explanation of consciousness, Nägeli is skeptical of the limits that Du Bois-Reymond sets for natural knowledge (36). The natural scientist cannot say anything against "immaterial principles" because all his reasoning is limited to the natural realm, so that he cannot determine anything beyond it. What he can say, however, is that such principles are superfluous, and indeed improbable, because they contradict the general course or structure of nature (36). Nature shows us continuity from the highest forms of human self-consciousness down to the most primitive forms of consciousness in the embryo. All organic beings are formed by the compounds of their chemical constituents; life and feeling are qualities that we now know arise from protein molecules under specific conditions (36). So it is safe to assume that mental powers and activities are manifestations of the interactions of their chemical elements. The assumption of an immaterial principle is therefore suspect because it is contrary to "the general analogy of nature" (36–37).

Nägeli notes that Du Bois-Reymond does not prohibit the possibility of a science of mental life and consciousness. True to his old physicalist program, Du Bois-Reymond thinks that it is in principle possible to determine the material conditions of mental life, so that we can correlate mental activities with precise chemical compounds and the laws of their interaction (37). What Du Bois-Reymond claims that we will never know, however, is how these compounds and their interactions *produce* consciousness; in other words, we cannot understand the *connection* between cause and effect (37). Nägeli grants that we cannot understand that connection; but he insists that in this regard there is nothing special about *mental-physical* interaction. Du Bois-Reymond fails to see that we cannot understand the connection between cause and effect *anywhere* in nature (38). We understand nothing about how the cause produces the effect in physical nature, so we cannot expect to understand it regarding the connection between minds and bodies. Following Hume, Nägeli maintains that causal relations are based upon nothing more than constant conjunctions and that we cannot grasp the necessity with which the cause produces the effect (38).

Nägeli closes his lecture with some general reflections about the relationship between natural science and metaphysics. Flatly contrary to Hartmann, he insists upon a strict separation between these disciplines. The natural scientist, the old student of Oken now realizes, has to refrain from mixing his investigations with metaphysics. He must avoid reference to the transcendent, i.e., anything whatsoever that stands above and beyond the finite and measurable (40). The method of the scientist must be materialist—but that does not mean that he must accept a *philosophical* materialism; rather, his materialism should be strictly empirical and methodological (40). This is not to say that the natural scientist should not philosophize at all, but it does mean that he must realize that he ceases to be a natural scientist insofar as he philosophizes. The scientist has to be humble: all that he will ever know is a grain of sand in the infinite expanse of nature, a brief second in the eternity of time. The eternal how and why of things will be forever inaccessible to him. Nevertheless, we should not despair, Nägeli urges. We should realize that, with the right methods, we can still make sure and steady progress, and that we can constantly push forward the boundaries of knowledge. And so Nägeli concludes his lecture on a more optimistic note than Du Bois-Reymond's. To counter his *Ignorabimus* he declares: "We know, and we will know!" (41).

6. DILTHEY ON THE VIRTUES AND VICES OF NATURALISM

No less than Eduard von Hartmann, Wilhelm Dilthey saw Du Bois-Reymond's lecture as a threat to his greatest ambitions. Ever since the 1860s Dilthey had been struggling to formulate the distinctive logic of the social and historical sciences.[32] He believed that there could and should be a science of the social and historical world just as there already was one of the natural world. Given that there had been so much progress in the the study of history, law, and anthropology since the beginning of the century, the time was now ripe attempt to develop a logic and methodology of the social and historical sciences. But Du Bois-Reymond's lecture threw cold water on such hopes. If the argument of his lecture were correct,

32 Dilthey announces his program in his inaugural lecture at the University of Basel, "Die dichterische und philosophische Bewegung in Deutschland 1770–1800," which was given in 1867. See Dilthey, *Gesammelte Schriften*, ed. Karlfried Gründer and Frithjof Rodi (Göttingen: Vandenhoeck & Ruprecht, 1961–), V, 12–27. Henceforth all references in parentheses are to this edition, which will be designated GS.

it would be impossible for there to be anything like a science of society and history. According to that argument, the paradigm of explanation is mechanical; and that paradigm cannot explain the first level of consciousness, sensation, let alone the more complex phenomena of history and society.

It comes as no surprise, therefore, that in his first major attempt to define the logic of the historical and social sciences, his 1883 *Einleitung in die Geisteswissenschaften*, Dilthey took issue with Du Bois-Reymond. In the second section of his book Dilthey countered Du Bois-Reymond's argument by finding an equivocation in his concept of the limits of natural science (9–13). The concept of the limits of science is ambiguous, Dilthey held. On the one hand, it refers to the incommensurability between two kinds of concepts, the concepts with which we describe consciousness and those with which we explain the physical world. These concepts are incommensurable because the former concepts cannot be reduced to the latter. On the other hand, the limits of science refers to the inexplicable, to what cannot be subsumed under natural laws or explained according to the mechanical paradigm. The problem with Du Bois-Reymond's argument, Dilthey claims, is that it confuses these issues. Because our concepts about mental life and consciousness are not reducible to those we use to describe the physical world, Du Bois-Reymond concludes that mental life and consciousness cannot be explained according to natural laws. But this is a non sequitur. It is still possible to provide a naturalistic explanation of mental life even if our discourse about it is incommensurable with those of the physical sciences (12).

Dilthey's point against Du Bois-Reymond is that he confuses a difference in perspective or explanation with a difference in reality itself. Because discourse about mental life is different from the laws with which we explain the natural world, he assumes that the phenomena of mental life cannot be explained according to those laws. A logical difference is reified and made into an ontological barrier. Dilthey later uses the old language of absolute idealism to explain his point about different standpoints (15). We can begin from inner experience and construct the entire world as a condition of self-consciousness, which was the standpoint of transcendental philosophy. Or we can begin from outer experience and derive self-consciousness from the laws of nature, which was the standpoint of natural philosophy. Both standpoints are legitimate, Dilthey implies.

This critique of Du Bois-Reymond does not conform to our popular image of Dilthey as an antinaturalist. But that is an image we would do well to abandon. It is important to see that Dilthey wants to uphold the possibility of a natural science of mental life, and that he thinks that it is mistaken in principle to limit natural explanation to the physical world alone. Time and again in *Einleitung in die Geisteswissenschaften* he stresses that a causal explanation of human life and consciousness is an essential part of the foundation of the historical and social sciences (27–28). Human beings are not simply disembodied spirits who exist in a special mental realm; rather, their intentions and thoughts are embodied in their actions and words, which are very much part of the natural world. We understand these intentions and thoughts, if only in part, when we subsume them under general laws and see them as part of nature as a whole (14–15, 42–44).

Yet Dilthey's disagreement with Du Bois-Reymond did not simply concern whether natural laws could explain the phenomena of mental life. That issue was for him really a sideshow. The deeper question concerned the exclusive authority of the mechanical paradigm of explanation. No less than Hartmann, Dilthey questioned whether that paradigm is the *only* one. Even though he allowed the application of that paradigm to mental life, he criticized the assumption that it is the *sole* paradigm. For Dilthey, the mechanistic paradigm is a necessary, not a sufficient, model of explanation for mental life. The incommensurability between our ordinary discourse about mental life and the concepts of the natural sciences is indicative of equally legitimate but heterogeneous perspectives upon it. When we talk about feelings, sensations, and thoughts in ordinary language we take a very different perspective from that of the mechanical paradigm; assuming that we could correlate these feelings, sensations, and thoughts with brain and nerve states, and then reduce these brain states to chemical interactions, that alone would still be only one perspective upon them. Dilthey's disagreement with Du Bois-Reymond on this score is never made explicit; but it is clear from his disagreement with the positivists that he would never have accepted the exclusive legitimacy of Du Bois-Reymond's mechanical paradigm. The attempt of the positivists to force the social and historical sciences to conform to the concepts and methods of the natural sciences, he writes in the preface to the *Einleitung in die Geisteswissenschaften*, ends in a distortion of their meaning and purpose (xvii).

What, exactly, is the logic of the social and historical sciences? And how, precisely, does it differ from that of the natural sciences? These were questions that preoccupied Dilthey for his entire career. His attempt to answer them began in the 1860s and continued into the 1890s. We will examine some aspects of Dilthey's theory of the social and historical sciences in the next chapter. Suffice to say here and now that for Dilthey the distinction in method between the social-historical and natural sciences is fundamentally a distinction between *explanation* (*Erklärung*) and *understanding* (*Verstehen*). In explanation we subsume natural events under universal laws; but in understanding we grasp *actions* according to intentions and context, and *thoughts* according to context and the rules of a language. Explanation and understanding, Dilthey maintains, have very different purposes and a very different logic. Whether this is really the case is a big question that we cannot explore here. It was a measure of the limits of Du Bois-Reymond's argument that it had failed to raise, let alone discuss, this important question. If there are social and historical sciences having a completely different perspective on the world from the natural sciences, then Du Bois-Reymond's account of the limits of *natural* knowledge does not begin to be an account of knowledge in general.

7. A MASK AND A MARTYR

More than a quarter century after Du Bois-Reymond's lecture in 1872, it continued to stir controversy and stimulate reflection. In 1898 a pseudonymous article appeared in the popular journal *Die Zukunft* that proposed to reconsider its central themes in the new cultural climate.[33] Much had changed since the original lecture, the

---

33   W. Hartenau, "Ignorabimus," *Die Zukunft* 25 (19.03.1898), 524–36, reprinted in *Der Ignorabimus-Streit*, pp. 233–51. All references here are to the original edition.

author felt, so that it was necessary to ask what one should think about it now. "The proud age of realism and natural science has now withered," he wrote. "Now the time of discoveries is past and physics works only for the reporter and the amusement of higher circles" (536). In his view, the late 1890s were the dawn of a new age where "science and art thirst for new ideas." This pseudonymous author—whoever he was—raised the most interesting questions about the limits of science in this new age. His article was one of the most bold and original of the *Ignorabimusstreit*. It introduces a new humanist standpoint, and it shows a more critical attitude toward natural science than all previous contributions.

"W. Hartenau"—so the author called himself—agrees with Du Bois-Reymond's account of the limits of natural science. It was perfectly correct for him to maintain that the problem of mental-physical interaction is irresolvable according to the physical-mathematical paradigm (525). It was one of the *more* beneficial consequences of Du Bois-Reymond's argument that the materialists were now chastened; but it was one of its *less* beneficial consequences that the positivists were now encouraged. Following Du Bois-Reymond, they believed that the natural sciences are the only kind of knowledge, and so they banished metaphysics or any other kind of thinking about the world (525). This last point reflects the core of Hartenau's critique. Like Dilthey and Hartmann, he questions, though from a completely different perspective, Du Bois-Reymond's assumption that the methods of natural science provide *the* model of knowledge (526).

We have to realize, Hartenau pleads, that the natural sciences do not satisfy our deepest longing for knowledge. We do not need natural science to resolve the most important questions about life. To know how to live we need knowledge of individual natural events, nothing more (526). The natural sciences never give us a guideline for our actions, never provide us with an ethic, and never teach us about what we need to know most: the final goal of our life. The natural sciences do nothing more than schematize, analyze, and dissect. The ultimate goal of explanation—just as Du Bois-Reymond said—is the analysis of an object into its ultimate particles. But let us suppose that this ideal is finally realized and that it results in a book, which we call *The Mechanical Theory of*

Natural Appearances. This would be "a printed tree of knowledge" with "withered leaves and wooden fruit." No one would want to read it. Why? Because this book would commit the greatest literary crime: it would be boring (527). No one would be interested in reading it because it would contain nothing about what moves the world now or in the future, nothing about humanity, morals, economics, society, and the nation, let alone the connection between mind and body. Nothing in the world would be changed by the publication of this book. It might extend our knowledge; but it will not deepen our insight into the essence of the world (527).

Much like a late nineteenth-century Rousseau, Hartenau asks what natural science has done for us. Why, he asks, do we need it? It makes no difference whether bread consists in atoms or not; it suffices only that we can eat it (528). The connection of things remains the same, no matter how we analyze it, and whether it is irreality or the ultimate degree of reality. To be sure, the natural scientists have made our lives more comfortable by showing us how to satisfy our desires; but they are blind in telling us what our ultimate values should be. The sciences have given us the Pandora's box of technology, which supplies us with endless comforts and inventions. But we are suffocating under technology; nowadays it is more difficult to find a need than to satisfy one (536). Science and art cry for new ideas and ideals; they have had enough of facts and forms.

Hartenau does his best to undermine the dogmatic realism behind the natural sciences. Their authority seems to rest on their claim to provide us with knowledge about the nature of things, the way things are in themselves. But this realism is naïve, Hartenau contends. We should not say that God created man and nature, because it is really man who creates nature and God (528). The objects that populate our world are not given but constructions; they are what we produce by applying our intellect to our sensations. All the atoms and forms of motion, in which we analyze things, are nothing more than an image or symbol of what is ultimate for us: sensations (529). We have no right to assume that there is some object or thing-in-itself behind the sensations because causality is only a formula for the continuity of appearances among one another. The chief question for the natural sciences has been how a bunch of chemicals came together in primal times to create thinking; but that question, Hartenau insists, is wrongly posed. The right question to ask is how we arrive at the idea of matter and its ultimate elements, and what does this idea presuppose (529). When we pose the question in this way, Hartenau argues, we see that natural science does not lie above us but below us. It cannot answer the fundamental questions about its epistemic status, about how it arrives at its knowledge. Once we raise these epistemological questions, Hartenau promises us, we will stand on the higher plateau of metaphysics and the deepest abyss of thought will open before us.

Hartenau takes these epistemological issues a proto-Kühnian step further to undermine the natural sciences' claim to objective truth. When we examine exactly the methods employed in the sciences, and all the questions that they raise, he argues, we can no longer say that there is a perfect correspondence between representation and object. We regard a proposition as true when the actions based upon it lead to the phenomena that we expect; but we do not trouble ourselves more about any contradictory data or any doubts we may have (530). To know the truth of even the simplest singular proposition raises questions that could go on ad infinitum. That this coin weighs the proper amount of gold depends on the accuracy of our instruments, the correctness of the weights, the measures for gold, the exact kind of gold in the coin, and so on. The complications are even greater for confirming a more general scientific law (531). It is utterly naïve of the scientist to think that one theory alone is the ultimate truth. Scientists change their doctrines no less than the metaphysicians. What is orthodoxy one day becomes rejected tomorrow (531–32). There is really no such thing as scientific truth, Hartenau insists, but only certain desiderata of truth, which we more or less approximate (532). We regard that theory as true that best simplifies the phenomena and that least encounters contradiction.

That the natural sciences cannot help us in the most important decisions of life Hartenau thinks is clear from the fact that our values ultimately must have a metaphysical or transcendent basis. I cannot perform a single deed whose effects last beyond my own life—like planting a forest, writing a book, caring for my children—without, so to speak, taking a step into a metaphysical realm (533). Many of my actions whose worth is not purely utilitarian I do because I have some belief in their value that transcends the natural world. My experience in life is a test of their value just like an experiment in physics. There is a great difference between an experiment in ethics and that in science: in science we determine what is true or good for everyone alike; but in ethics I determine what is good for myself. My own personality, my own individual decisions count; there is no intersubjective criterion like that used in the sciences (535).

Hartenau concludes his article with a plea to allow some other kinds of knowledge than those of the natural sciences. His ultimate aim, he reveals, is to vindicate metaphysics, the right to think about ultimate values and what each individual wants from life (535). There is no need to believe in a single metaphysical system that provides all the answers for everyone; but everyone still needs to think metaphysically because so much in their personal life depends on it. The belief in "nothing but natural science" has limited our horizons to such a degree that these fundamental questions have remained unanswered. There is a kind of thinking that is freer and richer than natural science, one of great value not despite but because of the fact that it is more personal. So against Du Bois-Reymond's *Ignorabimus* Hartenau proclaims in protest: "*Creabimus!*"

One question remains. Who was this Hartenau? The answer is surprising: no less than Walter Rathenau (1867–1922). He was one of the most prominent public figures in early twentieth-century Germany. Rathenau wrote the article when he was only an engineer; but he would later become a major industrialist, the chairman of the giant electrical firm AEG. During the 1914–18 war, he led the department for military supplies. After the war he became the foreign minister for the Weimar Republic, where it was his task to negotiate with the Allies the terms for reparation payments.[34] Conservative circles were outraged that Rathenau, a Jew, argued

---

34 On Rathenau's role in the Weimar Republic, see Erich Eyck, *A History of the Weimar Republic* (New York: Atheneum, 1970), I, 184–86, 192–93, 200–204, 206–21.

for compliance with these terms. In 1922 he was murdered by a clique of nationalists. Rathenau thus became an early martyr for the Weimar Republic.

8. HAECKEL'S LAST STAND

In 1899 the weary and wary Ernst Haeckel, who made his name and claim to fame championing Darwin in Germany, published his last will and testament, *Die Welträthsel*.[35] Haeckel called himself a child of his century, and now that that century was drawing to a close, he saw it as a fitting time to end his life's work. *Die Welträthsel* was to be the final statement of his philosophy, the culmination of all his labors and reflections as a natural scientist. The very title of Haeckel's work reveals the enduring effect of the *Ignorabimus-streit*. It was a reference to another writing of Du Bois-Reymond's, *Die sieben Welträthsel*, the sequel to his 1872 lecture.

Since his early years in Berlin, Haeckel had known Du Bois-Reymond.[36] Both had been students of the great physiologist Johannes Müller, though both were apostates, committed to the "physicalist program" for the explanation of life which Müller himself would never have approved. Despite their common ancestry and apostasy, the two did not like one another much. Du Bois-Reymond regarded Haeckel as too much of a metaphysician, as too eager to engage in speculation and not conscientious enough to do observation and experiment. Haeckel suspected that Du Bois-Reymond, in his capacity as president of the Academy of Sciences, was the reason for his failure to win a grant. In *Die Welträthsel* his animosity toward his former colleague is scarcely concealed. Haeckel complained about "the dogmatic fiats of the all powerful secretary and dictator of the Berlin Akademy of Sciences" (209).

Above and beyond these personal differences lay the deeper differences in their worldviews. *Die Welträthsel* was the last general

---

35 Ernst Haeckel, *Die Welträthsel* (Bonn: Emil Strauß, 1899). All references in parentheses are to this edition.

36 On the personal relationship between the two, see Laura Otis, *Müller's Lab* (Oxford: Oxford University Press, 2007), pp. 218–19.

statement of Haeckel's worldview, which he called "monism."[37] This is for Haeckel the doctrine that the universe is a unity and an indivisible whole, governed throughout by the same fundamental laws. Such monism is closely connected with Haeckel's naturalism, according to which everything in the universe is explicable, at least in principle, according to mechanical laws. The antithesis of his monism he calls "dualism," i.e., the doctrine that there is a supernatural realm in the universe above and beyond nature which is inexplicable according to such laws.

It is telling that, in the first chapter of *Die Welträthsel*, Haeckel pointedly contrasts his monism with the worldview of Du Bois-Reymond, whom he regards as the chief representative of dualism (18). In insisting that matter and mind are ultimately inexplicable, Du Bois-Reymond created a fundamental dualism in his universe, Haeckel charges. For Du Bois-Reymond, there is the natural world, which is explicable according to mechanical laws, and there is the supernatural world, which is inexplicable according to those laws. "The Ignorabimus lecture," Haeckel declares in no uncertain terms, "contains the decisive program of metaphysical dualism" (209).

The clash between Haeckel and Du Bois-Reymond regarding the limits of science and the knowability of the world could not be more drastic. In his *Die sieben Welträthsel*, his later apology for the *Ignorabimus* lecture, Du Bois-Reymond maintains that there are no less than seven world puzzles: (1) the essence of matter or force; (2) the origin of motion; (3) the genesis of life; (4) the design of nature; (5) the origin of sensation; (6) the origin of language; and (7) free will.[38] Du Bois-Reymond held that only (1), (2), (5), and (7) are "transcendent," i.e., in principle incapable of solution; the others are, at least in principle, capable of solution, though we are far from solving them in our present state of scientific knowledge. Since he saw these mysteries as the source and support of Du

37 Haeckel refuses to describe his position as "materialism" (23). He thinks his monism is closer to Spinoza's dual attribute doctrine, though it is striking that he makes the two attributes matter and energy (23, 249), from which the mental realm is to be explained. The reference to Spinoza is more a smoke screen to hide the materialist intentions behind Haeckel's philosophy.

38 Du Bois-Reymond, *Die sieben Welträthsel*, pp. 164–70.

Bois-Reymond's dualism, Haeckel rejected all of them, decisively so. None of them is really a mystery, he insisted. He claimed that the first six are resolvable in principle and that the seventh is no mystery at all, because there is really no such thing as free will in the sense assumed by Du Bois-Reymond, i.e., a power to act or not act for the same person under the same circumstances. Hence there are no mysteries in Haeckel's universe: to say that there is a single reality, a unified worldwhole, means for him that everything is in essence comprehensible, in principle explicable according to the laws of nature.

Haeckel's declaration of the intelligibility of the world, of the potential omniscience of natural science, would strike many as rashly arrogant and foolishly optimistic. But we have to place his declaration in context. It was really a statement of protest, a re-action against the treachery and timidity of his old friends and colleagues in the physicalist program. Now that they had grown old, they had lost their faith in science, and they were now seeing irre-solvable mysteries where they had once seen answerable questions. Haeckel's book was written in self-vindication against them, those who had once been proud naturalists themselves but who had now renounced the errors of their mechanist ways.[39] Rudolf Virchow (1821–1902), Karl Ernst Baer (1792–1876), Wilhelm Wundt (1832–1920), and, last but not least, Du Bois-Reymond himself had once conspired with Haeckel to create a world free of teleology and vital forces. But in their more mellow later years, they viewed their old physicalist program as a youthful dream. That left Haeckel stand-ing alone. He saw all his old friends and colleagues as traitors to the cause of science, which he alone was left to vindicate. They had given aid and comfort to their enemy—the theists, the idealists, and the spiritualists—who celebrated the turn against mechanism by the old physicalists as the sweetest vindication. Haeckel con-demned their treachery as evidence of timidity, even senility (118). So, although *Die Welträthsel* was meant to be a philosophy for the future, its author knew all too well that it was really a rear-guard

---

39 The battle against his old allies begins much earlier. The prelude to *Die Welträthsel* is his *Freie Wissenschaft und freie Lehre*, which is a critique of the apostasy of Baer, Virchow, and Du Bois-Reymond.

action, the last stand of an old-fashioned naturalist who now felt himself to be alone in the world.

Why was Haeckel so confident of his monism? Why was he so convinced of the weaknesses of Du Bois-Reymond's arguments? In those passages in *Die Welträthsel* that explicitly discuss Du Bois-Reymond's lecture (108–10, 206–13), Haeckel simply reaffirms his theory that the explanation of consciousness is a physiological or neurological problem, whose solution lies ultimately in the realm of physics and chemistry. Consciousness is only one part of the higher activities of the soul, which depend upon the brain (212). Experience shows us, Haeckel insists, that there is no immaterial substance and that all our conscious activities ultimately have their source in the brain (255). However, these were propositions that Du Bois-Reymond never doubted, and they hardly proved by themselves that consciousness is *only* a brain activity.

Yet there was a deeper disagreement between Haeckel and Du Bois-Reymond, one that explains Haeckel's confidence in monism as well as Du Bois-Reymond's confidence in dualism. This deeper disagreement concerns the nature of matter itself. Like Büchner, Haeckel argues that we must not conceive of matter in the classical Cartesian fashion as inert extension but as active energy, and indeed as a *nisus* or striving (259). If this is the case, then there is no real difference in kind between mind and matter: mind is only a more complex and developed form of the energies already inherent in matter. Du Bois-Reymond, Haeckel suggests much like Büchner before him, is still behind in his conception of matter, which he persists in understanding along old Cartesian lines. If we understand matter as inert mass, as Du Bois-Reymond does, then of course we cannot expect it to explain consciousness; but that for Haeckel is all the more reason to abandon such an antiquated view of matter.

Du Bois-Reymond knew that Haeckel held this theory of matter,[40] which he rejected utterly. In *Die sieben Welträthsel* he complained that Haeckel's hypothesis of animate molecules or atomic

---

40 Haeckel had expounded it in an earlier work: *Die Perigenesis der Plastidule oder die Wellenzeugung der Lebenstheilchen. Ein Versuch zur mechanischen Erklärung der elementaren Lebensvorgänge* (Berlin: Reimer, 1876).

souls was one of the worst legacies of *Naturphilosophie*.[41] Haeckel had violated one of the first rules of all philosophizing: *"entia non sunt creanda sine necessitate."* Haeckel could not explain how the unity of consciousness arose from the multiplicity of atomic souls. Rather than explaining consciousness, Haeckel simply read it into the molecules themselves, so his explanation is circular. For Du Bois-Reymond, Haeckel's theory was just another instance of how we project onto matter the very features of our own experience that we are to explain. It was ironic for him that Haeckel had spent so much time and energy lambasting an anthropomorphic conception of the world, because his own theory of matter was a singular instance of such anthropomorphism.

Haeckel responded to this criticism in *Die Welträthsel*, insisting that it was a distortion of his position to think that he ever attributed consciousness itself to the atomic souls. Their nature consisted in primitive forms of willing and feeling, which appeared only on a *subconscious* level (206). But he left aside the deeper question, which he felt he had answered elsewhere, about the evidence and justification for an animate or dynamic conception of matter.

In the end, the dispute between Haeckel and Du Bois-Reymond came down to their conflicting views of matter itself. Which view was correct was ultimately decidable only by the progress of science itself. Ironically, science itself has to determine its limits, which it is unwise for the philosopher to prognosticate or impose.

41 Du Bois-Reymond, *Die sieben Welträthsel*, pp. 1051–52.

4

TRIALS AND TRIBULATIONS

OF CLIO

I. HISTORY AS A SCIENCE

The nineteenth century is often dubbed "the age of history," just as the eighteenth century is often called "the age of reason." These names are clichés, of course, but they also have their core of truth. There are various reasons for calling the nineteenth century "the age of history." It is primarily because, at the beginning of the century, people were much more conscious of history as a force shaping society and state. One major lesson of the French Revolution was that people could not create societies and states according to the mandates of pure reason alone, and that social and political institutions were the product of a long and gradual development, which could not be abruptly arrested or changed if society and state were to function normally. But there is another reason for calling the nineteenth century the age of history: people became more self-aware that history is a determinant of human identity. The old belief, so commonly expressed in the eighteenth century, that human nature is constant and uniform throughout the ages, proved problematic. Because of increased anthropological and historical knowledge, it was realized that human nature changes with society and history, so that who we are depends deeply on when and where we were born and how we came into being.

There is one final reason that the nineteenth century is called the age of history: it is because history, as an intellectual discipline, became a science in its own right. As Friedrich Meinecke remarked nearly a century ago,[1] this was nothing short of an intellectual

---

1 Friedrich Meinecke, *Die Entstehung des Historismus* (Munich: Oldenbourg, 1965), p. 1.

revolution. At the close of the eighteenth century philosophers still espoused a mathematical paradigm of knowledge, according to which we know only what we prove, and according to which knowledge requires universality and necessity. This paradigm was common to both the Wolffian and Kantian traditions. It was made perfectly explicit by Kant when he famously declared that there is only as much science in a discipline as there is mathematics in it.[2] By such strict criteria, however, history cannot be science. None of its propositions is demonstrable; and they lack universality and necessity because they are about particular and contingent events. By the end of the nineteenth century, however, the mathematical paradigm had lost its grip. History became a science in its own right. For mysterious reasons, yet to be explained, demonstrability, universality, and necessary were no longer regarded as prerequisites of knowledge. Somehow, even historical propositions about particular and contingent matters of fact could be scientific.

How do we explain this revolution? It is easy to understand the social and historical forces pushing history toward scientific status. If history were such a powerful determinant of society, state, and human identity, then there better be a science of it. Otherwise, how could humanity control its own destiny? If human beings could not know history, they also could not direct it. Thus the demand for human autonomy, which fueled the criticism of religion and state, was also motivating the legitimation of history as a science.

But these social and historical forces alone were not sufficient to give history its *intellectual* or *philosophical* legitimation. They give a powerful motive for such legitimation; but they alone do not provide it. That philosophical side of the story is much more complex, involving many interweaving narratives. Here we will tell but one of them, the simplest and most basic.

This narrative begins in the middle of the eighteenth century. In 1752 the Wolffian philosopher Johann Martin Chladenius (1710–59) published his *Allgemeine Geschichtswissenschaft*,[3] a seminal but

2 Kant, "Vorrede," *Metaphysische Anfangsgründe der Naturwissenschaft*, IV, 470.
3 Johann Martin Chladenius, *Allgemeine Geschichtswissenschaft* (Leipzig: Friedrich Lanckischens Erben, 1752). After his death, Chladenius fell into oblivion. He was rescued by Ernst Bernheim in the beginning of the twentieth century.

largely forgotten text, which attempted to show how history can be a science. It would seem as a good Wolffian Chladenius should not dare to make a case for history as a science at all. For had his master not demonstrated that knowledge requires demonstrability, that it demands universality and necessity?[4] And had he not declared that history is the lowest form of knowledge?[5] Yet Chladenius was a bold man: he had devised an argument to show how history could satisfy even some of the stricter standards of his master. In his book he had shown how history, even though about particular and contingent events, is still a very rule- or norm-governed activity. There are many norms or rules for assessing evidence in history, Chladenius explained, and he went on to specify in great detail what these rules are and how they relate to one another. Before we make a claim to knowledge in history, Chladenius argued, we have to comply with these rules, which are strict and demanding, indeed universal and necessary, even if their application in particular cases is hard to determine. To a Wolffian, this was a compelling argument. For Wolff himself had made rule-following into the very criterion of rational activity.[6] So if history follows rules, and if following rules is rational, then history, too, should be rational, i.e., a science in its own right. Thus Chladenius had legitimated history even by the strict standards of his master, Christian Wolff, the most rationalist philosopher of them all.

On another level, though, Chladenius realized that historical propositions would never satisfy Wolff's strictest criterion: demonstrability. Although they are established by canons of evidence, historical propositions are still not logically necessary; they are still fundamentally contingent, so that it is logically possible that they are false. But here Chladenius did not attempt to bend and apply Wolff's criteria; rather, he questioned their relevance. It is absurd, he argued, to demand mathematical certainty of historical

---

See his *Lehrbuch der historischen Methode* (Leipzig: Duncker & Humblot, 1914), pp. 183, 223.

4   See Christian Wolff, *Vernünftige Gedanken von den Kräften des menschlichen Verstande und ihrem richtigen Gedanken in Erkenntnis der Wahrheit*, §2, in *Gesammelte Werke*, ed. Hans Werner Arndt (Hildesheim: Olms, 1965), I/1, 115.

5   See Christian Wolff, *Philosophia rationalis sive Logicae*, §22, in *Werke* II/1, 10.

6   See ibid., §§3–4, *Werke* II/1, 108.

propositions, which are not capable of it. As Aristotle taught, we must expect only as much exactitude as a subject matter permits.[7] Even if a historical proposition is contingent, it is still demonstrable by the kind of evidence appropriate for it, e.g., the number and reliability of witnesses, the coherence of testimony with other beliefs, and so on. While it makes sense to doubt an historical proposition if it does not meet these standards, it is pointless to doubt it if it does not meet a demand for logical necessity or mathematical certainty. Each science has its own sui generis standards, and we must not measure one by the standards of another.

It was by these sophisticated kinds of arguments, which both met and countered Enlightenment ideals of rationality, that Chladenius established the possibility of a science of history. But his science was really only a promise, an ideal, which Chladenius himself, more a philosopher than an historian, did nothing to realize. The promise was rapidly becoming a reality, however, virtually when Chladenius was writing. Unbeknownst to him, he was articulating an historical development that was taking place under his very nose. For by the middle of the eighteenth century in Germany, there had been an enormous expansion in historical research, which was becoming ever more rigorous and exacting.[8] Chairs in history were created in theological and law faculties in universities. History was growing because it was proving such a valuable means to legitimate church and state. It was history that could justify claims to throne and altar, titles to nobility and property. Germany was governed by a peculiar combination of Roman law and German customary law. But understanding Roman law required knowledge of Roman culture and history, just as understanding German customary law demanded knowledge of the

7 Aristotle, *Nicomachean Ethics*, Book I, chapter 3, 1094b.
8 On the study of history in eighteenth-century Germany, see Andreas Kraus, *Vernunft und Geschichte* (Freiberg: Herder, 1963), pp. 163–205; James Thompson, *A History of Historical Writing* (New York: Macmillan, 1942), II, 96–131; Konrad Jarausch, "The Institutionalization of History in 18th Century Germany," in *Aufklärung und Geschichte*, ed. Hans Bödeker (Göttingen: Vandenhoeck & Ruprecht, 1986), pp. 25–48; and Peter Hanns Reill, "Die Geschichtswissenschaft um die Mitte des 18. Jahrhunderts," in *Wissenschaften im Zeitalter der Aufklärung*, ed. Rudolf Vierhaus (Göttingen: Vandenhoeck & Ruprecht, 1985), pp. 163–93.

Middle Ages. And so it was that by midcentury, the University of Göttingen had established an eminent school of historians, whose major spokesmen—Johann Christian Gatterer (1727–99), Johann Stephan Pütter (1725–1807), and August Ludwig Schlözer (1735–1809)—wrote works on legal and church history conforming to just the kind of rigorous guidelines advocated by Chladenius.

Another major step toward the recognition of history as a science came with the foundation of the University of Berlin in the early nineteenth century. It was in Berlin that history became for the first time an independent faculty separate from theology and law. The first professor of history there was Barthold Georg Niebuhr (1776–1831), who gave his first lectures in the winter of 1810. By all accounts, Niebuhr's lectures, on Roman history, were a triumph. In 1825 Niebuhr was joined by Leopold von Ranke (1795–1886), whose own study of the early modern era was modeled on Niebuhr's work on Roman history. Together, Niebuhr and Ranke formed the so-called "critical school of history," whose ideal was applying exacting critical standards to historical research. The products of their labors were Niebuhr's *Römische Geschichte*, which was published in 1811–12,[9] and Ranke's *Geschichte der germanischen und romanischen Völker*, which first appeared in 1824.[10] Niebuhr's prefaces to his first and second editions, and Ranke's appendix to his book, laid out the thinking and ideals behind the new critical methods. They would, whenever possible, consult original sources; and all sources would have to be assessed for authenticity and accuracy. No source would be accepted simply because it had been handed down by tradition. In these works of Niebuhr and Ranke, Chladenius's ideals had again become reality.

And so Clio was born. Yet her struggles had only begun. For this new science faced a long struggle for recognition, an uphill battle to prove her legitimacy and very right to exist. Niebuhr and Ranke were concerned that Clio grow up to be autonomous, that she be independent from other disciplines and not the servant of law or

9 Barthold Georg Niebuhr, *Römische Geschichte* (Berlin: Realschulbuchhandlung, 1811–12).

10 Leopold Ranke, *Geschichte der germanischen und romanischen Völker von 1494 bis 1535* (Leipzig: Reimer, 1824).

theology as in the bad old days. Historical knowledge, Niebuhr and Ranke believed, should be acquired for its own sake, regardless of the agenda of church or state. The creation of an independent faculty of history in Berlin was an important step toward such autonomy. But it was also only a first step, because there were new dangers to the autonomy of this fledgling discipline. These came not from church and state, as in days past, but from a new and unexpected quarter: speculative philosophy. Fichte, Schelling, and Hegel all had a philosophy of world history, which they had formulated according to a priori methods. They saw empirical history as a mere underlaborer whose purpose was to supply materials for their more exciting speculative history. Compared to the speculations of the philosophers, the historians' work seemed tedious and laborious indeed. Why sweat over minutiae when the philosopher reveals, through sheer a priori excogitation, the goals and laws of world history? Here again the old struggle for survival in the academic division of labor came into play. If the historians were to vindicate their new faculty, they had to show that the methods of history were sui generis and reliable.

In the 1820s Berlin was riven into rival intellectual factions, "the historians" led by Schleiermacher and "the philosophers" led by Hegel.[11] While the historians stressed the autonomous value of history, the philosophers preached its subjugation under "the concept," the need to explain the meaning of history according to the system of philosophy. Niebuhr and Ranke belonged to the historicist faction, a fact not lost on Hegel, who condemned their critical history as a conspiracy to empty history of meaning by reducing it down to a multitude of disparate, if critically sifted, facts.[12] One of the most important episodes in the conflict between historians and philosophers was Ranke's 1831 lectures on universal history.[13] These lectures were an attempt to vindicate the autonomy of history, to

11 The best account of this dispute is still that of Ernst Simon, *Ranke und Hegel, Beiheft der Historische Zeitschrift* 15 (1928), pp. 16–119.
12 On Hegel's conflict with Ranke, see my "Hegel and Ranke," in *A Companion to Hegel*, ed. Stephen Houlgate and Michael Baur (Malden, MA: Wiley-Blackwell, 2011), pp. 332–50.
13 See Leopold Ranke, "Idee der Universalhistorie," in *Aus Werk und Nachlass*, ed. Walther Peter Fuchs (Munich: Oldenbourg, 1965), IV, 72–89.

spell out its distinctive goals and methods vis-à-vis philosophy. Philosophy and history, Ranke explains, have very different goals. While the philosopher sees the individual only as an instance of the universal, the historian examines the individual for its own sake. The historian's task is not to know the general laws that govern a particular thing, or what it has in common with other things, but what is unique about it, what makes it just this thing and no other. Using the language of Schelling, Ranke puts the difference this way: the philosopher sees the finite in the infinite, the particular in the universal, whereas the historian grasps the infinite in the finite, the universal in the particular. Corresponding to these different goals, the historian and philosopher have different methods, Ranke continues. The historian follows the analytic method, beginning from the particular and ascending to the universal, whereas the philosopher uses the synthetic method, beginning with the universal and descending to the particular. Ranke does not believe, however, that these methods are of equal epistemic value. He implies that the historian's method is more reliable than the philosopher's because it is based on solid facts, and because it does not reach general principles until they are first established in experience. The philosopher, however, begins with general principles, which might be false and whose legitimacy he cannot establish except through a priori means. In making this contrast in methods, Ranke was clearly aligning history with the methods of the empirical sciences against those of the philosophers. He was saying that history, because its methods are fundamentally akin to those of the empirical sciences, could provide results no less reliable.

Ranke's battle with Hegel in his 1831 lectures proved fateful. They did much to discredit Hegel's a priori methods in the philosophy of history. Not Marx, nor Kierkegaard, but Ranke was the most influential critic of Hegel's philosophy of history. Ranke's lectures had also articulated a theme that later defenders of history would strive to explain and justify in the course of the century: "the principle of individuality." The defining goal of history, Ranke held, is knowledge of the individual for its own sake and as an end in itself. This principle would later be adopted by many thinkers in the historicist tradition, who, following Ranke, regarded it as the distinguishing principle of history. We shall soon see how they used it to defend the autonomy of history. Our task now will be to describe Clio's struggle for autonomy in the second half of the nineteenth century.

2. HISTORICAL OBJECTIVITY?

It was an essential part of the promise of the new history that it be able to determine the facts of the past, that it could at least approach, through exacting critical methods, something like "objective knowledge." Only if this were so could history hope to claim the same status as the empirical sciences. Ranke gave voice to this important hope in the preface to his *Geschichte der germanischen und romanischen Völker* when he wrote that "strict presentation of the facts" was his "highest law" and that it was the purpose of his book simply to show "how things actually happened" (*wie es eigentlich gewesen*).[14] Ever since, Ranke's statement has been taken as the starting point for discussions about historical objectivity.

These discussions began in earnest in the 1850s. An important critic of Ranke's ideal of objective history was his contemporary and colleague in Berlin, Johann Gustav Droysen (1838–1908). In his lectures on historical method, which he first gave in 1857,[15] Droysen mocked Ranke's ideal of "eunuch-like objectivity." It is not possible in history, he argued, to describe facts as in the natural sciences. There are no hard and fast historical facts that exist independent of the historian, for the past has disappeared and now exists only in the mind of the historian. The facts constructed by historians very much depend on their interests and values, which vary with culture and epoch. All historical understanding is limited by the culture and the language of the historian, because these provide the terms into which he translates the words and the deeds of the past. There can no more be a single perfect understanding of the past, Droysen declared, than there can be a single perfect translation of

14 Ranke, *Geschichte*, pp. vi, vii.
15 Johann Gustav Droysen, *Historik. Die Vorlesungen von 1857*, ed. Peter Leyh (Stuttgart-Bad Cannstatt: Fromman-Holzboog, 1977). See also the later 1882/83 version of the lectures where Droysen continues his discussion: *Historik, Vorlesungen über Enzyklopädie und Methodologie der Geschichte*, ed. Rudolf Hübner (Munich: Oldenbourg, 1937).

a sentence. Just as the understanding of a sentence is relative to the
language into which it is translated, so understanding of the past
is relative to the perspective of the historian; and just as there are
as many legitimate translations as there are languages into which a
sentence is translated, so there are as many legitimate understand-
ings of the past as there are historical perspectives. And since these
perspectives are always changing, so will our understanding of history change. It is therefore necessary for each culture and epoch to
rewrite history, to rediscover its past and to translate it into its own
terms. The historian, Droysen was saying, has to take account of
the fact that he, too, is a product of history; and that means realizing that his results are only relative, the statement of the meaning
of history for his own culture and age.

Although Droysen was correct in pointing out the limits of historical objectivity, it was also important not to push these limits too
far, so that it seemed as if there could be no historical objectivity
whatsoever. There is a straightforward sense in which it is possible to attain, at least to some extent, historical objectivity. This is
the sense in which we can know just the facts in distinction from
hearsay, embellishment, assumption, interpretation, and distortion.
Courts of law require objectivity in this sense when they demand
that witnesses describe the facts alone; journalism also requires
such objectivity when reporters are told to determine the facts,
what, when, where, and how something occurred. The historical
skeptic pushes his critique too far if he concludes that there cannot be objectivity in this basic sense, as if no standards can be met
in courts of law or journalism. It was this simple sense of objectivity that Ranke had in mind in preface to his *Geschichte*. In the
appendix to that book,[16] Ranke engaged in a critique of previous
histories of the early modern era, especially Guicciardini's *Storia
d'Italia*, which for generations had been one of the most trusted
sources about Italian history. When he compared Guicciardini's
history to other documents and sources, Ranke found it filled with
inaccuracies and downright fabrications. It was not an eyewitness
account, as it presumed to be, but a compilation of other sources. If

16   Leopold Ranke, *Zur Kritik neuerer Geschichtsschreiber. Eine Beylage zu desselben romanischen und germanischen Geschichten* (Leipzig: Reimer, 1824).

the historian can determine such distortions and fabrications, then historical objectivity, at least in the basic sense intended by Ranke, is possible after all.

Droysen's critique of Ranke also raises difficult questions of its own. One question concerns historical relativism. Did Droysen mean to espouse a complete historical relativism, as if there are no objective facts in history at all and everything depends on the historian's perspective? There are passages in his 1857 lectures where he seems to accept just such a relativism, declaring historical truth to be only "relative truth"; but there are other passages where he shrinks back from such relativism, where he recognizes the need for "correctness" in determining whether a source is an accurate account of reality. For all his skepticism about objective facts, Droysen never abandoned the assumption that there is one fact seen from different perspectives; he never embraced the idea that there are as many facts as there are perspectives. Another question raised by Droysen's critique concerns ethnocentrism. One of the fundamental maxims of the new history was that the past should be treated for its own sake, according to its ideals and beliefs, and that the historian should refrain from judging it according to contemporary ideals and standards, as if past cultures were simply primitive or earlier versions of his own. Although Droysen was very aware of this danger, he does not think that it can be escaped; and so he attempts to make a virtue out of a necessity. The historian not only must but should write from his own historical perspective, from the values and needs of the present, he insisted, because only in that way will he make history relevant to his age and a living part of contemporary political struggles. It was for this reason that Droysen wrote his *Geschichte der Preußischen Politik* from the perspective of his own liberal nationalism.[17] It was a common criticism of that work, however, that it read contemporary nationalist ideals into the Prussian past, as if it were always the mission of Prussia to unite all of Germany. Not surprisingly, Ranke shared that criticism. It was the reason he gave for refusing to award Droysen's work an academic prize.

17 Johann Gustav Droysen, *Geschichte der Preußischen Politik* (Leipzig: Veit, 1855–86), 14 vols.

The question of historical objectivity arose again in the early 1880s with the publication of Wilhelm Dilthey's *Einleitung in die Geisteswissenschaften*.[18] The fundamental aim of that work, Dilthey explained, was to provide "an epistemological foundation for the sciences of the mind," where first and foremost among these sciences was history. Dilthey called his project "the critique of historical reason" because it would investigate the conditions and limits of historical knowledge. He saw his project as an extension of Kantian criticism to history, a realm of knowledge Kant had completely neglected. No less than Ranke, who was his teacher, Dilthey, too, was convinced that history could be a science and that it could provide objective knowledge like all the empirical sciences, even though its interests and subject matter were very different from them. Again like Ranke, Dilthey was determined to defend the autonomy of history, to show that it had its own aims and methods independent of philosophy and the natural sciences. Hence the critique of historical reason would show how the aims, methods, and subject matter of history differ from those of philosophy and the natural sciences.

So far, so good, and it all seemed a very laudable project. But there was an ambiguity in Dilthey's critique of historical reason that cast doubt upon itself and the very history it was to explain and defend. The genitive "of" was ambiguous: history was not only the object but also the instrument of criticism. The critique of historical reason would not only examine history through reason; it would also examine reason through history. For one of the major goals of Dilthey's project was to show how characteristic human activities—art, literature, religion, science, philosophy—arise from and depend upon their historical context. Thus the critique of historical reason aims to expose the ahistorical pretensions of reason. These pretensions appeared in the standpoint of critique itself, which claimed to speak for mankind as a whole and for all time, though its principles were really only the product of a specific

18 Wilhelm Dilthey, *Einleitung in die Geisteswissenschaften* (Leipzig: Duncker & Humblot, 1883). All references to Dilthey's work will be to *Gesammelte Schriften*, ed. Karlfried Gründer and Frithjof Rodi (Göttingen: Vandenhoeck & Ruprecht, 1961–). This edition will be abbreviated as GS.

CHAPTER 4

time and place. Among those who had such pretensions, Dilthey warned, was Kant himself, who had removed his transcendental standpoint from history, as if its norms and forms were a priori and eternal, originating from a self-sufficient noumenal subject, when they were really the product of history.

It was also obvious, however, that Dilthey's program applied to history itself. The historian's standpoint should also be the product of its own time and place, so that the interests and values behind it should depend on their place in history, just like any other intellectual activity or inquiry. But if this were so, what happens with objective historical knowledge? The only possible conclusion is that it, too, is an ahistorical pretension. These self-destructive implications of Dilthey's project were made clear to him by Wilhelm Windelband in a lecture published in 1883, "Kritische oder genetische Methode?"[19] "A critique of historical reason," Windelband warned, "is a very praiseworthy undertaking; only it must be a critique, and as such it needs a criterion."[20] This criterion must be a universal and necessary norm, Windelband argued, whose validity stands above the realm of history, because, otherwise, we are caught in the snares of relativism. Windelband then went on to explain that it is necessary to make a clear distinction between a *critical* method, whose main task is to assess the validity of claims to knowledge, and a *genetic* method, whose chief business is to determine the causes or origins of knowledge. Dilthey's project had confused these methods, Windelband charged, because it assumed that to determine the limits of historical knowledge is to ascertain its causes and origins.

Dilthey did not take these criticisms lightly. His response to them, which appears in several writings of the 1880s,[21] is that the neo-Kantian distinction between questions of validity and history, if generalized and applied too strictly, is artificial and misleading. It was precisely the purpose of historical criticism to break down the barrier between norms and facts, values and history, because it

19 Wilhelm Windelband, *Präludien, Aufsätze und Reden zur Philosophie und ihrer Geschichte*, Neunte Auflage (Tübingen: Mohr, 1924) II, 99–115.

20 Ibid., II, 120–21.

21 Wilhelm Dilthey, *Westermans Monatshefte* 57 (1884), 290–91, GS XVII, 469–70; *Ideen über eine beschreibende und zergliedernde Psychologie*, GS V, 149–50; and *Beiträge zum Studium der Individualität*, GS V, 267–80.

led to the illusion that the philosopher stood above history, that he was in possession of innate truths or a priori concepts that arose from an ahistorical transcendental subject. The neo-Kantians had failed to heed the fundamental lesson of the historical school: that what appears to be given and eternal to us now is the result of history. Dilthey was not questioning Windelband's basic point that the evaluation of the validity of a belief involves norms, which is distinct from determining its causes; but he believed that the neo-Kantians had taken that point too far when they went on to construct an ahistorical noumenal realm of norms. In doing so, they were either ignoring the question of the origin of their principles or they were presupposing a mysterious genetic account all their own. In either case, they were guilty of dogmatism by refusing to answer questions or by failing to examine their own assumptions. Perfectly valid points, though they still left Dilthey with Windelband's question: How can there be objective historical knowledge if the historian, too, is part of history?

Droysen's critique of Ranke, and Dilthey's response to Windelband, were only two of the chapters—though crucial ones—in the wider and longer debate about historical objectivity in the latter half of the nineteenth century. These debates eventually led to what later became known as "the crisis of historicism." Although this crisis has several meanings, one of its more important ones is that history could not justify itself as a science because it fell victim to its own methods of historicization. If those methods are applied without limits, the argument went, they would undermine the claim of history to provide a form of objective knowledge, and so to be a science. Thus the triumph of history—showing that everything is the product of history—became the downfall of history. This remarkable paradox later became the starting point for Heidegger and Gadamer, who would use it to make their case for the inescapable historicity of the human predicament.

3. THE BATTLE AGAINST POSITIVISM

The battle against speculative philosophy and the controversy about historical objectivity were only two episodes in Clio's struggle for independence and legitimacy. Another episode began in the

1850s and lasted until the end of the century. This time Clio had to prove herself against a very different enemy, one no less wily and imposing than speculative philosophy. This new foe was historical positivism, an import from England and France, which began to make headway in Germany in the 1850s. The chief champion of this positivism was Auguste Comte (1798–1857), whose *Cours de philosophie positive* first appeared in Germany in the 1840s;[22] but another advocate was John Stuart Mill (1806–73), whose *Logic* appeared in 1843 and in German translation in 1862.[23] Comte and Mill never disputed that history could be a science; and indeed they were eager to make it one, because they believed it to be the basis for a general science of society which would finally give mankind control over its own destiny. *Savoir pour prévoir, prévoir pour pouvoir*, as Comte loved to say. Yet Comte and Mill doubted that history had its own sui generis goals and methods; and they insisted that it model itself according to the natural sciences. They held that all explanation in the natural sciences is nomothetic (i.e., lawlike) in form, so that to explain an event means to subsume it under a general law. According to their paradigm of explanation, all explanation can be represented according to a syllogism, where the major premise states a general law (e.g., "All water freezes at zero degrees centigrade"), where the minor premise states a particular fact (e.g., "It was zero degrees centigrade in Syracuse last night"), and where the conclusion applies the law to the fact (e.g., "All water outside in Syracuse froze last night"). The same model of explanation, Comte and Mill hoped and believed, should be applied in history. The more we know the laws of history, the more we can control it. Though Comte and Mill wrote little history themselves, the English historian Henry Buckle began to apply their ideas in earnest in his *History of Civilization in England*.[24]

Positivism was a threat of which Ranke was blissfully ignorant in the 1830s. In his defense of history in his 1831 lectures he was

22 Auguste Comte, *Cours de philosophie positive* (Paris: Bachelier, 1830–42).

23 John Stuart Mill, *A System of Logic* (London: J. W. Parker and Son, 1843). It was translated by J. Schiel and published under the title *System der induktiven und deduktiven Logik* (Braunschweig: Vieweg, 1862–63).

24 Henry Buckle, *History of Civilization in England* (London: J. W. Parker and Son, 1857–61).

eager to ally history with the empirical sciences to do battle against speculative philosophy. History, Ranke argued, should follow the model of the empirical sciences by examining facts for their own sake, by refraining from speculation, and by adopting the analytic or inductive method. But Ranke was willing to take his analogy only so far. Never would he have wanted history to be completely like the empirical sciences, since this would forfeit the very autonomy he cherished and defended. Although he did not question the role of causal explanation in history, Ranke never believed such explanation to be its sole or central purpose. His fundamental principle of individuality means that the main purpose of history is not to construct general laws but to grasp the individual in all its uniqueness and difference. When Ranke first declared his principle, it was directed against Hegel and speculative philosophy. It was now the task of his successors to uphold it against the threat of positivism.

The first to do battle against historical positivism was Droysen. He had already begun to criticize it in the 1850s in his lectures on historics; but in the 1860s he wrote a full-scale critique in two important articles: "Die Erhebung der Geschichte zur Rang einer Wissenschaft," which appeared in 1863 in the *Historische Zeitschrift*, and which was a long review of Buckle's *History of Civilization in England*; and "Natur und Geschichte," which was published in 1868 in the first edition of his *Historik*.[25] In these articles Droysen deplores the methodological dogmatism of the positivists. Even if we accept that nomological explanation is possible in history, he argues, that does not mean that no other form of explanation is possible. "Is there only one way, one method of knowledge?" he asks. Droysen doubted that nomological explanation was the sole or chief goal of history. The main problem with positivism, Droysen argues, is that the subject matter of history is very unlike that of the natural sciences. The subject matter of the natural sciences is something given to our senses; we can observe it, and we can reproduce it in experiments. The subject matter of history, however,

<hr>

25 J. G. Droysen, "Die Erhebung der Geschichte zur Rang einer Wissenschaft," *Historische Zeitschrift* 9 (1863), 1–22; and "Natur und Geschichte," in *Grundriß der Historik* (Leipzig: Veit, 1868), pp. 63–74.

is not given, simply because it is the past, which no longer exists and cannot be reproduced. Droysen did not deny that the historian has to presuppose natural laws in the explanation of human actions; but he denied that this is his essential concern or purpose. The aim of the historian is not to know general laws, i.e., what makes events like one another, but to know unique and singular events, i.e., what makes them different from one another. History concerns the individuality of things, what makes them unique and different. It was precisely this individuality, however, from which the natural scientist would abstract in his search for universal laws. Here, though he would have been loath to admit it, Droysen was implicitly reaffirming Ranke's principle of individuality.

In the background of Droysen's polemics against positivism lay his own attempt to formulate an alternative model of historical explanation. In his 1857 lectures on historics,[26] Droysen began to outline a crude version of what later became known as the "method of understanding" or "*Verstehen.*" Though Dilthey is often regarded as the father of this method, Droysen had conceived it decades before him. The guiding principle behind Droysen's historics is an idea he inherited from Wilhelm von Humboldt: that language is the key to understanding the social and historical world. Humboldt had reasoned that human actions are governed and motivated by thoughts, which are embodied and expressed in language. If we are to understand these actions in all their individuality and uniqueness, we then have to understand exactly the language in which they are expressed. Hence for Droysen philology became the key to unlock the historical world. There was an important connection, therefore, between history and hermeneutics, the discipline of textual interpretation. That discipline had been developed before Droysen by Chladenius, Schleiermacher, and Boeckh; Droysen simply extended its guiding principles to history. All the techniques that we use for interpreting historical texts, he realized, could be applied to historical actions, whose meaning would be revealed only through the interpretation of the words that expressed and embodied them. A human action therefore could be understood on the analogy of a text. Just as we understand an ancient text when we translate its

26 See note 15.

language into our own, so we understand a past action when we translate the language that embodies and expresses the thinking of the agent. Understanding the past is therefore in large part translation, putting the thoughts of past agents into our own language. Given such a conception of historical understanding, it is easy to see the reasons for Droysen's resistance to positivism. Since the techniques and rules of textual interpretation are very different from those of nomothetic explanation, so will be the techniques and rules of historical understanding.

Droysen's protest against positivism was only the beginning. In 1883, in the preface to his just published *Einleitung in die Geisteswissenschaften*,[27] Wilhelm Dilthey remonstrated against the new positivist mentality, which would subjugate history and the social sciences to the goals and methods of the natural sciences. The historians had freed themselves from the tyranny of speculative philosophy only to be threatened by the natural sciences, he complained. It was Dilthey's aim to defend the autonomy of history and the social sciences, their right to have their own subject matter, their own goals and standards of investigation, independent of the natural sciences. Toward that end, he stressed the importance of establishing firm boundaries between disciplines. He therefore made a distinction between two kinds of subject matter or two different kinds of experience. While the social-historical sciences deal with *inner* experience, the natural sciences treat *outer* experience. Inner experience is what we are aware of through self-awareness, through the self-consciousness of our own activities; outer experience consists in our sense perception of the external world, the awareness of objects in space and time. Since these forms of experience are so different from one another, Dilthey argued, they more than suffice to separate the different sciences. He insisted that his distinction between the sciences was strictly *phenomenological*, corresponding to two forms of experience, and that it was not *metaphysical*, making claims about the entities behind these forms of experience. The distinction between inner and outer experience was not, therefore, intended to correspond to a dualism between mind and body. Dilthey also stressed that the distinction

27 GS I, xviii.

between the social-historical and natural sciences should not be methodological, i.e., between different forms of explanation. He acknowledged that the social-historical sciences use methods of abstraction and generalization no less than the natural sciences. Since human beings are so different from one another and their interactions and circumstances so complex, Dilthey doubted that laws in the social-historical sciences will have the same precision as those in the natural sciences; nevertheless, he stressed the importance of general causal laws in the social-historical sciences. The historical and social sciences, no less than the natural sciences, need to determine the interconnections between events; and these interactions are formulable in terms of laws of cause and effect.

A milestone in the reaction against positivism came in 1894 with Wilhelm Windelband's celebrated Rectoral Address in Straßburg, "Geschichte und Naturwissenschaft."[28] A neo-Kantian, Windelband was especially concerned to expand the criteria of science in the Kantian tradition so that it is not limited to mathematics and the natural sciences. The achievements of Ranke and Niebuhr, he declared, were no less than those of Helmholtz and Liebig, and it was important that the logic of the sciences be able to do justice to this fact. The critical philosophy should account for the logic of history no less than the logic of the natural sciences. So in his address Windelband made a distinction between two forms of empirical science: the natural sciences, which are *nomothetic*, i.e., concerned with discovering universal laws; and the historical sciences, which are *ideographic*, i.e., concerned with determining particular facts. While the natural sciences attempt to universalize and explain as many facts as possible under a single law, the historical sciences aim to individuate and to account for the differences between things. Windelband intended his distinction to be primarily formal or methodological and not material or in subject matter, because a critical epistemology should stress more *how* we know than *what* we know in the world itself. But he realized a purely formal distinction is difficult to make, partly because the natural sciences are sometimes interested in individual events, and partly because

28 Wilhelm Windelband, *Geschichte und Naturwissenschaft* (Straßburg: Heitz, 1894), reprinted in *Präludien*, II, 136–60.

the historical sciences are sometimes concerned with making or at least applying general laws. The point of his distinction between the ideographic and the nomological is ultimately more pragmatic than methodological, i.e., it is a distinction between different goals rather than methods of inquiry. Although each science could use individuating and universalizing methods, that did not affect the crucial question: What *use* or *interest* did each science have in applying the method? Was its chief *goal* to know the universal law or the particular event? Windelband believed that history and natural science are equal and independent kinds of science ultimately because they have equal but independent cognitive objectives: to know either the particular or the universal, the unique events and personalities of history, or the general laws of the cosmos.

Windelband's Rectoral Address was the occasion for an interesting exchange between Windelband and Dilthey. Implicit in Windelband's lecture was a criticism of his fellow opponent of positivism, Dilthey. Windelband took exception to Dilthey's phenomenological distinction between the historical and natural sciences for two reasons. First, it made the distinction in subject matter rather than method. Such a distinction was not in accord with Kant's critical principle that there is only as much form and structure in an object as the mind creates in it, which means, Windelband insisted, that the distinction should be primarily in terms of method rather than subject matter. Second, Dilthey's emphasis upon inner experience gave great importance to psychology, though it was increasingly becoming a nomothetic discipline. So if Dilthey wanted his realm of inner experience to be inaccessible to nomothetic explanation, he would have to endorse methods of introspection, which are notoriously unreliable.

To these criticisms, Dilthey responded that the distinction between the sciences really could not be formal or methodological, because the social-historical sciences use nomothetic methods no less than the natural sciences.[29] Economics, for example, was especially concerned with the formulation of nomothetic laws. But if we are not to distinguish these sciences through their methods, how are we to distinguish them? Dilthey responded to this ques-

29 See Dilthey, *Beiträge zum Studium der Individualität*, GS V, 241–58.

tion with a revised version of his distinction between forms of experience. He now made it clear that this distinction is not between distinct kinds of *events* or *actions* but between distinct kinds of mental or intellectual *content* or *meaning*. The aim of the social-historical sciences is not to provide a description of mental *events* or *activities* as they pass through consciousness—hence Windelband's objection against introspection misses the mark—but to identify and analyze the *content* or *meaning* of our inner experience. This is not a distinction between objects because one and the same object can have a different meaning or content depending on the perspective of the inquiry; for example, the same physical object can be the content of chemistry, physics, and physiology. What determines the content is the system of relations into which we analyze the object; and which system we formulate depends on the specific inquiries and perspective we make.

After his exchange with Windelband, Dilthey continued to reflect on the difference between the social-historical and natural sciences, which eventually led him to some of his most interesting and influential views about the sui generis status of the social-historical sciences. Since Dilthey saw inner experience as the distinctive subject matter of the social-historical sciences, and since he saw psychology as the discipline concerned with such inner experience, he gave psychology a crucial role among all the social-historical sciences. All these sciences were forms of psychology, which was their master discipline. But Dilthey took onboard Windelband's point that psychology is becoming an increasingly nomothetic science like other natural sciences. He therefore made a distinction between two different kinds of psychology, which appears in his 1894 *Ideen über beschreibende und zergliedernde Psychologie*.[30] This is a distinction between a mechanical or explicative and a descriptive or analytical psychology. While mechanical psychology begins with psychic elements and determines the law-like relations between them, descriptive or analytical psychology begins with the whole of our inner experience and proceeds to analyze it into its separate parts. In other words, mechanical psychology applies an analytic

30 Wilhelm Dilthey, *Ideen über eine beschreibende und zergliedernde Psychologie*, GS V, 139–240.

method, proceeding from parts to whole, whereas descriptive or analytical psychology (despite the name) moves from wholes to parts. The main concern of mechanical or explicative psychology is *explanation*, the subsumption of particular mental events or activities under general laws, whereas the chief aim of descriptive or analytical psychology is *interpretation* or *understanding*, understanding the *content* or *meaning* behind these events or activities. Ironically, this was a distinction between method, the very kind of distinction once advocated by Windelband and repudiated by Dilthey. But by making his distinction between explanation and interpretation, between laws and content or meaning, Dilthey gave the methodological distinction a new and much deeper meaning than Windelband had imagined. The ideographic, Dilthey was saying, is not only about individuals but about content and meaning.

Dilthey's final formulation for the subject matter of history, which appears in his late work *Aufbau der geschichtlichen Welt in den Geisteswissenschaften*,[31] is that it concerns what he calls "lived experience" (*Erlebnis*). This concept was an explication and elaboration of what he originally meant by "inner experience." Lived experience is essentially what someone lives through in the course of his life. It involves all aspects of a person's life, not only perception and cognition but also volition and emotion. Hence lived experience comprises the whole of what we perceive, feel, and desire. Since it is a unity of cognition, emotion, and volition, it involves no sharp distinction between value and fact; what we live through, Dilthey insisted, is determined by our values, which are constitutive of our lives. Another fundamental element of lived experience, Dilthey explains, is temporality. Lived experience is not simply the whole of what we perceive, feel, and desire at any single moment but also what we perceive, feel, and desire through the whole course of our lives. The whole character of lived experience is determined by the consciousness of the passing of time, by the awareness of a past, present, and future, and a sense of our own mortality. Dilthey's concept of lived experience greatly enriched and extended his account of the subject matter of history and the social sciences.

31 See especially the draft "Abgrenzung der Geisteswissenschaften," GS VII, 70–75. See also the earlier drafts, GS VII, 304–10, 310–17.

Rather than seeing experience as simply the consciousness of the cognitive subject, Dilthey added the dimensions of emotion, volition, and temporality. The only means of doing justice to lived experience, Dilthey implied, was through narrative, an intellectual structure completely different from nomothetic explanation. Only narrative could account for the importance of individuality that Ranke, Droysen, Windelband, and Dilthey all saw as the characteristic concern of history.

4. POSITIVIST MISUNDERSTANDINGS OF HISTORICISM

Although Ranke, Droysen, Dilthey, and Windelband would often quarrel among themselves about the logic of historical interpretation, there were still notable common features among them. They all held that the purpose of history is knowledge of the particular; they all insisted that history should be an empirical science; they all resisted the speculative philosophy of history of the idealist tradition; and they all opposed the positivist nomothetic paradigm of explanation. For these reasons they have often been placed in a single tradition, which is sometimes called "the German historical," "historicist," or "hermeneutical" tradition. This tradition has often been regarded as the philosophical alternative to positivism, which became dominant in Anglophone philosophy after the Second World War. We cannot do justice here to the debate between positivism and historicism, which raises many complex philosophical issues. But, in a history like this, we should address some misunderstandings about the historicist tradition that arose during the positivist polemics against it.

Because of their common antipositivist stance, Ranke, Droysen, Dilthey, and Windelband have all been lumped together as if they represented a single philosophical position. There were, however, important differences between them, as our account of the disputes between them illustrates. The most important of these differences concern historical understanding itself. Although they all agree that history is about the individual, they have very different conceptions of what it means to understand the individual. Ranke saw such understanding as the *intuition* of the individual, the contemplation of its unique qualities, which was much like the experience of a work of art. Droysen regarded understanding as the translation of the language of the historical agent into a contemporary language. Dilthey likened understanding to the reconstruction of lived experience, to re-creating the narrative of a person's life. And Windelband conceived understanding as normative, the subsumption of an action not under laws but under social, political, and ethical norms. The historicist tradition has often been identified with the hermeneutical tradition;[32] but these traditions have distinct histories, and they converged only in Droysen and Dilthey. Ranke and Windelband, despite their many affinities with Droysen and Dilthey, had little understanding of hermeneutics.

In their polemics against the historicists, the positivists would often create a caricature of their opponents. They portrayed historicism as a species of "aestheticism," "intuitionism," or even "irrationalism," because the historicists portrayed the understanding of the past as a form of intuition, empathy, or sympathy, where the historian reproduced or reenacted what happened according to his own imagination.[33] The objections against such a theory are obvious: that it is too subjective, allowing the historian to read his own attitudes and feelings into his subject matter; that imagining or re-creating the past, in all its complexity and confusion, is not the same as understanding it; that it is impossible for us, who are the product of a completely different culture, to get inside the minds of people in the past. And so on. Although these objections are plausible, they are also problematic, because they were directed against a bogeyman, a position that no one really held. Although Ranke,

32 This misunderstanding has its source in Hans-Georg Gadamer, *Wahrheit und Methode*, in *Gesammelte Werke* (Tübingen: Mohr, 1990), I, 203.

33 See Carl Hempel, "The Function of General Laws in History," *Journal of Philosophy* 39 (1942), 35–48; Otto Neurath, "Sociology and Physicalism," in *Logical Positivism*, ed. A. J. Ayer (New York: Free Press, 1959), 282–317, esp. 295, 298; Theodore Abel, "The Operation Called *Verstehen*," *American Journal of Sociology* 54 (1948), 211–18; and Edgar Zilsel, "Physics and the Problem of Historico-Sociological Laws," in *Readings in the Philosophy of Science*, ed. H. Feigl and M. Brodbeck (New York: Appleton-Century-Crofts, 1953), 714–22, esp. 721. Although Popper distanced himself from the positivists, he shared a similar account of the historicist method of *Verstehen*. See *The Poverty of Historicism* (London: Routledge, Kegan & Paul, 1957), p. 138.

Droysen, and Dilthey would sometimes portray understanding in terms of intuition and reenactment, they always insisted that such intuitions should be the *result* of historical research, which would employ all the conceptual tools of history. Such intuitions were not meant to be the replacement for discursive tools, viz., concepts, judgments, and reasoning, but the product of them.

It is also a misinterpretation of the historicist tradition to present it as if it were completely opposed in principle to the use of nomothetic explanation. Ranke, Droysen, Dilthey, and Windelband all recognized that nomothetic explanation has an important role to play in historical understanding. Although they held that the purpose of history is understanding the individual, they also stressed that we could not do so without placing the individual in context and connection with other things, a task which inevitably involved subsuming the individual under general laws. The quarrel of the historians with nomothetic explanation is only that it cannot be the sole end or purpose of historical inquiry. Since the end of the historian is to understand the individual as such, it follows that his work is very different from that of the natural scientist, whose chief aim is to create a system of universal laws. Construed simply as a pragmatic difference about the ends of inquiry, the dispute between historicist and positivist loses much of its point and meaning. It ceases to be a debate about the logic of explanation or understanding in history and becomes instead only a difference in the ends of inquiry. There cannot be much dispute about the propriety or legitimacy of having different ends of inquiry, however. It is hard to quarrel with the claim that, even if methods of inquiry are very alike, their ends can be very different.

Still, the debate might seem to have some life in it insofar as the positivist insists that nomothetic explanation is the *sole* form of understanding in history. Surely there is still a dispute here, someone might say, because this is a point that the historicist denies and the positivist affirms. But even in this regard, the debate between historicist and positivist melts away once we recognize that they are talking past one another. The positivist thesis that covering laws should be the sole paradigm of explanation in history is plausible only if we presuppose that we already know the historical facts. The positivist assumes that the past is just given to us and that it is only a matter of explaining the general laws that govern it. But it is precisely this assumption that the historicist finds so problematic. Ranke, Droysen, Dilthey, and Windelband always stressed that the past has disappeared, that it no longer exists, and that it has to be reconstructed for us. It is precisely in this respect that history differs from the natural sciences, where the facts of experience are still present for us. All the historicist's tools of interpretation and criticism are designed to reconstruct these facts; but these activities are very different from nomothetic explanation. They involve unearthing evidence, determining the authenticity of sources, interpreting and translating documents, assessing whether there is sufficient evidence for a conclusion, and so on. It was for these reasons that the historicists resisted the positivist thesis that everything is reducible to "covering laws" or nomothetic explanation.

Once we realize this, we can see that the historicist and positivist were really talking about different things. The positivist was talking about history *a parti objecti*, i.e., history as the totality of past human actions; the historicist was talking about it *a parti subjecti*, i.e., history as the totality of what human beings have said or written about the past. Even if the positivist thesis is true for objective history, so that all historical events have to be explained nomothetically, it hardly follows that it is true for subjective history. Nomothetic explanation would be at best a goal the historian reaches at the end of his inquiries; before he gets there, he first has to apply methods and techniques to assess what has been said or written about history; and in engaging in these activities he is hardly just formulating and applying covering laws.

5

THE PESSIMISM

CONTROVERSY

I. A FORGOTTEN CONTROVERSY

In the 1960s budding young philosophers were told that philosophy does not have anything to do with the question of the meaning or value of life. That was a popular misconception about philosophy—so we were told—that we should get out of our heads right away, because philosophy is essentially a science, a technical discipline concerned with the logic of language. Philosophers who towed this positivist line in the 1960s will be pleased to know that nearly a century earlier many neo-Kantians and positivists held a similar conception of their discipline. They will be less pleased to know, however, that their neo-Kantian and positivist forebears soon admitted the error of their ways. They quickly realized that they had to address this question after all, not only if they were to have an audience but also if they were to justify their basic moral and political convictions. In the late 1870s and early 1880s, as we have seen,[1] neo-Kantians and positivists were forced to depart from their narrow agenda concerned exclusively with the logic of science and to discuss the grand question of the meaning and value of life.

That philosophers in the 1870s and 1880s were forced to move away from their rigid scholastic agenda was due to the work of a single man: Arthur Schopenhauer. By the early 1860s he had become the most famous philosopher in Germany. His works not only had an appeal to the general educated public, but they also proved powerful competition for philosophy professors whose

---

1   See chapter 1, section 5.

agenda was limited to the logic of the sciences. Schopenhauer had performed a remarkable feat that was the envy of the professors: he had made philosophy relevant again, so that it was asking basic questions of concern to everyone alike, not only professors interested in abstruse matters of logic. Schopenhauer's grand question was simple, pressing, and inescapable: Is life worth living? That was a question every reflective person had to face sometime in his or her life. Compared to it, the logic of the sciences seemed scarcely important or relevant.

Schopenhauer's challenge to his age arose not only from the question he raised but from the answer he gave to it. That answer was his pessimism. The central thesis of Schopenhauer's pessimism is as simple as it is shocking: that life is *not* worth living. Nothingness is better than being, death is preferable to life. Rarely, if ever, in philosophical history has life received such a damning verdict. It was as if Schopenhauer were telling people: you are better off dead and there is no point to your struggles. All your deeper aspirations—all your strivings to create a better world—are null and void.

From the shock of Schopenhauer's pessimism there arose one of the most intense philosophical controversies of the late nineteenth century: the *Pessimismusstreit*. According to some contemporary accounts, pessimism quickly overshadowed materialism as the most pressing and important issue of the age.[2] Pessimism swiftly became the talk of the town, the subject of literary salons, and even the object of satire.[3]

The pessimism controversy had two main phases. The first phase arose in the 1860s with Schopenhauer's rise to fame, when many articles, pamphlets, and books were published attacking his pessimism. If Schopenhauer had many detractors, he also had some

2   Theodor Tautz, *Der Pessimismus* (Karlsruhe: G. Braun'schen Hofbuchhandlung, 1876), pp. 6–7; Edmund Pfleiderer, *Der moderne Pessimismus* (Berlin: Carl Habel, 1875), pp. 7–8.

3   See M. Reymond, *Das Buch vom bewußten und unbewußten Herrn Meyer*, which was part of his *Das Buch vom gesunden und kranken Herrn Meyer* (Bern: Georg Frobeen & Cie., 1877). Herr Meyer, Reymond's hapless antihero, holds a literary salon where Hartmann's pessimism is discussed.

able defenders.[4] The second phase began in 1870 in reaction against Eduard von Hartmann's *Philosophie des Unbewussten*, which had reaffirmed but qualified Schopenhauer's pessimism. During the 1870s alone hundreds of reviews, scores of articles, and dozens of books were published on Hartmann's pessimism.[5] The torrent continued unabated throughout the 1880s; it began to weaken only in the 1890s. Though Hartmann's pessimism was the focus of the second phase of the controversy, no one was under any illusions that Schopenhauer was his spiritual father.

Despite its great philosophical and cultural importance, the pessimism controversy has been largely forgotten. It had one great historian in the late nineteenth century: Olga Plümacher. Her *Der Pessimismus in Vergangenheit und Gegenwart*,[6] which was first published in 1883, remains the single attempt to explain and describe the various viewpoints and episodes of the controversy. Today, if the controversy is remembered at all, it is solely through its most famous participant: Friedrich Nietzsche. In his day, however, Nietzsche was known as only one among many contributors to the controversy.[7] But these other contributors also had many interest-

4 The chief defenders were Julius Frauenstädt, *Briefe über die Schopenhauer'sche Philosophie* (Leipzig: Brockhaus, 1854); Julius Bahnsen, *Der Widerspruch im Wissen und Wesen der Welt* (Berlin: Theobold Grieben, 1880) and *Zur Philosophie der Geschichte* (Berlin: Duncker, 1872); Phillip Mainländer, *Philosophie der Erlösung* (Berlin: Theobold Grieben, 1880); and Paul Deussen, *Die Elemente der Metaphysik* (Bonn: Marcus, 1876).

5 O. Plümacher, "Chronologische Verzeichniss der Hartmann-Literatur von 1868–1880," in *Der Kampf um's Unbewusste* (Berlin: Duncker, 1881), pp. 115–50. On the first decade of the reception of Hartmann's philosophy, see his own article "Die Schicksale meiner Philosophie in ihrem ersten Jahrzehnt (1869–1879)," in *Philosophische Fragen der Gegenwart* (Leipzig: Wilhelm Friedrich, 1885), 1–25.

6 O. Plümacher, *Der Pessimismus in Vergangenheit und Gegenwart* (Heidelberg: Georg Weiss Verlag, 1883). A second edition appeared in 1888. See also her "Die Philosophie des Unbewussten und ihre Gegner," *Unsere Zeit* 15 (1879), 321–45. Plümacher was also the author of a book on two thinkers in the Schopenhauer school, *Zwei Individualisten der Schopenhauer'schen Schule* (Berlin: Duncker, 1882). She also wrote the article "Pessimism" for *Mind* 4 (1879), 68–89, which is a critique of James Sully's *Pessimism: A History and a Criticism* (London: Henry King, 1877).

7 See Plümacher, "Die Philosophie des Unbewussten und ihre Gegner," pp. 329–30; and Otto Siebert, *Geschichte der neueren deutschen Philosophie seit Hegel* (Göttingen: Vandenhock & Ruprecht, 1898), pp. 243–45.

ing things to say and, for philosophical as well as historical reasons, we do well to remember them.

In its heyday, 1870–90, the pessimism controversy ranged over a wide variety of topics and issues. Virtually any aspect of life relevant to its value was discussed. Among the chief topics were pleasure, work, art, love, suicide, freedom, and death. A full discussion of the various topics would be the subject for a whole book. Our task in this chapter, which is only introductory, is to recount *some* thinkers and themes. We will focus chiefly on those thinkers who have been forgotten, and we will leave aside Nietzsche, not because he is unimportant but because his work has already been so intensely studied by others.

But before we examine the pessimism controversy itself, we need to have some idea of the meaning and justification of Schopenhauer's pessimism, which was the initial cause and constant background of the controversy.

2. SCHOPENHAUER'S PESSIMISM

If anyone deserves the title "philosopher of pessimism," it is Arthur Schopenhauer. It is impossible to have a gloomier outlook on life. The darkest outlook is that which likens the world to hell. But Schopenhauer did not hesitate to make the comparison. "We do not have to seek hell below the earth," he writes in the second volume of *Die Welt als Wille und Vorstellung*, "because we already are living it here and now" (II, 744; P 580).[8] A passage from the *Paralipomena* is even more direct: "The world is *hell*, and we humans are its tormented souls and its devils" (V, 354).

Schopenhauer's pessimism is best understood as his answer to Hamlet's famous question: "To be or not to be?" Schopenhauer's answer is clear and unhesitating: that it is better not to be. "The essential meaning of the world famous monologue in *Hamlet*," he wrote, "is

---

8   All references to Schopenhauer's works in parentheses will be to *Sämtliche Werke*, ed. Wolfgang Freiherr von Löhneeysen (Stuttgart: Insel, 1968). "I" and "II" refer to the first and second volumes of *Die Welt als Wille und Vorstellung*. "P" refers to the English translation of this work by E.F.J. Payne, *The World as Will and Representation* (New York: Dover, 1969).

this: That our life is so miserable that complete non-existence would be preferable to it" (I, 445; P 324). Another statement for Schopenhauer's pessimism is provided by the myth of Silenus, which he retells in the second volume of *Die Welt als Wille und Vorstellung* (II, 752; P 587). As the story goes, King Midas chases Silenus, a satyr and companion of Dionysus, through the forest; when he finally catches Silenus, he asks him what is the best life for man. Silenus answers with a shrill laugh: "not to be born, not to be, to be nothing." It was Schopenhauer's mission on earth to proclaim that dark message: "The purpose of our existence is indeed to declare nothing more than the knowledge that it is better we never existed" (II, 775; P 605).

Pessimism for Schopenhauer is the only honest and adequate answer to the problem of evil. As soon as we realize that there cannot be any justification for all the suffering and injustice of the world, he insists, we must become pessimists. The sheer scale, constancy, and intensity of human suffering, and the fact that the wicked prosper while the virtuous suffer, make it necessary to admit that it would have been better had the world never existed (II, 738–39; P 739). The mere existence of evil is sufficient to disprove theism, Schopenhauer argues, because no omniscient, omnipotent, and benevolent God would ever permit it. The only kind of God that could be demonstrated from the suffering and evil of life, Schopenhauer insists, would be an evil tormenter who derives joy from the suffering of his creatures.

Usually Schopenhauer appraises the value of life in strict eudemonistic terms, as if its purpose were to make us happy; and he invites us to measure its pleasures against its pains. According to this criterion, he argues, life is not worth living because its pains vastly outweigh its pleasures, its sufferings greatly overshadow its joys (IV, 343). If we were purely rational beings, who decide strictly according to our advantage, we would prefer nothingness over being simply because life creates more pain than pleasure (II, 742; P 579–80). Hence Schopenhauer compares life to a bad business venture where the losses outweigh the gains, and where we never recover our initial investment (II, 734, 742; P 574, 579–80). Rather than comparing life to a gift, he thinks that we should liken it to a debt (II, 743; P 580). Paying off the interest takes our entire life; and we pay off the principal only with death.

Schopenhauer's pessimism rests partly upon empirical evidence about the prevalence of evil and suffering in the world. It is important to see, however, that Schopenhauer refuses to rest his case on empirical evidence alone, even though he thinks that it is overwhelmingly in his favor. In §§57–59 of *Die Welt als Wille und Vorstellung* he states "a priori" arguments for his pessimism. The intent of these arguments is to prove one central thesis: "that all life is suffering" (*alles Leben Leiden ist*) (I, 426; P 310). If this is indeed the case, then pessimism will be well-founded, the sole rational attitude toward life.

Schopenhauer's arguments in behalf of his thesis come straight from the playbook of classical philosophy, from the Epicurean and Stoic traditions. The Epicureans and Stoics had argued that the life of human desire is inherently frustrating and that it cannot bring true happiness, which consists in tranquility or equanimity. Such happiness can be attained, they taught, only through virtue, self-discipline, and withdrawal from the world. To a remarkable extent, Schopenhauer follows their arguments, their conception of happiness, and even their strategy for attaining it. Where he departs from his classical forebears is in his greater pessimism: he denies that we can attain lasting happiness in this life.

Schopenhauer's argument in §§57–59 consists in his analysis of human desire. The essence of a human being, he maintains, consists in willing or striving. This willing or striving manifests itself in desire or need, which is some felt deficiency or lack. When we perceive this deficiency or lack, Schopenhauer argues, we feel pain (*Schmerz*), by which he means not so much physical pain (pangs, aches, stabs) but discomfort, frustration, or unease. We strive to satisfy these needs (viz., for food or sex), so that the discomfort, frustration, or unease ceases. Although we sometimes satisfy these needs, the pleasure in their satisfaction never lasts very long but takes the form of momentary relief. The problem is that needs regenerate, so that the discomfort, frustration, or unease recurs. Since needs are constant and the source of suffering, and since the pleasure of satisfying them is very brief, life consists in more pain than pleasure, more suffering than happiness.

This argument is, however, only the opening of Schopenhauer's indictment. He adds another argument to bolster his case. The suffering of life, Schopenhauer maintains, arises not simply from deprivation, from the feeling of need alone. It also comes from another potent source: boredom. If need gives rise to an excess of *activity*, the toil and trouble of striving, boredom comes from an excess of *inactivity*, the restlessness and discontent of doing nothing at all. Boredom is just as much a source of suffering as need, Schopenhauer insists. When we are bored, we are desperate: we do not know what to do with ourselves; our very existence is a burden.

The analysis of desire has shown that our lives oscillate between need and boredom. Whether we feel one or the other depends on how slowly or quickly we satisfy our needs. If we satisfy them too slowly, we prolong feelings of deprivation; but if we satisfy them too quickly, we suffer boredom. In either case, we suffer, whether from too much or too little activity. These horrible states feed off one another. When we are bored, we long to chase after the objects of our desires; but in the midst of that chase, which quickly exhausts us, we long for nothing more than rest, which immediately gives rise to boredom again.

With this argument, Schopenhauer had come closer to his goal of proving all life is suffering. Our lot consists in suffering, it seems, whether we satisfy our needs or not. If we satisfy them, we suffer boredom; and if we do not satisfy them, we suffer deprivation. But what, one might ask, about those moments when we do satisfy our needs? Surely there are some moments of joy, however brief, that add to life's value. Schopenhauer, however, has a response to this point, one that deprives even these moments of any positive worth. In §59 of *Die Welt als Wille und Vorstellung* he argues, following Epicurus, that pleasure is only a negative quality, i.e., it arises only from the removal of the deprivation of need. Pleasure is not a positive quality in itself, one that is different from pain, for the simple reason that it is only the absence of pain. We only feel pleasure, Schopenhauer argues, when we return to our normal condition after feeling need. Once we are in that normal condition, however, we do not have any special feeling of pleasure. We appreciate what we have only when we lose it.

So in the calculus of life's costs and benefits, only the pains, which constantly add up, count because they alone have a positive value; the pleasures, however, are equal to zero.

If all this were not enough, Schopenhauer adds another argument just to bleaken life's prospects a little bit more. This argument, which appears briefly in chapter 40 of the second volume of *Die Welt als Wille und Vorstellung* (735; P 575) and in §153 of *Paralipomena*, once played a central role in Stoic and Epicurean arguments against the life of desire. The main contention of this argument is that we inevitably acquire new needs, which grow in intensity, so that it becomes increasingly harder to satisfy them (V, 347). This adds a completely new dimension to the life of desire, because it is not only that the same needs regenerate but that we acquire new ones, which have no natural limit and which grow the more we satisfy them. Schopenhauer's example for this kind of need is ambition. We are not satisfied with just a little recognition; we demand more and more, until we achieve fame; and once we are a little famous, we want to be more so. Schopenhauer could have chosen other examples, such as money and power, which were favorite targets of the Stoic and Epicurean traditions. Of these too we can say that the more we have of them, the more we want them, where there is no limit to how much we want. But the greater our wants, the harder it becomes to satisfy them, so that the feeling of discontent only grows.

To appreciate Schopenhauer's arguments for pessimism, it is crucial to consider his views about sex, which he outlines in a famous essay in volume 2 of *Die Welt als Wille und Vorstellung*, "Metaphysik der Geschlechtsliebe."[9] Here Schopenhauer makes it clear that sex is the strongest drive in human nature, one even more potent than self-preservation given that people often sacrifice themselves for love and children. The sex drive is not only the strongest but also the most pervasive, playing a decisive but subconscious role in motivating virtually all our actions. But this most potent and pervasive of drives, Schopenhauer argues, is blind and irrational, the source of endless suffering which we are powerless to resist. We surrender to it even if it is ruinous for us, and even if its satisfactions are fleeting and momentary. We think that love will bring us the greatest of pleasures; but no sooner do

---

9 Arthur Schopenhauer, "Metaphysik der Geschlechtsliebe," WWV II, 678–727.

we satisfy its urgings than disillusionment begins. Thus we flee nothing with greater haste than the bedroom the morning after. Rather than learning any lessons, we persist in our folly because our desires regenerate and we cannot resist them. Although we think that we are the agents behind our quest for love, we are really only the instruments of a higher power that controls us and uses us for its purposes. This higher power is the will to life; and its purpose is nothing more than existence itself, the mere continuation of life. There is no purpose to sex other than procreation; and there is no purpose to procreation other than the survival of the species. The will to life could not care less for the happiness of the individuals who serve it. Each individual lives for the sake of the species; and once it performs it procreative task, it is discarded and left to die.

When we consider all these arguments, it is difficult to resist Schopenhauer's conclusion that life is indeed suffering. Though there are moments of pleasure—sexual climaxes, quenched thirsts, sated bellies—they are fleeting, few, and far between; and never do they outweigh our usual fate: the deprivation of need, the desperation of boredom, and the pointlessness of sex. During most of our day we struggle to satisfy needs, to stave off boredom, or to still sexual urges, only to find that we are doomed to repeat our efforts tomorrow. We know that we are caught in a cycle of torment; but we find it hard, if not impossible, to escape, because we long for the very things that trap us. It is as if we were, as Schopenhauer put it, "lying on the revolving wheel of Ixion . . . and drawing water from the sieve of the Daniads" (I, 280; P 196).

3. THE NEO-KANTIAN CRUSADE

The most strident and tireless critics of Schopenhauer in the second half of the nineteenth century were the neo-Kantians. They were also, by far, the most numerous. Almost every major neo-Kantian had some stone to hurl against Schopenhauer's pessimism. From the mid-1860s until the early 1900s, Kuno Fischer (1824–1906), Otto Liebmann (1840–1912), Jürgen Bona Meyer (1829–97), Friedrich Paulsen (1846–1908), Rudolf Haym (1821–1901), Alois Riehl (1844–1924), Johannes Volkelt (1848–1930), Hermann Cohen

(1842–1918), and Wilhelm Windelband (1848–1915) wrote articles, essays, or book chapters about it. By the late 1870s, pessimism had replaced materialism as the Kantians' *bête noire*.

Why, though, were the neo-Kantians so provoked by Schopenhauer's pessimism? Prima facie a good Kantian should not be troubled by it. As we have seen, Schopenhauer had measured the value of life mainly by eudemonic standards, and he found it wanting because it brings more suffering than happiness. But such a conclusion should not have ruffled a single Kantian feather. For Kant himself had famously argued in the *Grundlegung zur Metaphysik der Sitten* that the natural end of human life is not happiness, and that we would all be much happier if we were led by instinct and not endowed with reason.[10] The proper criterion to measure the value of life, Kant held, is moral rather than eudemonic. Our lives are worth living just insofar as we are able to contribute to the moral ideal of the highest good, i.e., to create a social and political order where personal happiness and moral desert are in perfect harmony. No matter how much one suffers in striving toward such an ideal, one's life will still have been worth it.

Yet, on a deeper level, a good Kantian had strong reasons to be very disturbed by Schopenhauer's pessimism. For there was a quietistic message behind it that made all human endeavor pointless, even when measured in strictly moral terms. In the fourth book of *Die Welt als Wille und Vorstellung* Schopenhauer had argued explicitly for a quietism, according to which it is hopeless trying to change the human condition, which is ineradicable suffering. Human nature always remains the same, locked in the same vain struggle to satisfy its desires; the state cannot educate or reform human beings and it cannot make them happy; all that it can do is protect one person from harming another. Since we cannot change the world, we are better-off resigning ourselves to it and renouncing the very will that attempts to improve it. The only path toward some measure of tranquility is to withdraw from the world, to escape from it in aesthetic and religious contemplation. Hence the striving toward the highest good was, in Schopenhauer's view, only

10   Immanuel Kant, *Grundlegung zur Metaphysik der Sitten, Schriften*, ed. Preussische Akademe der Wissenschaften (Berlin: de Gruyter, 1902–), IV, 395.

so much wasted labor. We are like Sisyphus pushing his rock up the hill, only for it to roll back down again.

It was chiefly this quietism that motivated the neo-Kantians to take up arms against Schopenhauer's pessimism. Schopenhauer had undercut the motivation to pursue their chief political ideal: the creation of a republican constitution founded on the principles of liberty, equality, and independence. Most neo-Kantians were staunch liberals who, despite the disappointment of 1848, still believed in the value of constitutional government and national unity. However, they did not believe, like Kant and Hegel, that republican and liberal ideals would be achieved through the sheer mechanism of history. They were more disciples of Fichte than Kant in one important respect: they held that man made his own history and that he could achieve his political ideals only through direct political engagement.[11] But it was this Fichtean activism that seemed undermined by Schopenhauer's quietism, which whispered its discouraging message into the ears of all those who were committed to changing the world. Nothing could be more opposed to the activist's agenda than Schopenhauer's ethic of denial of the will, renunciation of life, resignation to the ways of the world. For the neo-Kantians this was tantamount to surrender to the forces of darkness. Since so much was at stake, Schopenhauer's pessimism would have to be defeated and destroyed, root and branch.

One central strategy in the neo-Kantian campaign against Schopenhauer's pessimism was to undermine its claim to philosophical or scientific status. In one form or another, Windelband, Paulsen, Liebmann, Meyer, and Riehl all followed this strategy.[12]

11   On the Fichtean dimension of the neo-Kantian movement, see Klaus Köhnke, *Entstehung und Aufstieg des Neukantianismus* (Frankfurt: Suhrkamp, 1986), pp. 186–94; and Hermann Lübbe, *Politische Philosophie in Deutschland* (Munich: Deutscher Taschenbuch Verlag, 1974), pp. 194–205.

12   See Windelband, "Pessimimus und Wissenschaft" (1876), *Präludien*, 9th ed. (Tübingen: Mohr, 1924), II, 218–43; Friedrich Paulsen, "Gründen und Ursachen des Pessimismus," *Deutsche Rundschau* 48 (1886), 360–81; Otto Liebmann, "Trilogie des Pessimismus," in *Gedanken und Thatsachen* (Straßburg: Karl Trübner, 1902), II, 265–66; Jürgen Bona Meyer, *Schopenhauer als Mensch und Denker* (Berlin: Carl Habel, 1872), pp. 44–45; and Alois Riehl, *Zur Einführung in die Philosophie der Gegenwart*, Fünfte Auflage (Leipzig: Teubner, 1919), p. 187.

They contended that there could no proof for Schopenhauer's doctrine, either empirical or a priori, and that it was ultimately more a statement about his personal attitude than a genuine metaphysical fact about the world. According to this line of argument, whether life is worth living is a question of value, and so it is a matter for each individual to decide on the basis of his or her own experience. Who was Arthur Schopenhauer to tell everyone that their lives are pointless or worthless? That was a matter for each individual to decide for him- or herself. In advocating his pessimism as if it were some kind of deep metaphysical or psychological truth, Schopenhauer had made a fundamental confusion between fact and value. Windelband, who developed this line of argument most fully and rigorously, contended that there could be only one way to make an objective thesis about the value of existence: if we knew the purpose for which the world was created, then we could tell whether it is good or bad; it would then be a matter of simply seeing whether it fit its purpose or not. But there is no way of knowing what the purpose of life is in itself, and that is because metaphysics is impossible, just as Kant rightly taught.

One variation of this strategy, which was pursued by Paulsen and Meyer,[13] is that Schopenhauer's pessimism could be scientific or philosophical only if there were a kind of hedonic calculus, i.e., a method of comparing the pleasures and pains of this life and determining which outweighs the others. Although they knew that Schopenhauer never claimed to be in possession of such a calculus, they still maintained that it is a presupposition of his argument, because it is only by showing the predominance of suffering over happiness, of pain over pleasure, that he can justify his thesis that life is not worth living. But such a presupposition, Paulsen and Meyer argued, is absurd for the simple reason that it is impossible to make such comparisons. Pleasures and pains are very heterogeneous, and to determine their value we have to assess not only their quantities but also their qualities. Paulsen pointed out that it is impossible to determine for even a single ordinary day in a person's

13   Paulsen, "Gründen und Ursachen des Pessimismus," pp. 361–62, 367; and Jürgen Bona Meyer, "Weltlust und Weltleid," in *Probleme der Weltweisheit*, Zweite Auflage (Berlin: Allgemeine Verein für Deutsche Literatur, 1887), pp. 263–64.

life whether pleasures or pains predominate. For that to work, we would have to assign numerical values to the most heterogeneous pleasures and pains. But how do we measure, Paulsen asked, the pleasure of a good breakfast against the displeasure of having burned soup for dinner? And how do we determine the pleasure of reading a good book against the displeasure of hearing disturbing background noise? If we cannot calculate the sum of pleasures and pains on a single day, then how can we do so for a whole human life? And then for human life in general?

Another prevalent theme in the neo-Kantian polemic against Schopenhauer was the inadequacy of his theory of pleasure and desire. Paulsen, Meyer, and Volkelt were the main exponents of this theme.[14] They contended that Schopenhauer assumes that pleasure is *extrinsic* to action, as if it were a reward attained at the end of activity; but he fails to see that it is often *intrinsic* to action, that it derives from and is simultaneous with its very doing. There is a very big difference between the *pleasure of gratification*, which comes at the end of an action, and the *pleasure of doing*, which comes from acting itself. The sensation of satiety after a full meal and the feeling of rest after exertion are pleasures of gratification; the enjoyment of playing the piano or reading a good book is a pleasure of doing. Schopenhauer's concept of pleasure is too narrow, derived entirely from pleasures of gratification, as if they were the sole kind of pleasure. This mistake is a crucial premise to his pessimism, however, because it assumes that the active pursuit of pleasure has to be painful, a source of suffering, when it can be entirely enjoyable.

Another mistake of Schopenhauer's theory of pleasure, several neo-Kantians argued,[15] is its assumption that pleasure has solely a negative significance, as if it were nothing more than freedom from the pain of desire. We can feel pleasure, they pointed out, even if we have not felt pain, or even desire, beforehand. Are there not

14 Paulsen, "Gründen und Ursachen des Pessimismus," p. 365; Meyer, "Weltlust und Weltleid," p. 269; Johannes Volkelt, *Arthur Schopenhauer, Seine Persönlichkeit, seine Lehre, sein Glaube* (Stuttgart: Frommann, 1900), p. 214.

15 See Windelband, "Pessimismus und Wissenschaft," p. 237; Riehl, *Einführung*, pp. 182, 189; Paulsen, "Gründen und Ursachen des Pessimismus," p. 363; Meyer, "Weltlust und Weltleid," pp. 258, 270; and Volkelt, *Schopenhauer*, p. 216.

pleasant surprises in life? In any case, Schopenhauer's argument for his thesis is a non sequitur: the mere fact that desire attempts to satisfy some need does not mean that its satisfaction consists only in the removal of the need. There could still be positive elements of feeling in the satisfaction.

The most weighty neo-Kantian objections against Schopenhauer's pessimism concerned the chief conception behind it: the will. Liebmann, Meyer, and Riehl doubted that this concept could be given any definite meaning at all. Schopenhauer's will was supposed to be groundless, a mere striving, urge, or impulse, having no definite motive or purpose. But what kind of will is that, Liebmann asked,[16] that does not have an end or motive? If I will, I have to will something; my will needs a specific object. Meyer could not understand Schopenhauer's claim that the inner nature of a human being consists in the will.[17] We are supposed to know this through some kind of immediate intuition; but though it is true that self-consciousness is always of some form of *acting*, it does not follow that it is of some form of *willing*; after all, some forms of acting are just thinking. Riehl pushed home these kinds of criticisms many years later.[18] He maintained the concept of a will is only an abstraction that we derive from particular acts of will. In depriving the will of motives and ends, Schopenhauer was confusing it with simple instinct or desire, which need not have a conscious purpose; the will, however, must have such a purpose as a distinctly human form of volition.

No less problematic for the neo-Kantians was the metaphysics Schopenhauer based on his theory of the will. In the second book of *Die Welt als Wille und Vorstellung* Schopenhauer had put forward the bold thesis that the will is the inner nature not only of human beings but of all things, whether animate or inanimate.[19] Whoever knows that the will is his inner nature, Schopenhauer said, will want to generalize this for everyone and everything else, so that its inner nature, too, consists in the will. For Liebmann,

---

16   Otto Liebmann, *Kant und die Epigonen* (Stuttgart: Schober, 1865), pp. 191–92.

17   Meyer, *Schopenhauer als Mensch und Denker*, p. 32.

18   Riehl, *Einführung*, p. 177.

19   WWV I, 165 (P 106); and I, 169–70 (P 109–10).

Meyer, Haym, and Riehl, however, this was a speculative leap of astonishing proportion. "Never have the basic limits of speculation been treated with more nonchalance," Liebmann wrote.[20] For his part, Meyer found Schopenhauer's inference to be bolder than anything undertaken by the most speculative *Naturphilosoph*.[21] And Riehl found Schopenhauer's concept of will so mysterious that he could not understand how it could explain the entire world; here was a true explanation *obscurum per obscurius*.[22]

Fischer, Meyer, Haym, Riehl, and Volkelt were quick to point out the main difficulty in Schopenhauer's theory of redemption.[23] Schopenhauer had maintained that the will is the guiding force behind the intellect, which is essentially only a tool to determine the means for its ends. But he also maintained that human beings can deny the will, and ascend above all its pointless striving, through an act of pure intellectual insight. But how could the intellect liberate us from the will if it is also only its servant? Or do we somehow will to free ourselves of the will? How, indeed, does the will negate itself if it is constantly affirming itself as a power of infinite striving?

Such, in abstract, was the neo-Kantian polemic against Schopenhauer's pessimism. It was a polemic of extraordinary passion, length, depth, and breadth for a movement that first convinced itself that the sole aim of philosophy is to examine the logic of the sciences. But when we keep in mind the neo-Kantians' political agenda, not to mention their need to address the interests of the public, the polemic becomes all too understandable.

4. DÜHRING ON THE VALUE OF LIFE

A major voice in the pessimism controversy in late nineteenth-century Germany was Eugen Dühring (1833–1921). He wrote a widely read book on the topic, *Der Werth des Lebens*, which was first

20 Liebmann, *Kant und die Epigonen*, p. 194.
21 Meyer, *Schopenhauer als Mensch und Denker*, p. 38.
22 Riehl, *Einführung*, pp. 178–79.
23 Kuno Fischer, *Schopenhauers Leben, Werke und Lehre*, 2nd ed., Band IX of *Geschichte der neueren Philosophie* (Heidelberg: Carl Winter, 1898), p. 514; Meyer, *Schopenhauer als Mensch und Denker*, p. 45; Haym, *Schopenhauer*, pp. 31–32; Riehl, *Einführung*, pp. 183–84; Volkelt, *Schopenhauer*, pp. 262–64.

published in 1865[24] and went through eight editions.[25] One careful reader of the book was Nietzsche, who took copious notes on it in the summer of 1875.[26]

Like so many in his age, the young Dühring was profoundly impressed and influenced by the "Frankfurt pessimist." He admired Schopenhauer's clarity, rigor, and style, and especially his stand against university philosophy. It was Schopenhauer's great merit, Dühring declared, to have dragged philosophy out of its scholastic cocoon to confront the greatest question of them all: to be or not be. That question was for Dühring nothing less than "the chief theme of philosophy."[27] Yet despite his admiration for Schopenhauer, Dühring was challenged by his pessimism, which he regarded as utterly dangerous, indeed as "the greatest evil of all."[28] Pessimism sapped people of the very will to live, the courage and energy needed to face and fight the problems of life and the evils of the world. The primary purpose of Dühring's *Der Werth des Lebens* was to combat this evil.

Today, Dühring is very much forgotten. He is best known as the hapless target of Engel's famous polemic, *Anti-Dühring*.[29] But it was not for nothing that Engels chose to attack Dühring, who was one of the most controversial figures of German intellectual life in the late nineteenth century. Starting in the mid-1860s, he became involved in a number of protracted and bitter disputes with his colleagues at the University of Berlin for his outspoken views on an array of topics, such as the originality of Helmholtz's discovery of the law of conservation of energy, university philosophy,

24 E. Dühring, *Der Werth des Lebens. Eine philosophische Betrachtung* (Breslau: Eduard Trewendt, 1865).

25 The second edition appeared in 1877 with Fues Verlag in Leipzig. The later editions appeared in 1881, 1891, 1894, 1902, 1916, and 1922 with O. R. Reisland, which had taken over Fues Verlag.

26 Friedrich Nietzsche, *Sämtliche Werke*, VIII, 131–85. These notes are mainly a careful paraphrase of Dühring's text, with occasional critical remarks. They were written when Nietzsche was still under the influence of Schopenhauer. One can find many anticipations of Nietzsche's later philosophy in Dühring's book.

27 Dühring, *Der Werth des Lebens* (1865), p. 1.

28 Dühring, *Der Werth des Lebens* (Leipzig: Fues, 1877), pp. 219–20.

29 Friedrich Engels, *Herrn Eugen Dührings Umwälzung der Wissenschaft* (Leipzig: Genossenschaftsbuchdruckerei, 1878).

and the rights of women.[30] When, in 1877, he was removed from his lectureship, he accused his enemies of violating his academic freedom. The dispute then went public in a dramatic fashion, with articles in newspapers taking sides for and against him, and with massive protests by students against his dismissal. Despite the outcry, Dühring never regained his position and had to eke out a bare living as an independent writer. Fittingly enough, he cast himself in Schopenhauer's old role: the solitary, independent, and persecuted thinker, who had the courage to blow the whistle on university philosophers. For the remainder of his long life, he nurtured and vented his grudges against a host of enemies, whether they were university philosophers, reactionary politicians, communists, or, worst of all, the Jews. Along with Heinrich von Treitschke, Dühring has the dubious distinction of being a founder of the anti-semitic movement in the late nineteenth century.[31]

However disgraceful, Dühring's reputation does not diminish his important place in the history of nineteenth-century philosophy. Despite his hatred and small-mindedness, Dühring redeemed himself through a singular accomplishment: he was the founder of German positivism, the grandfather of Schlick, Carnap, Neurath, and Reichenbach. The founding text of German positivism is one of his early works, his *Natürliche Dialektik*.[32] Many of the signal themes of logical positivism make their first appearance in this work: faith in the unity of science; the rejection of metaphysics; the orientation of philosophy around the sciences, especially physics and mathematics; the defense of empiricism and the rejection of the synthetic a priori; the quantitative and mathematical paradigm

---

30   Dühring discusses the disputes at great length in his autobiography, *Sache, Leben und Feinde* (Leipzig: H. Reuther, 1882). A second expanded edition appeared in 1902 with Thomas Verlag (Leipzig).

31   Dühring wrote three anti-semitic tracts: *Die Ueberschätzung Lessings und dessen Anwaltschaft für die Juden* (Karlsruhe: Reuther, 1883); *Die Judenfrage als Frage der Racenschädlichkeit für Existenz, Sitte und Cultur der Völker* (Karlsruhe: Reuther, 1881); and *Der Ersatz der Religion durch Vollkommeneres und die Ausscheidung alles Judäerthums durch den Modernen Völkergeist* (Karlsruhe: Reuther, 1881). In *Sache, Leben und Feinde* the Jews are a pathological obsession, whom Dühring blames for his every misfortune.

32   Eugen Dühring, *Natürliche Dialektik* (Berlin: Mittler, 1865).

THE PESSIMISM CONTROVERSY

of reasoning; the concept of a pseudo-problem; and so on. It was no accident that Dühring was a great admirer of August Comte, the French founder of positivism, whose works he had read in his youth.[33] In his opinion, there were two great philosophers who paved the way for modernity: Feuerbach and Comte.[34]

Although Dühring was often critical of Comte,[35] he never broke with the main direction and spirit of his thought. Although he described his own philosophy as "the philosophy of reality" (*Wirklichkeitsphilosophie*) partly to distinguish it from positivism, it was really only a more radical form of positivism. Dühring's chief criticism of Comte is that he had not taken his scientific rationalism far enough, that he had insisted on limits to knowledge and left an unknowable realm as the last refuge for religion and pessimism. His own philosophy of reality is so-called because it emphasizes a realistic attitude toward the world (just like positivism), and because it refuses to acknowledge the existence of any world beyond that explicable by science (more positivist than positivism). The philosophy of reality is therefore positivism (i.e., scientific rationalism) taken to its ultimate limits. What the methods of the sciences could not explain simply did not exist. Though Dühring never takes explicit issue with Du Bois-Reymond during the *Ignorabimus* controversy, we can safely assume what his position would have been.

What, we might well ask, does Dühring's positivism have to do with his views on the value of life? *Prima facie* nothing, but *secunda facie* everything. Positivism means first and foremost for Dühring having an affirmative attitude toward existence, toward "factuality" or "positivity." The positivist sees the facts of this life as the ultimate reality, as the sole form of existence, so that we should not trouble ourselves about some other kind of reality above or beyond them. We should seek redemption in this life alone, and we should make

33 See *Sache, Leben und Feinde* (1902), pp. 77, 109. Dühring's chief discussion of Comte is in his *Kritische Geschichte der Philosophie*, Vierte, verbesserte und vermehrte Auflage (Leipzig: O. R. Reisland, 1894), pp. 505–25.

34 E. Dühring, *Cursus der Philosophie als streng wissenschaftlicher Weltanschauung und Lebensgestaltung* (Leipzig: Erich Koschny, 1875), p. 486.

35 See, for example, his many criticisms of Comte in *Cursus der Philosophie*, pp. 42, 59, 75, 135, 298, 410.

the most of our life on Earth, which is our sole and singular life. The highest good has to be sought in the here and now.

Dühring regarded his philosophy as first and foremost a guide to life, a strategy for making life worth living.[36] Of all such guides, positivism is the most effective, he believed, because it alone adopts a realistic and practical attitude toward life's problems and evils. While the optimist turns a blind eye to the dark side of life, and while the pessimist advises resignation to it, the positivist alone squarely faces it and does everything in his power to conquer it, so that we can live in a better world. So, contrary to its popular image, positivism does not mean for Dühring accepting the ultimate reality of facts but the readiness to change them, so that reality comes closer to our ideals.[37]

The more he wrote about the value of existence, the more Dühring became convinced that it is ultimately a political problem.[38] Life can have little value if it is lived under political oppression and if a person has to struggle to earn the mere means of subsistence. If life is a miserable affair for the great mass of people, that is not because of desire as such, as Schopenhauer thought, but because of the historical system of ownership and production. Hence the solution to the existential problem lies with political action. The proper form of that action, Dühring insisted against the communists, lies with reform rather than revolution. Making a distinction later appropriated and turned upside down by Engels, Dühring stated that the positivist is not a *utopian* socialist, who wants to destroy existing institutions for the sake of some ideal, but a *scientific* socialist, who accepts the reality of existing institutions while striving to reform them.

The basis for Dühring's views on the value of life lay in his chief work on logic and epistemology, his *Natürliche Dialektik*, which he published in January 1865, only months before *Der Werth des Lebens*.[39] Dühring himself stressed the close connection between

36 Dühring, *Cursus der Philosophie*, p. 546.
37 Ibid., p. 14.
38 Ibid., pp. 369–70, 539.
39 Dühring, *Natürliche Dialektik*. The preface is dated January 1865, while the preface to the first edition of *Der Werth des Lebens* is dated April 1865. The publication of two major works in such a short time is remarkable; but Dühring explained

these works. They relate to one another, he later wrote, "as head and heart."[40] Any theory about the value of life, Dühring believed, requires a logical and epistemological foundation. The task of *Natürliche Dialektic* was to provide just that foundation.

The central task of Dühring's book is "how to conceive the infinite" (7). All the conundrums and confusions of metaphysics, we are told, ultimately revolve around this thorny problem (7, 109). There is nothing wrong in principle with the idea of the infinite, Dühring assures us, if it is taken as the simple idea of repeating a quantity without limit (112). The idea of an infinite series, which we construct with the idea of a number greater than any given number, is not self-contradictory. All the problems with the concept of the infinite arise, however, when one assumes that the entire series of infinite things *exists*, or that *there is* some definite thing that is infinite (114–15). Both assumptions are problematic because they are hypostases, reifications of a rule of understanding. The infinite is not an existing series of things, still less a special kind of thing, Dühring insists, but solely a method of counting things (115, 117). More exactly, it is that *procedure* that allows us to construct a new quantity by adding to any given quantity. Or, in mathematical terms, the infinite is not a number but the *rule* that allows us to create a new number by adding another number to any given one (123). The concept of a *definite* infinite number is indeed contradictory, because if it were a definite number we could still conceive one greater than it, so that it would no longer be infinite at all (121).

It is from this simple logical point that Dühring draws weighty conclusions against metaphysics. Central to metaphysics since classical times, in his view, was its concept of the unconditioned, which attempts to complete the series of conditioned things by postulating the existence of something unconditioned. But, however venerable, this concept commits, Dühring argues, the same kind of fallacy that we find with the infinite in pure mathematics (125–26). It is like assuming that there is an infinite number. The concept postulates the existence of some thing that is infinite,

---

in his autobiography that both were the product of a decade of thought. See *Sache, Leben und Feinde* (1902), p. 111.

40   Dühring, *Sache, Leben und Feinde* (1902), p. 115.

when the infinite is not a thing but simply the procedure for constructing a series of things. We have to realize, Dühring teaches, that the urge to explain the whole of experience by postulating the existence of something beyond it arises from an illusion: the hypostasis of rules of explanation. We explain definite things in experience by other definite things which are their causes, where there is no limit to this procedure for anything in experience; but we then take this rule and apply it to experience in general, as if there were some general thing to explain all of experience, just as there is always a specific thing to explain other specific things in experience. But we cannot get beyond our experience to grasp the cause of experience as a whole: "We are lacking an Archimedean point to lift the world from its axis" (144). The assumption that there is some general thing unifying the world is the hypostasis of a purely formal rule of explanation, one that demands systematic unity in our conception of the world (83–84, 137–38). Because we must provide a unified explanation of the world does not entail, however, that there is some thing that unifies everything.

Having exposed the illusion inherent in metaphysics, Dühring saw himself in a position to debunk Schopenhauer's program for its revival (141). All Schopenhauer's talk about "the riddle of existence" or "the puzzle of the world," he argues, is pure mystification and obfuscation. There is really no riddle or puzzle at all, because the question is based on a false assumption. It assumes that there is something outside the world—the will or the thing-in-itself—that can explain the entire world, even though we have no reason to assume that there is any such thing at all. The confusion or mystification comes from nothing more than hypostasis, the reification of a rule of the understanding that demands unity in explanation.

Dühring's positivist program grew directly out of his critique of metaphysics. This program is essentially Kant's critique of metaphysics taken to its ultimate limit: the elimination of the noumenal or otherworldly as hypostasis. The central principle of the positive philosophy, as Dühring first announces it in *Natürliche Dialektik*, states that "Factuality (*Tatsächlichkeit*) is the ultimate basis of all positing; it is the simple form upon which all knowledge has to be led back in the final instance" (57–58). This means that the facts of experience should be taken as simple and primitive, that they should not be explained by some transcendent principle beyond or behind them. This principle is for Dühring not simply epistemo-logical, a verificationist thesis that limits knowledge to experience, but it is more fundamentally ethical or existential, because it is a principle of immanence, according to which all meaning or value comes from within human life itself; it contains the implicit in-junction that we must not make meaning or value depend upon another world beyond this life. It is for this reason that Dühring makes positivism a philosophy about the value or meaning of life. Its central doctrine, as he later put it in the second edition of *Der Werth des Lebens*, is that "human existence is a complete and suffi-cient reality in itself" (61).

Having laid down his fundamental principles in *Natürliche Dialektik*, Dühring was ready to apply them to the question of the value of life in his *Der Werth des Lebens*.[41] The critique of meta-physics, and the principle of immanence, had set the basic param-eters for his theory of the value of life. The critique of hypostasis had eliminated the classical ideas of the unconditioned, e.g., the ideas of God and the soul, which had been the pillars of the tradi-tional Christian view about the meaning of existence. There was no longer a providential order in which the individual could find his place; and there was no more an eternal soul to find redemption in another world. Somehow, then, Dühring had to show that this life, despite all its suffering and sorrow, is still worth living. Since there is no life beyond this one, we have to prove that there is value and meaning here and now.

Dühring's views on the value of life in *Der Werth des Lebens* de-pend not only on his critique of metaphysics but also on his ethics or general theory of value, which he sets forth in chapters 1 through 3 of the first edition.[42] Regarding the basis of ethics, Dühring is a

41 All references in parentheses in this section will be, unless otherwise noted, to the first edition.

42 *Der Werth des Lebens* (1865): Capitel I, "Das Leben als Inbegriff von Emp-findungen und Gemüthsbewegungen"; Capitel II, "Der Unterschied als der eigen-tliche Gegenstand des Gefühls"; and Capitel III, "Die Grundgestalt in der Abfolge der Lebenserregungen," pp. 13–51. Heavily revised, in exposition if not content, these chapters were condensed into a single chapter for the second edition. See Dühring, *Der Werth des Lebens* (1877), pp. 61–85.

straightforward empiricist. The source of value lies for him not in the principles or ideals of reason but in the feelings and sensations of experience. To know whether something is of value, we must be able to sense or feel it (13). We approve what gives us positive feelings, we disapprove what gives us negative ones. Reason alone cannot give normative force to moral principles or ideals, Dühring argues, because they must receive their content from sensation and feeling (20). Not only the reason or justification for a moral principle but also the incentive or motive to act on one comes from feeling or sensation (16). If a person felt nothing, he would have no motive to act, and so he would do nothing.

Dühring offers no argument for his ethical empiricism.[43] We are served bald statements and bold assertions. Part of the reason for his position rests on his general empiricism, which he had already defended in his *Natürliche Dialektik*. According to that work, *all* principles, not only moral ones, receive their content from experience. There are no synthetic a priori principles, whether moral or metaphysical. In *Der Werth des Lebens* Dühring also affirms the classical empiricist tenet that feelings or sensations cannot err. Like a true Epicurean, he maintains that feelings or sensations cannot be mistaken for the simple reason that they do not judge. Since sensations and feelings refer to nothing beyond themselves, they have no cognitive component and so cannot be right or wrong (110). If they sometimes seem to lead us astray, that is only because of the ideas or beliefs that accompany them, not because of the feelings themselves. No sensation as such is illusory: "it is what it is, entirely and complete" (38).

Since feeling or sensation (*Empfindung*) is the sole source of value, Dühring makes it the criterion to judge the value of life: "Existence has its charm and worth through the totality of affections in which it develops" (13). It might seem from such empiricism that Dühring must be a eudemonist, holding in classical fashion that the highest good depends on happiness, which consists in pleasure. It is striking, however, that Dühring does not take this position,

---

43 Not at least in the first or second edition of *Der Werth des Lebens*. His chapter on Kant in his *Kritische Geschichte der Philosophie*, pp. 399–437, criticizes the emptiness of the Kantian categorical imperative (412–13).

at least not in the first edition of *Der Werth des Lebens*.[44] He holds that the value of life depends not only on our pleasant feelings but on the whole life of feeling, which includes pain as well as pleasure. What makes for a worthwhile existence is the total play of passions, which comprises not only pleasant but also painful sensations (16). Not only the heights but also the depths of sensation or feeling are essential for vitality, the intensity and fullness of living, upon which all well-being depends. Likening the life of feeling to the rising and falling of a wave, Dühring stresses that the entire movement, the whole undulation, is important for a complete life (30). "Take away our love and our hate and you make existence itself into a barren desert" (17).

To explain exactly how and why the value of life depends on the whole play of feeling, Dühring sets forth a general theory of feeling in the second and third chapters in the first edition of *Der Werth des Lebens*. The fundamental principle of this theory is what Dühring calls "the principle of difference." This principle means that feelings arise from, and are in proportion to, change or difference in stimulus. If the stimuli in life are constant, or if they change in a strictly regular way, then they do not give rise to new feeling. Hence to have a valuable life, one rich and intense in feeling, one must have change and variety in its stimuli: "The multiplicity of risings and fallings of feeling is the indispensable requirement for a valuable existence" (30).

From this theory, Dühring drew important conclusions about the value of existence. First, we should value not only pleasure itself, conceived as the end or reward of activity, but also the activity of trying to achieve it. We could never value constant, uninterrupted pleasure, which would quickly prove dull and enervating; we also need the stimulus and excitement involved in striving and struggle. Ironically, then, the obstacles to the enjoyment of life, and the attempt to overcome them, are a crucial value of life itself. As

---

44 In the second (1877) edition, there is a passage where Dühring seems to affirm the classical eudemonist position. He states, p. 192, that the source of all privation (*Ungemach*) lies in pain (*Schmerz*). In the *Cursus der Philosophie*, however, Dühring reaffirms his theory of feeling and draws the noneudemonist conclusions from it. See pp. 361–66.

CHAPTER 5

Dühring later formulated this point: "the evaluation of life has to proceed from the principle that the natural resistance to the enjoyment of life is not an evil but a necessity, without which an enjoyable life is impossible."[45] Second, we should enjoy certain experiences and situations only once and not strive to repeat them.[46] We value experiences and situations, though we are not self-conscious of it at the time, because they are unique and irrepeatable. The problem with repetition has nothing to do with the content of the experiences themselves, Dühring insists, but simply the fact of repetition itself. What is the case for individual experiences can then be generalized for life itself, so that we value it for its uniqueness and brevity; from this perspective, death itself becomes a necessity. We find true self-satisfaction with existence only when we recognize how all its moments are unique, irrepeatable, and irreplaceable.

To appreciate the novelty of Dühring's theory, it is important to place it in a broad historical perspective. In stressing the importance of vitality, the whole play of passions, Dühring was breaking with not only eudemonism but also the entire classical tradition. Both the Epicureans and Stoics had placed the greatest value on equanimity, or peace of mind, which rests upon regulation of the passions. Dühring questions, however, not only our power to control the passions but also the value of equanimity itself. A completely peaceful life, where we are never distressed or dissatisfied, he avers, would be a complete torment (16).

Having adopted feeling and sensation as his criterion of value, Dühring again had to face the challenge of Schopenhauer, who had also adopted such a criterion in advancing his pessimism. Fully aware of this threat, Dühring duly examines Schopenhauer's theory of feeling and desire in several chapters of the first edition of *Der Werth des Lebens*.[47]

Dühring agrees with Schopenhauer that the gap or tension between subjective need and the objective world is fundamental to

45 Dühring, *Cursus der Philosophie*, p. 361.

46 Dühring drew this conclusion most explicitly in his *Cursus der Philosophie*, p. 366.

47 Kapitel II, "Der Unterschied als der eigentliche Gegenstand des Gefühls," pp. 28–39; Kapitel V, "Die Liebe," pp. 87–124; and Kapitel VI, "Der Tod," pp. 125–47.

our existence (50) and that there is an element of need and dissatisfaction involved in all human striving (93). Still, he thinks that Schopenhauer fails to appreciate the intrinsic value of striving and the necessity for that gap or tension, which is a *sine qua non* for a valuable existence. Furthermore, he contends that Schopenhauer overstates the amount and duration of pain involved in need. He assumes that pain is constantly present throughout the striving to satisfy need, while it is usually present only at the onset. Need arises only slowly and gradually, so that its first stirrings are only slightly painful (94). If Schopenhauer overrates the pain of human striving, he underrates its pleasure. Pleasure does not have a strictly negative significance as freedom of pain but is a positive quality of its own.

The most important feelings to give value to life, Dühring maintains, are not physical but social. This was a point overlooked by Schopenhauer, who focuses so much on physical pleasure and pain and on a person's private life. But physical pleasure and pain are virtually nothing to us compared to the joy and suffering that come from our relations to others (69). There is an enormous leap, Dühring claims, from the physical pain we suffer from some wound to the mental pain caused us by humiliation or dishonor (24).

Of the social feelings, Dühring thinks that two are especially important in giving value to life: honor and love. Both feelings are in need of revaluation from their current reputation, he thinks. Honor is our feeling of self-worth as it depends on the approval of others (81). Rather than a source of injustice, a form of competition or *amour propre* that strives to outdo others, honor is only the claim of the self for justice, the demand that one receive the recognition one deserves. It is only in virtue of its power, the need to feel self-worth, that someone is inspired to great achievements. In insisting that honor is "a motive of moral action that cannot be prized enough" (83), Dühring was breaking with Schopenhauer and the Epicureans, who had seen the drive for honor as a major source of discontent.

Love is no less important than honor in giving value to life, and it, too, stands in need of revaluation, Dühring insists. Schopenhauer has exaggerated the pains of love, as if erotic desire were an affliction. But love does not consist chiefly in pain, or even in a mixture of pleasure and pain, Dühring argues, but essentially in pleasure. The only pain of love is "the soft draft of a slight unease."

Nature has made the yearning of love such an intense pleasure that we hardly detect the element of pain contained in it (92). Schopenhauer gave love a mainly instrumental value, the means toward reproduction. But this only goes to show, Dühring claims, that Schopenhauer fails to understand its intrinsic value (94). He has no conception of erotic love, which is a pleasure in itself. Love is valuable for its own sake, and it is not merely a means to the end of procreation (124). Of course, there is often the terrible disappointment of love; but this is not an argument against the feeling itself so much as the romantic notions and high expectations that surround it (120–21).

In stressing the importance of the whole play of passions for the value of life, and in calling for a revaluation of passions such as hate and honor, Dühring clearly anticipates Nietzsche's later revaluation of all values in the 1880s. The foreshadowings of Nietzsche are even more apparent in Dühring's analysis of justice, which he traces back to the feeling of revenge. Justice, he explains, arises from the life of feeling, and more specifically when someone's honor is injured. That injury gives rise to the demand for retribution and restitution, which alone restores what has been taken away (72). In his 1875 notes on *Der Werth des Lebens* Nietzsche paid careful attention to Dühring's theory, remarking that it was reason to question Schopenhauer's own theory of justice.[48] In his *Zur Genealogie der Moral* Nietzsche would expound a theory of the origin of justice very similar to that of Dühring, whom he called the *"Berliner Rache-Apostel."*[49] Though Nietzsche later drew very different conclusions from a similar concept of justice, we should not let this obscure the influence of Dühring.

5. HARTMANN'S PESSIMISM

Many of the neo-Kantian polemics, and the first edition of Dühring's *Der Werth des Lebens*, appeared in the 1860s, which marks the first phase of the pessimism controversy. With the 1870s, however, a new phase begins with the publication of Eduard von

---

48 See Nietzsche, *Sämtliche Werke* VIII, 152–53, 176–78.
49 See Nietzsche, *Zur Genealogie der Moral, Sämtliche Werke* V, 370, §14.

Hartmann's *Philosophie des Unbewusstens*, which was first published in 1869. In several chapters of that book Hartmann defended a more moderate version of Schopenhauer's pessimism.[50] Because Hartmann's version was seen as the latest and improved version of pessimism, critics tended to focus on it rather than Schopenhauer's earlier version. The guiding assumption was that squashing Hartmann's pessimism would also smash Schopenhauer's. Two flies with one swatter.

Although Hartmann tended to distance himself from Schopenhauer in his later years, there cannot be any doubt that he was greatly indebted to the Frankfurt scrooge. Much of his argument for pessimism should be seen as a defense of Schopenhauer against Dühring and the neo-Kantians. It is indeed telling that Hartmann's statement of pessimism in the *Philosophie des Unbewussten* constantly cites Schopenhauer, approvingly, and that he declared all discussions of Schopenhauer's pessimism had still failed to refute him.[51]

Still, Hartmann was never Schopenhauer's devotee or disciple. It was perfectly correct for him to protest against the frequent characterization of his philosophy as Schopenhauerian.[52] He later insisted that he was more influenced by Schelling and Hegel than Schopenhauer.[53] His own position he once described as a *synthesis*

50 See Eduard von Hartmann, *Die Philosophie des Unbewussten*, Zweite vermehrte Auflage (Berlin: Carl Duncker, 1870). The discussion of pessimism appears in chapters C.XI–XIII, 564–681. Hartmann also wrote many articles and an entire book on pessimism. The book is his *Zur Geschichte und Begründung des Pessimismus* (Berlin: Carl Duncker, 1880). Also see his "Zur Pessimismus-Frage," in *Philosophische Fragen der Gegenwart* (Leipzig: Wilhelm Friedrich, 1885), pp. 78–120. See also the articles cited in the following notes.

51 See his article "Ist der pessimistische Monismus trostlos?" in *Gesammelte Philosophische Abhandlungen zur Philosophie des Unbewussten* (Berlin: Carl Duncker, 1872), 71–85, esp. 71, 74.

52 See his discussions of Schopenhauer's pessimism, "Ueber die nothwendige Umbildung der Schopenhauerschen Philosophie," in *Gesammelte Philosophische Abhandlungen*, pp. 25–56; and "Mein Verhältnis zu Schopenhauer," in *Philosophische Fragen der Gegenwart*, pp. 25–38.

53 Notably in the "Vorwort zur zehnten Auflage" of his *Philosophie des Unbewussten* (Leipzig: Haacke, 1902), p. xiii. The influence of Schelling is apparent from Hartmann's early *Schelling's positive Philosophie als Einheit von Hegel und Schopenhauer* (Berlin: Otto Loewenstein, 1869).

of pessimism and optimism, as an attempt to correct and complement the one-sidedness of Schopenhauer's pessimism with Leibniz's and Hegel's optimism.[54] Just how Hartmann synthesizes these viewpoints—and whether he did so successfully—requires some discussion, however. His theory of the value of life is subtle and sophisticated, though of doubtful consistency.

Hartmann summarized his syncretic theory in a single paradoxical proposition: "that this is the best of all possible worlds; but it is worse than none at all."[55] In that one proposition he had combined—so be believed—the better points of both optimism and pessimism. Hartmann unraveled the paradox thus: to say that this is the best of all possible worlds does not mean that existence is better than nonexistence. It is still possible for all possible worlds to be bad; it's just that some are worse than others and that ours happens to be the least bad. So to claim that our world is the best possible really only means that it is the least bad, the best possible with respect to all other worlds, all of which are bad. Hartmann did not accept Schopenhauer's argument, then, that this is the *worst* possible world, an argument he dismissed as sophistry (573).[56]

What makes this world the best possible, Hartmann thinks, is that the unconscious cosmic will achieves its ends with the greatest possible wisdom and efficiency. Hartmann attributes to this will some of the traditional attributes of God: omniscience, omnipotence, and omnipresence (554–56). Given that the world exists, it is not possible for it to be organized in a wiser and more efficient manner. Hartmann thinks that it is a great error on Schopenhauer's part not to see the purposiveness and rationality of nature (20). Schopenhauer's doctrine that the cosmic will implants into us a futile striving for happiness raises questions about the purposiveness of nature. This cannot be the best organized world if the cosmic will dooms us to the frustration of our deepest urges.

The core of Hartmann's pessimism lies with his statement that existence is worse than nonexistence, that nothingness is better

54 See his "Ist der pessimistische Monismus trostlos?" p. 78.
55 Ibid.
56 All references in parentheses, unless noted otherwise, are to the page numbers of the second edition of *Philosophie des Unbewussten* (1870).

than being. Hartmann wagered, like Schopenhauer, that no sane person would choose to live his or her life over again; he or she would prefer instead annihilation, complete nothingness, which at least brings eternal peace. The existence of the world is a complete surd, a total mystery, the result of an irrational act of the cosmic will (669). For the "what" and "how" of the world it is possible to give reasons; but for its "that," its sheer existence, it is not possible to give any reason at all (669–70). Given that the world exists, the will orders it in wise and efficient ways; but it would have been better if nothing existed at all.

The reason that nothingness is better than being, Hartmann argues, is because life brings more suffering than happiness. Pessimism is for Hartmann essentially the doctrine that happiness is unattainable in life. Happiness consists in pleasure, or in the preponderance of pleasure over pain; and misery consists in pain, or in the preponderance of pain over pleasure. But the very nature of human desire and physiology, and the essential facts of human life, inevitably result in more pain than pleasure. For this contention, Hartmann brings forth a slew of arguments, which we can only baldly and crudely state here.[57] (1) Human beings are more sensitive to pain than pleasure. (2) Pleasure is subject to diminishing returns but not pain, which only increases in intensity. (3) The possession of the great goods of human life—youth, security, health, and freedom—consists not in pleasure but in the absence of pain. We take these goods for granted; and we feel pleasure in having them only after regaining them. (4) The pleasure in the satisfaction of our desires is much shorter in duration and intensity than the misery of their frustration. (5) The chief desires—hunger and sex—are the source of more suffering than happiness. Hunger takes us below 0 in the scale of pleasure; and when it is satisfied, it only brings us back to 0. Because of their inevitable disappointments, sex and marriage give rise to more sorrow than pleasure. (6) The desires for power, honor, and money are inexhaustible; the more we get of them, the more we want them, but the greater our wants, the less

57 Hartmann himself provides his own summary, *Philosophie des Unbewussten*, pp. 630–31, but it is not the most accurate summary of his arguments from pp. 564–629.

likely they are to be satisfied. Although Hartmann disagrees with Schopenhauer's theory that pleasure has only a negative value—he points out that there are pleasures not preceded by any pains—he still thinks that most pleasures arise indirectly from the diminution of pain (575). Furthermore, he contends that, practically speaking, Schopenhauer is correct (578–79). All that we can achieve in this life is something negative, i.e., the diminution of pain; but we cannot achieve anything positive, i.e., the predominance of pleasure over pain. Summarizing these arguments, Hartmann draws the damning conclusion that life is not worth living. If (1) the best life consists only in the absence of pain; if (2) the absence of pain is equivalent to 0 on the scale of happiness; and if (3) complete absence of pain is unattainable for anyone in life, then (4) the value of life falls *below* 0. Life is then worse than nothingness, which consists in the absence of all sensation, and which therefore stands only at 0 (586).

Hartmann divides his discussion of the value of life into three main illusions. The first illusion is that "Happiness is attainable in the present stage of development of the world" (573). This is an illusion, Hartmann argues, because, as we have just seen, happiness in a positive sense is unattainable, and because pain and suffering far outweigh pleasure and contentment in this life. The prevalence and persistence of this illusion in human beings, Hartmann maintains, are due to hope, which is almost always disappointed—nine times in ten, he estimates—but which forever reasserts itself. The reason for its persistence, despite experience, is that it is grounded in our instinct for self-preservation. If we had no hope for a better future, we would not be able to bear this life and would commit suicide. The second illusion is that "Happiness is attainable for an individual in a transcendent life after death" (635). This is an illusion, too, Hartmann explains, because if our world did not exist, there would be no will; and if there were no will, there would be nothingness (642). In other words, there is no world beyond ours, another world that is better than our own; the only world is our horrible one, that which is created through a single irrational act of will. The prevalence of this illusion arises from egoism, which wants to assert our individual existence beyond the grave; those who are denied individual happiness in this world seek compensation in another (642). Although Hartmann is critical of Christianity for fostering this illusion, he still thinks that it marks an important step beyond paganism, because it at least sees that this life is a vale of tears and that the highest good is not attainable in it (635, 643). The third illusion is that "Happiness lies in the future through the world-process" (645). Here Hartmann criticizes those philosophers (Lessing and Hegel) who believe in human progress and who find the meaning and purpose in life in contributing to the ends of world history. He maintains that, however much humanity progresses, it will never get rid of the greatest sources of human misery: sickness, age, dependence on the will of others, sexual frustration, and hunger (650). The state has only a negative ideal—to protect our rights to life and liberty—but it cannot help us achieve the best life or make us happy (658). The best we can ever accomplish through political activity is security, health, and freedom; but that brings us at best only to 0 on the scale of pleasure (659). Hartmann does not dispute the enormous technical progress that has been made through the arts and sciences; but he insists that it at best only makes life easier and never brings happiness (659). However far we progress in medicine, agriculture, and chemistry, this will still leave us with the difficult question: "What content should we give our lives?" (660).

Despite all these arguments on behalf of pessimism, Hartmann never wanted to give it the final word. Though he held that hope is illusory in nine cases out of ten, he still refused to smother hope for that single case (670). Pessimism is not, he insisted, a doctrine of despair, because, by revealing all the miseries of the world, it gives us a strong incentive to improve it. Although we cannot achieve happiness in this life, we can still, at least to some degree, diminish the amount of suffering, and that alone gives us all the motivation we need to change things (629). One of the most important points in which Hartmann takes issue with Schopenhauer concerns his quietism, i.e., his thesis that all attempts to improve the human condition are futile. He insisted that his own pessimism, unlike Schopenhauer's, includes social and political programs for the improvement of the human condition (650).

Hartmann described his own syncretic position as a synthesis of "eudemonistic pessimism" with "evolutionary optimism."[58] The

---

58 Hartmann, *Zur Geschichte und Begründung des Pessimismus*, pp. ix–x, 36.

eudemonic pessimist held that it is impossible to achieve happiness in this life and that life consists essentially in suffering; but the evolutionary optimist held that it is still possible to make progress in diminishing human suffering and in achieving greater morality and perfection. Such a synthesis Hartmann saw as an attempt to complement and correct Schopenhauer's pessimism with Hegel's optimism. Hartmann was enough of an Hegelian to believe in progress in world history, in the gradual development of greater self-consciousness and the growth of reason. He saw history as a struggle between the irrational will and reason, between unconsciousness and consciousness, where reason and consciousness gradually take control over subconscious feelings and impulses (670, 327–28). The more the realm of consciousness and reason grows, the more we learn to limit our desires and to take control over our lives, and the less we are frustrated by the vain pursuit of pleasure. Hartmann's enduring optimism surfaces in his belief that reason and consciousness will ultimately prevail over the unconscious will (330, 675). The penultimate chapter of *Philosophie des Unbewussten* then closes with an almost Nietzschean "*affirmation of the will to life*" (675; his emphasis).

6. HARTMANN'S SELF-DEFENSE

Philosophie des Unbewussten proved to be, despite its unwieldy size and prose, one of the most successful philosophical works of the 1870s, and indeed of the entire nineteenth century. By the end of the decade it had already gone through eight editions, and it would go through eleven in Hartmann's lifetime.[59] Hartmann's book spawned a flood of polemical literature, most of it hostile and some of it defamatory. Hartmann himself struggled to reply to his critics, but he could not cope with the sheer scale of the polemics against him. In desperate need of allies, he was aided in his battle by his wife, Agnes Taubert, whose *Der Pessimismus und seine Gegner*

---

59   On the many editions and their sales, see the memoir by Hartmann's publisher, Carl Heymons, *Eduard von Hartmann, Erinnerungen aus den Jahren 1868–1881* (Berlin: Duncker, 1882).

became one of the central texts in the controversy.[60] Taubert had a fearsome polemical and philosophical talent, which she wielded effectively in defense of Hartmann's pessimism.

One of the most common objections against Hartmann's pessimism is that it undermines morals, not only the motivation to improve the world but also the motivation to continue living when struck down by misfortune. If we cannot achieve happiness—so the objection went—what point is there in going on living or striving to make the world a better place? This question emerged early in the 1870s; but in the early 1880s a Dutch religious society, *Godgelaerde Genootenschap te Haarlem*, announced a prize essay on the topic of pessimism and morals, which gave rise to several books and essays.

Hartmann's first response to this objection was to take the moral high road: although pessimism does indeed undermine egoism, the selfish striving for personal happiness, it supports morality, which demands that we act for the sake of principle alone.[61] When the pessimist demonstrates that we cannot achieve personal happiness, he undermines the motivation to act contrary to moral principle for the sake of selfish interests. If *per contra* the eudemonistic optimist were correct that we can achieve happiness in this life, then the self-interest in one's own pleasure would be the irresistible motivation for all human action, undermining the possibility of morality. Pessimism is therefore the chief weapon against egoism or selfishness, which is the main enemy of all morality. So, far from undermining morality, eudemonistic pessimism is the necessary presupposition of it. Hartmann's second response to this objection was to stress that his pessimism is eudemonic rather than moral. In other words, while it denies that it is possible to achieve happiness in this life, it affirms that it is possible to attain greater human

60 A. Taubert, *Der Pessimismus und seine Gegner* (Berlin: Duncker, 1873). Since she published under her maiden name, it was not known that Taubert was Hartmann's wife; since she published under the initial of her first name, it was not even known that she was a woman. Most writers assumed that she was a male student or friend of Hartmann.

61 See Hartmann's articles "Ist der pessimistische Monismus trostlos?" pp. 71–89, esp. 77–78; and "Ist der Pessimismus schädlich?" in *Zur Geschichte und Begründung des Pessimismus*, pp. 86–100.

perfection and morality. Following Kant, Hartmann stressed that these propositions are indeed interdependent: that the price we pay for greater progress toward perfection and morality is the loss of happiness, which was more prevalent in the primitive stages of human history. The moral optimist has to be, therefore, a eudemonistic pessimist. Once again, then, eudemonic pessimism proves to be the necessary presupposition of morality.

Another common objection against Hartmann's pessimism was that it is pseudoscientific, resting upon an impossible comparison of incommensurable values. If we consider all the different values in life, it becomes impossible to compare and summarize them, so that we can never say that misery preponderates over happiness. Hartmann's response to this objection was mainly to dig in his heels and to stress the purely quantitative aspects of pleasure and pain.[62] Pessimism is a purely scientific outlook because it rests upon the pure empirical fact that the sum of painful sensations is greater than the sum of pleasant ones. Hartmann readily admits that sensations have a qualitative dimension which makes them incommensurable with one another; but he still insisted that in determining their pleasure or pain alone we can abstract from their qualitative aspect and consider their quantitative aspect alone, i.e., their duration and intensity. Just as we can determine whether on a given tabletop the weight of the pears is greater than that of the apples, so we can determine whether different sensations bring more pleasure over pain. If the sum of pleasure in the world is negative, then we have to accept pessimism, which is entirely an inductive truth from experience. Hartmann later explained that there are three fundamental presuppositions involved in arriving at this truth.[63] (1) That one gives each sensation a value strictly corresponding to its actuality in consciousness, independent of memory and moral values. (2) That pleasure and pain relate to one another as positive and negative quantities, irrespective of their qualitative aspects. (3) The quantity of pleasure and pain is determined by the product of their intensity and duration. Regarding the qualitative

---

62   See "Ist der Pessimismus wissenschaftlich zu begründen?" in *Zur Geschichte und Begründung des Pessimisus*, pp. 65–85.

63   See section 2 of "Zur Pessimismus-Frage," pp. 91–102.

dimension of experience, Hartmann took a somewhat equivocal stand: that we can abstract from it entirely, because it is not relevant to the assessment of pleasure and pain; or that we can reduce it down to its quantitative dimension, because higher pleasures are simply greater in intensity and duration than are lower ones. But neither position seemed tenable: we do take into account the quality of feelings in evaluating the value of life; and that quality is not reducible to its qualitative dimensions alone. Take the case of the artist or saint who believes that life is worth living only because of "higher feelings"—aesthetic inspiration or religious ecstasy—and who is ready to suffer pains of great intensity and duration to have them.

In 1880 Hartmann hit upon a remarkable strategy to foil his many neo-Kantian critics. He would demonstrate that the true father of pessimism was not Arthur Schopenhauer, as everyone thought, but Immanuel Kant. If he could show this, his neo-Kantian critics would have to reappraise their hostile attitude toward pessimism. And so Hartmann wrote a long article, "Kant als Vater des Pessimismus," which appeared as chapter I of his *Zur Geschichte und Begründung des Pessimismus.*[64] Hartmann's thesis seems as implausible as his strategy desperate. But by exhaustively combing through and citing from the Kantian corpus, he managed to make a solid case for his thesis that Kant was indeed a "eudemonistic pessimist," i.e., someone who held that it is not possible to achieve happiness in this life. Hartmann was perfectly correct that Kant had denied happiness is the purpose of life and that he had doubted the likelihood of achieving happiness in this world. Of course, it is not plausible to claim that Kant was a moral pessimist, because he had maintained that it is possible to achieve progress in history toward human perfection and morality. But Hartmann did not dispute that Kant was a moral optimist and insisted that he was one, too. Kant's theory of the value of life was very much the precedent for his own, Hartmann claimed, because it too combines eudemonistic pessimism with evolutionary optimism. Kant had taught the goals of history—the growth of culture and the perfection of human faculties—are attainable but only at the ex-

64 Hartmann, *Zur Geschichte und Begründung des Pessimismus*, pp. 1–64.

pense of happiness. Flatly contrary to the common neo-Kantian objection that pessimism undermines morals, Hartmann further argued that it is essential for Kant's project for cleansing ethics of eudemonism.[65] For pessimism shows that happiness cannot be attained in this life, thus undermining the motivation to act on happiness instead of the moral law. Predictably, rather than silencing his neo-Kantian critics, Hartmann's article provoked them, and he soon found himself engaged in even more polemics.[66]

7. THE VALUE OF WORK

In response to his critics, Hartmann held that the case for pessimism has to be based on induction, on the consideration of particular cases. His was to be a scientific pessimism, not one based on metaphysical principles. But that line of reply pushes the case for pessimism deep into empirical territory. It means that the pessimist can draw his dreary conclusions about the value of existence only after an examination of particular aspects of human life. Withholding all general principles, he has to consider these aspects for their own sake. Hence the pessimist controversy began to discuss a wide array of special topics bearing on the value of life.

One such topic, which became an intense battleground between pessimists and their critics, was work (*Arbeit*). Clearly work is a crucial theme in the pessimist's portrait of life. Our days are filled with work, nine to five for many of us, so if work proves to have a negative value in the general accounting of life, the scales will be tipped heavily in the pessimist's favor. Mainly for this reason, Hartmann's analysis of work in the *Philosophie des Unbewussten* is very bleak, even cynical.[67] There can be no doubt, Hartmann declares, that work is an evil for whoever must engage in it. Nobody works if they do not have to, and we do it only to avoid a greater evil, whether that be poverty or boredom. So work is not an end in itself, only a means to other ends. Usually work is the price some-

---

65   Ibid., p. 18.
66   See his "Zur Pessimismus-Frage," pp. 112–20. On p. 113 Hartmann refers to the many articles written against his.
67   Hartmann, *Philosophie des Unbewussten* (1870), C.XII, pp. 584–55.

one must pay to have a secure existence; but that is not a positive but a negative good, i.e., one to avoid greater evils, and, furthermore, it is a good that we must purchase through much pain (unlike health and youth). We also must not underestimate, Hartmann adds, the misery that work often imposes upon us. He then cites Schopenhauer's lines about the factory work of five-year-olds, who sit twelve to fourteen hours a day doing repetitive tasks and who thus "buy very dearly the mere pleasure of drawing breath." The best we can do with work, Hartmann thinks, is to get used to it, to make it habitual, so that we become just like the cart horse that learns to bear its load.

For Hartmann's critics, this was an unduly grim, wildly inaccurate conception of work. Rudolf Haym, a neo-Kantian critic, thought that Hartmann's conception was suitable only for the galley slave and that he completely neglected the satisfaction work gives us in exercising our powers and in realizing our will.[68] Work, Jürgen Bona Meyer, another neo-Kantian critic, responded,[69] is not simply a means to other ends but it is a pleasure in itself, because it activates our powers, directs our energies, and satisfies our human need for "the good, beautiful and true." Of course, there is toil and trouble connected with work; but these negative factors do not outweigh the positive ones, and eventually they become part of the pleasure. By exaggerating the negative aspects of work, Hartmann falsifies one of the chief sources of human happiness: pleasure in acting (*Freude am Thun*).

None of these objections impressed Agnes Taubert, Hartmann's wife and staunchest defender.[70] She was skeptical whether the pleasure in work came strictly from work itself. There are so many other sources of that pleasure, she argued, that it is not likely that it comes simply from working alone. One must consider the greater evils that work avoids, viz., the absence of boredom and idleness; the means it provides for obtaining many other things, viz., the

68 Rudolf Haym, "Die Hartmann'sche Philosophie des Unbewussten," *Preußische Jahrbücher* 31 (1873), pp. 41–80, 109–39, 257–311, here p. 267.

69 Jürgen Bona Meyer, *Weltelend und Weltschmerz, Eine Rede gegen Schopenhauer's und Hartmann's Pessimismus* (Bonn: Marcus, 1872) p. 17.

70 Taubert, *Der Pessimismus und seine Gegner*, III, "Die private Güter und die Arbeit," pp. 33–36.

happiness of one's family; and the anticipation of the products of work (33–34). When we consider all these factors, the pleasure in work itself seems to evaporate, so that we have to acknowledge, Taubert insisted, "the activity of work in and for itself is onerous and unpleasant" (35). In responding to Haym and Meyer, Taubert went on to mention another important factor that diminished the value of work in modern life: the division of labor. In the past a craftsman could derive great pleasure from creating something for which he contributed all the parts and labor; in producing it, his talents and skills would be exercised. But such work had been superseded by modern mass forms of production, which made each worker engage in a single monotonous task. It is impossible for a worker in the modern factory to take pleasure in his work when he does one small task over and over again, and when he has little role in its design and mode of production. If Haym only considered the consequences of labor in modern forms of production, Taubert tartly retorted, he would not have made his tasteless comment about galley labor.

An important voice in these exchanges about the meaning of work was Johannes Volkelt, a young neo-Kantian and social democrat, whose *Das Unbewusste und der Pessimismus* appeared shortly after Taubert's *Der Pessimismus und seine Gegner*.[71] Volkelt, like Haym and Meyer, felt that Hartmann had given a much too negative portrait of work and its value in life. Work was the means by which we exercised and became self-conscious of our own powers; and in exercising and becoming self-conscious of them, we gain a sense of our self-worth, which is a great source of inner pleasure. Of course, work involves challenges, obstacles, and difficulties; but it is precisely in overcoming them that we develop our powers and grow in self-confidence and self-consciousness. Volkelt did not underestimate, however, the problems posed for work in modern methods of production. All the problems raised by Taubert he fully recognized. Work had become dull, routine, mindless, and even degrading in the modern division of labor. But, Volkelt explained, these problems are not intrinsic to work itself but only

71 Johannes Volkelt, *Das Unbewusste und der Pessimismus* (Berlin: Henschel, 1873), pp. 287–92.

its present form. Many of them will disappear in the socialist state of the future. Although there will still be forms of mass production and a division of labor, working hours will be shorter and working conditions much better; more important, everyone will receive a liberal education where they learn to develop all their faculties and not only those needed on the factory floor. There would be not only bread for everyone but, as Heine put it, "roses and myrtle, beauty and pleasure."

For Taubert, however, the socialist state was no solution to the problems of modern work and production.[72] She shared Hartmann's conviction that a socialist state, which promises happiness for everyone, is an illusion. There will always be social and economic inequality, because resources are always scarce and because people are born with very unequal capacities to attain them. A socialist state, which would control all aspects of the economy, and which would impose social and economic opportunity, would be a threat to property, liberty, and talent. Remarkably, Taubert and Volkelt had a very similar diagnosis of the social problem: the modern economy had increased the standard of living for everyone, especially the working classes; but it had also increased their needs and expectations beyond the means of the government and economy to satisfy them.[73] This created a crisis, because the people now demanded more than they could ever possibly have. Nevertheless, despite their common diagnosis, Volkert and Taubert had very different solutions to the problem. For Volkelt, the solution is socialism; but for Taubert, it is pessimism, because only it could expose the illusions of socialism, the pointless striving for happiness in life.

An interesting take on Taubert's solution to the social problem was given by Georg Peter Weygoldt in his *Kritik des philosophischen Pessimismus*.[74] Weygoldt shared Taubert's conservative views, and

---

72 See Taubert, *Der Pessimismus und seine Gegner*, "X: Die Glückseligkeit als historische Zukunftsperspektive," pp. 101–22, esp. 114–16.

73 See Johannes Volkelt, "Die Entwicklung des modernen Pessimismus," *Im neuen Reich* II (1872), 952–68. Taubert cites p. 967 of this article, which outlines Volkelt's very similar take on the social problem, but she takes exception to the conclusions that Volkelt draws from it.

74 G. P. Weygoldt, *Kritik des philosophischen Pessimismus der neuesten Zeit* (Leiden: Brill, 1875), pp. 101–4.

he, too, was a critic of socialism. He believed that the demand for higher wages and better working conditions had become excessive, the result of socialist agitators among the workers. Because of the increased expectations and demands of the working class, and because of the limited means of satisfying them, discontent was growing and revolution was on the horizon. But for Weygoldt, pessimism is not the solution to that looming danger but part of its cause, chiefly because the pessimists had painted such a bleak portrait of labor. Work has an intrinsic value, and people should work because it is a pleasure. But because the pessimists have portrayed work as an evil to be avoided, they have encouraged the workers to demand higher reward for their sacrifices. Nowhere are the dangers of pessimism more evident, Weygoldt contended, than in its conception of work. By describing work in such negative terms, the pessimists have only encouraged the very evil they so deeply fear: revolution.

In 1884, seven years after Taubert's death in 1877, and well after the initial dust had settled, Olga Plümacher provided a new analysis of the concept of work from a pessimist perspective.[75] She took a broad and mature view of the topic, one which attempted to take into account all that the critics had written but also one which could reveal the strengths of the pessimist's case. Plümacher began with a general definition of work. In its initial natural form, work is a species of movement, one where the goal lies not within but beyond the movement itself (210–11). Insofar as movement expresses a physiological need, and insofar as it provides for a person's needs, it can be an important source of pleasure. To that extent, Plümacher conceded, Hartmann was "perhaps" wrong to underestimate the degree of pleasure that could be involved in work (211). However, it is wrong to assume, as the optimists did, that the sheer activity of work is intrinsically pleasant. Work is often unpleasant for many reasons: it involves more movement than necessary for a person's needs; it requires too much of one kind of movement; or it inhibits other forms of movement (211). All too often work develops only one side of our nature, leaving the other sides frustrated or atrophied. Although Plümacher conceded that Hartmann might have exaggerated the negative aspects of work, she stressed that he never meant to demean

75 Plümacher, *Der Pessimismus in Vergangenheit und Gegenwart*, pp. 210–16.

its value. He had always emphasized its importance as a means for realizing higher social ends; and in that respect he had given work a much greater value than had his critics, who measured its worth solely in terms of the pleasure it gave to the individual (212). Critics like Weygoldt were completely unfair, then, when they charged Hartmann and Taubert with demeaning the value of work.

Recognizing the value of work does not mean, Plümacher was eager to explain, that we should regard it as an intrinsically pleasant activity (212, 214). The moral, social, and cultural value of work is one thing; its eudemonic value for the individual is quite another. To be sure, people often take pleasure in knowing their work to be of moral, social, and cultural value; but that is often small compensation for their trouble and toil; and in many cases all the effort and struggle in trying to do good come to nothing because circumstances make it impossible to realize one's plans (212). For the philosopher, who takes a broad historical perspective, work plays an important role in advancing social ends and world progress. But for the individual, who sees only particular ends in concrete circumstances, work is often just a grueling and unpleasant task (214).

Plümacher admits that work sometimes could be very rewarding and pleasant. But to be so, she insists, three conditions have to be fulfilled: (1) the activity of one's vocation is in balance with the individual's desire for action; (2) the activity also promotes the individual's personal ends; and (3) the activity has a higher meaning as something socially useful (212). But these conditions are rarely fulfilled; in most cases, where a worker has to earn the means of subsistence, the demands of work exceed the natural need for movement and require a great expenditure of physical and psychic energy. The sad truth of the matter is that, for the great majority of people, work means sacrificing one part of one's life to gain another. Of the work of the great majority, that old dictum is sadly true: "If you do not put your life into it, you will never get it back" (213).[76] It was for this reason that the goal of the great majority is not work but leisure, i.e., they work only so that they do not have to work anymore (215).

76 Plümacher implies this is an old saying, which is in the original German: "*Und setzt ihr das Leben nicht selber ein, nicht wird euch das Leben gewonnen sein.*"

Plümacher regarded this situation as "a tragic contradiction of cultural life," and not as the temporary result of an historical form of political or economic organization. She had sympathy with the condition of the workers, whose wages could barely cover their needs and whose work was often exhausting and meaningless to them (213). But she could see no social or political solution to it, and seemed to disapprove of social democracy as a remedy (213). In one remarkable passage she seems to admit that the social problem is the result of social, economic, and political organization. She writes that "in our cultural situation" the poor work too much for their reward; but then it turns out that this is the result of climate and geography. With her experience in Tennessee in mind, she writes that in many parts of the southern United States people can earn a living from the soil without much trouble or labor.

Work, Plümacher explained, is not something accidental or arbitrary in the human predicament but something necessary and natural. It lies in the plan of the world as much as breathing in the plan of an organism. This plan is not something imposed upon us but lies deep within our inner natures (214). In this respect the optimists are right to speak about "the blessings of work"; hence Hartmann, Plümacher implied, was one-sided in seeing work only in negative terms as something we want to avoid (214). Nevertheless, though work, in one respect, fulfills our inner selves and our natural needs, in another respect, it demands self-denial and even self-destruction (214). The fact that work is a blessing does not speak against but for pessimism, Plümacher insisted, because that blessing demands nothing less than "the forgetting of one's self and one's existence," "self-alienation through the mechanical expenditure of energy" (215).

8. AESTHETIC REDEMPTION

In the course of their polemics again Hartmann's pessimism, Jürgen Bona Meyer and Rudolf Haym had both made a point of mentioning the many pleasures in life that Hartmann had left out of his equations. Almost en passant both of them cited the pleasure we derive from nature (*Naturgenuss*) and stressed its importance for human well-being.[77] It seemed a serious omission that Hartmann had never considered this pleasure, especially given the importance that had been bestowed upon it since the romantic era. For Schiller, Goethe, Herder, and the romantics, contact with nature regenerates and inspires human beings. One escapes the drudgery and despair of life, which are the products of culture, by turning to nature. While culture divides us, nature restores us, making us whole again. But if this is so, the pessimist's case against life needs significant qualification.

Even though made *en passant*, this objection did not go unnoticed. It was fully appreciated by Taubert, who devoted a chapter to it in *Der Pessimismus und seine Gegner*.[78] It was true, Taubert admitted, that Hartmann, in calculating the pleasures of life, had failed to consider those we derive from nature. But then, she added, he also did not mention the suffering often caused by nature, viz., volcanoes, earthquakes, hurricanes, floods, and so forth. And that suffering is often very great indeed. In Japan millions have lost their lives from earthquakes; in Bengal ten thousand people a year die from tiger attacks; and in sailing across the Atlantic, thousands of ships have been lost. So, as these facts attest, nature does not only heal us; she also destroys us. If any objection is to be made against Hartmann, then, it is that he failed to consider such a weighty argument in favor of his pessimism (56).

If we find nature beautiful, Taubert went on, that is only because we read our feelings and purposes into it (58, 61). The peace, tranquility, and harmony of nature are really only illusions that we create to calm and charm ourselves. The "laughing meadows" conceal as much suffering as "the torment of the cities"; and "the peace of the night" is the occasion for predators to stalk their prey. A view of a forest from the distance might be beautiful and uplifting; but it is an illusion to think that its denizens are happier than people in cities. There is terror, need, and struggle in the forest just as in the city.

77 Meyer, "Weltelend und Weltschmerz," p. 20; Haym, "Die Hartmann'sche Philosophie des Unbewussten," p. 275. The same point was made in much greater detail by Johannes Volkelt in his *Das Unbewusste und der Pessimismus*, pp. 294–98. Though published in the same year as Taubert's work, Taubert does not mention it.

78 Taubert, *Der Pessimismus und seine Gegner*, VI, "Der Naturgenuss," pp. 55–62.

Taubert regarded pleasure in nature as a fiction because it is, in her view, more a cultural construction than a natural feeling (56–57). Pleasure in nature is a very modern phenomenon, she pointed out, the product of the romantic age and Rousseau's rebellion against modern culture. We derive pleasure from nature only when we want to return to it; and we want to return to it only after we have become alienated from it in the first place. That alienation has been the product of modern urban life, which has enclosed man in a shell of art, technology, customs, and laws. The ancient Greeks felt no longing for nature, because they were already part of it; and the medievals did not want to become one with nature, because they saw their resting place in heaven. It was only after the infliction of the wounds of modern urban life that people began to long for nature. This only goes to show, Taubert believed, that pleasure in nature is really negative in value: we appreciate it only if we do not have it (57). Nature cannot be regarded, therefore, as a constant source of pleasure even for those who live close to it.

But even if we admit that nature is the source of pleasure in the modern age, Taubert added, it still should not be given much weight in calculating the general value of life. Why? The problem is that this pleasure is becoming more and more rare and inaccessible for most people in the modern age. Nature has been so polluted by modern industry and technology, it has been so trammeled and spoiled by human habitation, that there are few places left on Earth that offer people tranquility and beauty (59). If we want to find unspoiled nature, we have to travel far to see it; and the farther we have to travel, the more stress we have to endure before we get to it. We have to ask ourselves whether traveling to exotic locations to enjoy nature is worth all the trouble; in most cases, it would be more relaxing simply to stay at home (60). What is the pleasure of the Alps if, to enjoy its occasional vistas, one has to endure poor food, rough roads, and dirty hotels? As the reader can see, all the arguments for stay-at-home vacations were already well in place in the nineteenth century.

So far the thrust of Taubert's case against Haym and Meyer is to show that pleasure in nature should not be given much weight on the scales of the value of life. That we take pleasure in nature is a fact that we should not dispute. But that pleasure is not natural or universal; it is not positive and constant; and it is not accessible or common. But, beside these points, Taubert had another kind of argument up her sleeve to show that pleasure in nature should not count as evidence against pessimism. The pessimist is in a better position than the optimist, she contended, to explain why we take pleasure in nature in the first place. That pleasure has its source in our longing to become one with the universe, in our striving to lose our individuality and to rest in peace "in the harbor of nothingness" (57). If life were truly beautiful and desirable, as the optimist assures us, we would never feel this longing; we would not strive to lose our individuality; we would not feel separated from nature; and we would not want to return to her (58). The longing and striving to return to nature stand as evidence for the sorrow and suffering of our normal existence, where we are caught in the toils and troubles of our own individuality. So the pleasure we take in nature, properly examined and explained, turns out to be one of the strongest proofs for pessimism.

The dispute about pleasure in nature was only a foreshadowing, however, of a much bigger issue dividing Taubert and her critics. Haym's complaint about Hartmann's neglect of pleasure in nature had its source in a much broader and deeper criticism: that Hartmann had ignored the aesthetic dimension of life. Hartmann, he insisted, had "stubbornly closed his eyes to the aesthetic element" (273), and he had done his utmost "to reduce the aesthetic to a minimum" (275). For Haym, this was a major weakness of Hartmann's pessimism, because the aesthetic dimension of life is proof that it is not a scene of sorrow and suffering. Beauty is a source and sign of pleasure, and the omnipresence of beauty is therefore proof of the happiness of life. As Haym wrote: "The existence of beauty in the world, and the sense for it, is the guarantee of all pleasure that exists, and it is an undisputable original phenomenon of pleasure. . . . The enjoyment of art is in truth striking testimony of happiness, which flows in streams through the veins of the earth" (274).

Never one to shirk a challenge, Taubert engaged Haym's criticism in the very next chapter of *Der Pessimismus und seine Gegner.*[79]

---

79 Taubert, *Der Pessimismus und seine Gegner*, "VII: Die Glückseligkeit als ästhetische Weltanschauung," pp. 63–84.

Haym, she charged, had simply confused aesthetic pleasure with happiness. It is one thing to enjoy beauty; it is quite another to equate such enjoyment with happiness, with contentment in life. Even if one sees beauty everywhere, it does not follow that the world is a happy place. After all, beauty lies more in the mind of the perceiver than in things themselves. The conflation of beauty with the happiness of the world becomes especially apparent, Taubert claimed, from the highest form of art, from tragedy, which depicts not the happiness but the suffering of humanity (64). The purpose of art is to take us beyond the realm of ordinary life, where there is so much sorrow and suffering, and into a higher realm, where we can enjoy forms for their own sake (65). It is art that gives human beings some consolation about the misery of life and that reconciles them to life through the magic of aesthetic illusion (66–67).

Such views about the power of art sound strikingly Nietzschean, though it was probably only a coincidence that Nietzsche's *Geburt der Tragödie* had appeared only a year earlier.[80] Unlike Nietzsche, Taubert did not think that art could provide a path of redemption, a remedy for all the sorrows and suffering of life. She doubted the possibility of "an aesthetic redemption of the world, i.e., an overcoming of suffering through beauty" (77). The problem with such a program, in her view, is that the aesthetic dimension of life is too rarified, accessible only to an elite few, the artist and the highly educated. The great masses of people are too poor and ignorant to appreciate beauty, and so this antidote for their toils and troubles lies out of reach. Haym, for his part, was not so skeptical about the powers of art. Though he admitted that beauty is fully appreciable by only a few, he still insisted that beauty is omnipresent in life and that everyone can take pleasure in it, at least to some degree (274). But Taubert believed that Haym was too naïve and idealistic, that he had little conception of the poverty and weaknesses of the masses. He had underestimated how poor most people are and how little time, energy, and money they have for the pleasures of

80 Friedrich Nietzsche, *Die Geburt der Tragödie aus dem Geiste der Musik* (Leipzig: Ernst Wilhelm Fritzsch, 1872). Taubert never mentions Nietzsche in her book.

art (77). He was like Queen Antoinette recommending that the people should eat cake when they could not afford bread (76).

The exchange between Taubert and Haym raised the question: Why not aesthetic education? Why not educate the people so that they can appreciate art? In that case the pessimist's reckoning about the value of life would have to be reformulated, throwing much more pleasure into his equations. Aesthetic education was indeed the idea behind Haym's thesis: "Happiness is in truth an ethical-artistic task" (276). Haym's point is that beauty is not something given in human life but something we create by making our lives works of art. Through such an aesthetic education we give our lives a much greater value than they would otherwise have. Hartmann had treated beauty and happiness as a given, as if they had to be handed down to us by fate, and he had failed to appreciate the simple point behind the old adage that everyone is the forger of his own happiness.

Aesthetic education, though, was not an ideal for which Taubert had much patience. She willfully misread Haym's remarks about it, interpreting them as a proposal for a eudemonistic ethic.[81] Haym had no such intention, and all her criticisms about his attempt to attach rewards to virtue were beside the point. We should not be misled by Taubert's apparent sympathy with the masses, as if she deplored their poverty and lack of education. The truth of the matter is that Taubert did not sympathize with the people but feared them. She stated that they are not really interested in art and the realm of the ideal, and that they are content with eating, drinking, and material well-being (77). Worst of all, their ambitions were to take the property of the elite and privileged. Goaded by socialist agitators, their goal was complete social and political equality, a world where there would be no place for art at all (77).

Nearly a decade after Taubert's exchanges with Haym, Olga Plümacher revisited the aesthetic question in her *Der Pessimismus in Vergangenheit und Gegenwart*.[82] The charges against Hartmann

---

81 See Taubert, *Der Pessimismus und seine Gegner*, VIII, "Die Glückseligkeit als Tugend," pp. 79–84.

82 Plümacher, *Der Pessimismus in Vergangenheit und Gegenwart*, Zweite Ausgabe, VI Cap., pp. 233–37.

for ignoring the aesthetic dimension of life had not abated, and the optimists continued to maintain that taking it into account would tip the eudemonic scales in their favor. Art and pleasure in nature—so the argument went—made life more pleasant than painful, and therefore worth living after all. Plümacher, however, remained skeptical of this argument. She insisted that pessimism does not exclude aesthetic contemplation and that it can take into account the pleasure derived from it (227). But the question remains whether aesthetic pleasure really counts that much in weighing the general amount of pleasure versus pain in the world. The aesthetic realm, Plümacher conceded, is indeed very wide, extending to all kinds of objects and experiences. But the problem is that the pleasure of beauty is, for most people, very weak, fragile, and uncommon (231). To appreciate the fragility and weakness of beauty, one only had to go to a concert with a toothache, visit an art gallery with a stomachache, or watch a sunset while seasick (231–32). So even if the aesthetic realm is wide, the conditions for enjoying it are narrow (231). Such pleasure requires disinterested contemplation, which is a rare state of mind, one hard to attain and sustain in life (232). The aesthetic attitude demands tranquility and peace of mind, which are easily upset by those passions, such as longing, fear, dread, and anxiety, which are inevitably involved in the usual business of life. Whoever insists upon having an entirely aesthetic existence would have to abandon the normal feelings of life and renounce "two thirds of the richness of the life of the soul" (232). So, unlike Nietzsche, but like Taubert, Plümacher did not think that life could be made worth living as an aesthetic phenomenon.[83] Art was at best a faint and fleeting escape from the suffering of life, upon which no hope for enduring redemption could be based.

83 Plümacher does not respond to Nietzsche in *Der Pessimismus in Vergangenheit und Gegenwart*, though she does briefly refer to him on p. 176. She had certainly read him. In an early article, a survey of Hartmann's foes, she took into account Nietzsche's critique of Hartmann in *Unzeitgemässe Betrachtungen*. See "Die Philosophie des Unbewussten und ihre Gegner," 321–45, esp. 329.

9. LOVE

It was an old truth dear to Christianity and Romanticism that the value of life depends on, more than anything else, love. Life was held to be worthwhile only if we love others and are loved by them. Novalis, epitomizing this core belief of Christianity and Romanticism, once wrote: "The heart is the key to the world and life. One lives in this helpless condition to love, and to be committed to others. . . . So is Christ, seen from this standpoint, certainly the key to the world."[84] What made life worth living, for Christians and romantics alike, was love. No matter how much evil and suffering there were in the world, love conquered all and redeemed everything.

So if the pessimist were to make his case against the value of life, he had no choice but to tackle the theme of love. Whether love is really so valuable and redeeming clearly depends on one's conception of it. What, after all, is love?

Schopenhauer had taken his stand on this question in his famous essay on the metaphysics of sexual love in the second volume of *Die Welt als Wille und Vorstellung*.[85] There he had argued that love is rooted in sexual desire and that its chief purpose is procreation, the propagation of the species. Because it is based on instinct, a drive of nature over which we have no control, love has no moral value. Love, Schopenhauer insisted, is filled with illusions. While the lover believes to be pursuing his self-interest, he is really in thrall to the sexual instinct acting through him. The lover is enchanted by the beauty of the beloved, though beauty is really only the bait to capture him. We think that love is a matter of reciprocity, of giving and receiving; but the lover really does not care about the interests of the beloved and cares only about satisfying his desires. While the lover thinks that he will be forever happy in the arms of the beloved, his passions quickly fade after sexual

84 "Teplitzer Fragmente," no. 62, in *Novalis: Werke, Tagebücher und Briefe Friedrich von Hardenbergs*, ed. Hans-Joachim Mähl and Richard Samuel (Munich: Hanser Verlag, 1978), II, 396.

85 Schopenhauer, "Metaphysik der Geschlechtsliebe," WWV II, 678–727.

satisfaction and soon disillusionment prevails. All these illusions arise from the fact that we are not self-conscious, that we are not aware of the will of nature which acts through us and which uses us as instruments to preserve the species. Because he was so bent on exposing these illusions, Schopenhauer called his own attitude toward love "a crude realism"; but its crudity was also its honesty, which he believed so much better than all the idealist and moral afflatus surrounding love. When we see love from this broad metaphysical perspective, Schopenhauer concluded, we can see that it does not redeem life but simply perpetuates it, keeping in motion the cycle of desire and suffering. Love brings a short moment of ecstasy in sexual orgasm; but that hardly compensates for all its despair and disillusionment. A wise man, seeing the cause of love and all the sorrows it brings, would strive for self-renunciation and extirpation of sexual desire.

In *Philosophie des Unbewussten* Hartmann explicitly and emphatically endorsed Schopenhauer's metaphysics of sexual love.[86] That metaphysics was as important to his pessimism as it had been to Schopenhauer's. Hartmann differs from Schopenhauer only in the bluntness and clarity of his exposition and in introducing a Darwinian element into his theory. Love, on the face of it, Hartmann wrote, appears completely absurd. What is it that people are after? Why are they going to all this trouble? Why are they so gripped by their desires? The more one thinks about it, the more one feels like a sober man in a party of drunks. All the mystery of love disappears, however, once we admit the hard and honest truth about it: that its goal is sexual satisfaction, not just with any individual but with just this particular individual (190). Whenever sexual desire abates, so does love itself (189). Love is the instinct to mate with another particular individual to produce the best possible offspring for the species. Though we think we are making a conscious choice, the selection of another partner is really natural selection working through us, striving to find the most suitable mate to create the best offspring (192, 193). The reason that love

---

86 Hartmann, Kap. B.II: "Das Unbewusste in der geschlechtlichen Liebe," *Philosophie des Unbewussten* (1870), pp. 181–98; and "Hunger und Liebe," 3 in Kap. C.XII, "Die Unvernunft des Wollens und das Elend des Daseins," pp. 586–99.

seems so mysterious to us is simply because we are unconscious of its goals. We think that we are pursuing our own self-interest, because we desire nothing more than to be with the beloved; but we also know that it cannot be solely our self-interest when we have to sacrifice so much of ourselves for the beloved, and when we are so often disappointed and disillusioned after the satisfaction of our desires. When, however, we become wise to nature's purpose with us, the mystery of love disappears; yet despite our better knowledge, we still find ourselves pushed again by recurring desires, though with decreasing enthusiasm (595–96).

The importance of this theory of love for Hartmann's pessimism should be clear. If love is only sexual desire, and if the satisfaction of this desire is momentary, the intense but brief pleasure of orgasm, then love does not weigh much in the hedonic calculus of life (598). Against its momentary pleasures, we have to weigh its many troubles and disadvantages. There is all the stress and frustration we endure *before* we satisfy our desires; and there is all the disillusionment and disappointment *after* we satisfy them. The sadness of disillusionment lasts much longer than all the happiness of our illusions (592). For the female, the intense pains of childbirth far outweigh the passing pleasures of sex (590). Although love affairs sometimes lead to marriage, few marriages are happy, and those that are happy are so not because of love but because of friendship between the partners (593).[87] On all these grounds, reason advises us to abstain entirely from love; but then the torment of repressed desires makes abstemiousness an even greater evil than indulgence (599). Ultimately, then, reason must advise an even more drastic remedy: extermination of the drive, i.e., castration. That is the only possible result from the eudemonological standpoint, Hartmann admits (599). If there is anything to be said against it, that must be from some moral standpoint beyond the self-interest of the individual.

---

87 It is noteworthy that Hartmann distinguishes love from friendship, which he says are "himmelweit verschiedene Dinge," *Philosophie des Unbewussten*, p. 187. Plümacher, however, claims that Hartmann made "*Liebesfreundschaft*" an important element of marriage. But Hartmann, at least in the second edition of *Philosophie des Unbewussten*, would have regarded this concept as a contradiction in terms.

It should not be surprising that the reaction against this theory of love was swift, strong, and severe. No other aspect of pessimism created such indignation and hostility among its critics. For its theist critics, Schopenhauer's and Hartmann's theory of love clashed with their deepest convictions and ultimate values. Some of Hartmann's first theist critics were so shocked, their moral senses so offended, that they accused Hartmann of advocating promiscuity, free love, and prostitution. By reducing love down to sexual desire, Hartmann seemed to be advocating the pursuit of sexual desire for its own sake, regardless of moral restraints. Thus Gustav Knauer, one early theist critic, said that Hartmann's views about love were surrounded by "the pestilential air of prostitution" and that they were "laden with the egoism of old bachelorhood."[88] Another early theist critic, Ludwig Weis, wrote that Hartmann's treatment of love was "spiced with a tickling of the palate and the arousal of the senses" and that for this reason his philosophy should have all the success of Offenbach's pieces for the theater.[89] Both Knauer and Weis insinuated that Hartmann's work sold so well only because it aroused pornographic interests, especially among young women.

Taubert swiftly condemned these early critics.[90] They were moralizing like principals of a girl's school, and they had little appreciation for the fact that Hartmann was trying to get to the truth about love without the blinkers of moral scruples. First and foremost philosophers had an obligation to tell the truth, even if it were difficult for people to admit on moral grounds (37–38). Taubert did not dispute that there might be people who were attracted to Hartmann's writings for salacious motives; but that hardly discredited the writings themselves, still less the author (39). That Hartmann was not

88 Gustav Knauer, *Das Facit aus E.v.Hartmann's Philosophie des Unbewussten* (Berlin: L. Heimann, 1873), pp. 48–49.

89 Ludwig Weis, *Anti-Materialismus oder Kritik aller Philosophie des Unbewußten* (Berlin: F. Henschel, 1873), p. 129. This work is volume 3 of his *Anti-Materialismus* (Berlin: F. Henschel, 1871–72). Regarding Offenbach, Weis was probably referring to the scandal created by the *Galop infernal* of Act II, Scene 2, of Offenbach's *Orphée aux enfers*, which contains the famous *cancan* dance.

90 Taubert, *Der Pessimismus und seine Gegner*, Kap. IV, "Die Liebe," pp. 37–50. See also her long review of Weis's *Anti-Materialismus*, which appears as an appendix to her book, pp. 147–64.

condoning, let alone recommending, free love and prostitution was clear, Taubert pointed out, from some passages in the third edition of *Philosophie des Unbewussten* where he explained that following instinct leads to marriage, and that free love and prostitution are a corruption of instinct (40–41).[91] All the moral indignation about Hartmann's theory of love is entirely beside the point, Taubert argued, because it was never his intention to treat the *ethical* meaning of love (42). Hartmann's aim is to determine only the *eudemonic* value of love, i.e., he wants to see whether and how its miseries outweigh its joys. Having thus defended Hartmann, Taubert went on to give her own views on love, which are more positive than Hartmann's about its eudemonic value. While she did not dispute Hartmann's main finding that love creates more suffering than happiness, she weighed it more heavily on the eudemonic scales than he by stressing its importance in overcoming loneliness (46). Besides science and art, love alone could at least give us "a dream of happiness," which was sometimes enough to get us through "the night of life" (46).

Though Taubert's defense was widely read, it hardly staunched the flow of criticism against Hartmann. While later critics did not stoop to the level of Knauer and Weis, they were still indignant about Hartmann's reduction of love to sexuality. The conservative theist critic Weygoldt thought Hartmann's theory faulty on eudemonic grounds alone, because the miseries Hartmann found in love do not arise from love itself but only from contemporary social mores.[92] Hartmann had judged the metal from its dross, Urania from *Venus vulgivaga*, Weygoldt claimed. That young men nowadays suffer from repressed sexual drives has much to do with contemporary mores, which prevent early marriage. That young women, too, feel sexual frustration has more to do with lax morals than their natural desires. And that there are so many unhappy marriages has nothing to do with love itself but with the low morals of the age, which allow flirtation and *mariages de raison*. Paul

91 Taubert cites *Philosophie des Unbewussten*, dritte beträchtlich vermehrte Auflage (Berlin: Duncker, 1871), pp. 192, 209. These passages were probably added by Hartmann to respond to critics like Weis and Knauer.

92 Weygoldt, *Kritik des philosophischen Pessimismus*, pp. 105–7.

Christ, another conservative theist critic, said that he could not read Hartmann's theory without a deep inner indignation.[93] Like Weygoldt, he thought that much of the unhappiness of love came from a lack of morality and reason, and that it had nothing to do with love itself. Of course, there are many illusions in love; but it is the responsibility of everyone to learn to control them and to keep them within realistic limits. Every happy marriage—and there are more of them than Hartmann wanted to admit—stood as a refutation of Hartmann's theory. Experience shows us that in happy marriages there is no disillusionment but only fulfillment. Hartmann's theory is dangerous for morals, Christ believed, because it encourages people to seek sexual satisfaction alone in their personal relationships. And the Darwinist strands of Hartmann's theory, which stressed the importance of racial improvement, raised serious moral questions: could it not lead to abortion and mistreatment of those who were not born so perfect? Remarkably, the social democrat critic Johannes Volkelt agreed with his conservative colleagues, Weygoldt and Christ, that contemporary social conditions are responsible for much of the misery of love.[94] But his solution to this problem was very different from theirs: a new socialist order rather than a return to old customs and beliefs. In a socialist republic, Volkelt was convinced, there would be much less sexual misery: there would be fewer unhappy marriages, because divorce would be easy; there would be much less sexual frustration because men and women could marry young and whomever they really loved; and there would be little prostitution because there would be public careers for women as well as men and because there would be no standing armies (soldiers being the main customers of prostitutes).

Whatever the merits of these later criticisms, it is important to see that they could at best affect only one half or side of Hartmann's thinking about love. For, besides his theory about love as sexual instinct, Hartmann harbored another very different theory about love. This other theory is latent in his monism, and it was

93   Paul Christ, *Der Pessimismus und die Sittenlehre* (Haarlem: De Erven F. Bohn, 1882), pp. 164–66.
94   Volkelt, *Das Unbewusste und der Pessimismus*, p. 309.

only a matter of developing its implications. It is an important implication of that doctrine, Hartmann thought, that each individual is essentially one with all other individuals, and that each fully realizes itself only when it forfeits those aspects of its individuality that separate it from others and only when it recognizes its identity with all others. There is a single universal will in all of us, which makes up our inner identity; and it is our task as moral agents to make this identity, which is normally subconscious, fully self-conscious, so that we understand the moral consequences of our actions. When I become self-conscious of this will, I know that whatever I do to others I also do to myself and that whatever others do to me they do to themselves. Schopenhauer had given great importance to this theme in Book IV of *Die Welt als Wille und Vorstellung*.[95] The same theme was no less important for Hartmann, who developed its implications into another theory of love. While the theme is not explicit in the first two editions of *Philosophie des Unbewussten*, it appears in a later article, "Ist der Pessimismus trostlos?"[96] Here Hartmann writes about "the mystical roots of love" which come from the longing for identity with all other beings. This longing for identity with all other individuals, we learn, is really a form of love: "All love is in its deepest root longing; and all longing is the longing for unification [with others]" (86). In this unity people do not retain their individuality but surrender it, Hartmann stresses. "Whoever has not felt the longing for self-annihilation in the loved person does not know what love is" (87). Taubert developed this theme in *Der Pessimismus und seine Gegner*, stressing how love is "homesickness," the longing of the lover to surrender its individuality and to become one with the absolute (47).

Clearly this mystical theory of love is very different from the instinct theory. While the mystical theory sees the goal of love as the absolute, the instinct theory finds it in procreation. The mystical theory demands the surrender of individuality, whereas the instinct

95   WWV I, §§63, 66, 484, 508–9.

96   Eduard von Hartmann, "Ist der Pessimismus trostlos?" *Philosophische Monatshefte* 5 (1870), 21–41. Reprinted in *Gesammelte philosophische Abhandlungen zur Philosophie des Unbewussten* (Berlin: Duncker, 1872), pp. 147–65. All references in the text are to this later edition.

theory affirms it, because the goal of love is achieved through physical sex. In the mystical theory the individual penetrates through the veil of Maya and finally discovers the truth about the world; but in the instinct theory the individual is subject to all kinds of illusion, the abolition of which leads to self-renunciation but not identification with the universe as a whole. Whatever its merits, the very different logic of the mystical theory deflects some of the criticisms of the instinct theory. No one could charge the mystical theory with egoism or immorality, the most common complaints against the instinct theory.

Some of Hartmann's critics, however, were not blind to the mystical theory, which they found as faulty as the instinct theory. Johannes Volkelt questioned that the two theories, having such different logic, could ever be reconciled.[97] Bona Meyer saw in the mystical theory not a negation of egoism but a superegoism because the individual sees him/herself as the universe as a whole.[98] The reason he or she seeks identity with others is still egoistic because he or she wants *self*-redemption. Hugo Sommer, a disciple of Lotze, thought that the mystical theory rested on a simple logical mistake.[99] Assuming that there is an essential identity of all beings, that has little or nothing to do with love, for love arises despite this essential identity, not because of it. Love occurs only in the interaction between individuals, and only in the recognition and respect of each other's individuality. It demands that we take pleasure in the well-being of another not because he or she is the same as we are but because he or she is different from us.

Such, in summary, were some of the fundamental issues of the pessimism controversy. There were other issues, such as the nature of pleasure, the advisability of suicide, and the morality of pessimism,

97 Volkelt, *Das Unbewusste und der Pessimismus*, pp. 305–8.

98 See Meyer, "Weltlust und Weltleid," pp. 291–92. Meyer makes this criticism only in this revised version of his original article "Weltelend und Weltschmerz." It is noteworthy that he made it after corresponding with Hartmann.

99 Hugo Sommer, *Der Pessimismus und die Sittenlehre* (Haarlem: de Erven F. Bohn, 1882), pp. 125–26.

the full treatment of which would involve a book much larger than this one.

When, with the benefit of hindsight, we look back over the pessimism controversy, it is impossible not to view it without a sense of loss. The discussion was pursued at a high level of philosophical subtlety and sophistication by Schopenhauer, Dühring, Hartmann, the neo-Kantians, Taubert, Plümacher, and Hartmann's many critics. Rarely has so much intellectual energy been focused on an issue of such great existential importance and of such wide public interest. Yet the pessimism controversy has been largely forgotten, and the issues it raised about the value of life have not been much discussed in contemporary philosophy. This is a pity, because the pessimism controversy shows us that the question of the value of life was capable of very exacting philosophical treatment; the topic raised classical philosophical issues about pleasure, desire, work, love, good and evil, and the role of art in life, which no serious philosopher can ignore.

The great question of the value of life not only deserves but demands reexamination. It remains an urgent question for us today, even after decades of discussion, not least because Schopenhauer's pessimism still stands as a challenge to the modern secular world. If there is no God or providence to redeem suffering and evil, then what makes existence worthwhile? Hartmann was correct to declare in 1870 that Schopenhauer's pessimism was still unrefuted; but the same point is still true today. Schopenhauer's pessimism is unbearable and must be false; but it is still an open question why it is so and what makes our lives, so filled with evil and suffering, worthwhile. Philosophy should return to that fundamental question.

APPENDIX

TWO FORGOTTEN WOMEN PHILOSOPHERS

Contemporary history of philosophy demands, fairly and properly, that the historian take into account women philosophers from the past. There are two forgotten female philosophers of the late nineteenth century to whom I wish to draw attention here and to rescue from oblivion. Both were major contributors to the pessimism controversy. Although their writings were well-known in their day, both authors were assumed to be men because both published under their first initials only.

One of these authors was Agnes Taubert (1844–77), the wife of Eduard von Hartmann. Although, during the pessimism controversy, Taubert defended the views of her husband, she had a fearsome polemical talent all her own, and she did not hesitate to state her own views or criticize her husband in print. She wrote two contributions to the pessimism controversy: *Philosophie gegen naturwissenschaftliche Ueberhebung* (Berlin: Duncker, 1872); and *Der Pessimismus und seine Gegner* (Berlin: Duncker, 1873). Both books were widely reviewed. The first book was a defense of Hartmann's metaphysics against critics who appealed to the authority of natural science. Its theme, which we can roughly translate as "natural scientific presumption," seems to have been her own coinage; the idea that natural science could overextend itself would have been novel in an age of natural science. The second book became a focal point of much controversy in the early 1870s. According to Carl Heymons, Hartmann's publisher, Taubert played a major role in the organization and strategy of the dispute with Hartmann's critics.[1] Tragically, Taubert died May 1877, only thirty-three years old, of "an attack of a rheumatism of the joints."[2]

---

1 Carl Heymons, *Eduard von Hartmann, Erinnerungen aus den Jahren 1868–1881* (Berlin: Duncker, 1882), p. 49.

2 According to Heymons, *Erinnerungen*, p. 47, she suffered from "*heftigen Anfällen eines Gelenkrheumatismus.*" This is late nineteenth-century medicine.

The other female philosopher was Olga Plümacher née Hüner-wadel (1839–1895).[3] Plümacher wrote two major contributions to the pessimism controversy: *Der Kampf um's Unbewusste* (Berlin: Duncker, 1881); and *Der Pessimismus in Vergangenheit und Gegenwart* (Heidelberg: Georg Weiss Verlag, 1883; 2nd ed., 1888). The bibliography appended to the first book is still the only complete one and unsurpassed. The second book is still the only history of the pessimism controversy, also unsurpassed. Both works show a complete mastery of the polemical literature and great intellectual acumen in discussing the issues. It has been said that had Hartmann's critics read her, they would not have bothered to make criticisms in the first place.[4] Plümacher wrote an article on Hartmann's pessimism for *Mind*,[5] which served as the introduction to his ideas for an Anglophone public. Plümacher's achievement is all the more remarkable considering that she had no formal university education, that she was a mother, and that she spent much of her life in a Swiss colony in the backwoods of Tennessee.[6] It is sad that her library, most of her correspondence, and her personal documents have disappeared.[7] She died in Tennessee in 1898. Her gravestone still exists there.

Why Taubert and Plümacher have been forgotten is not much of a mystery. Their chief contributions to German intellectual life were to the pessimism controversy, which has been largely

---

3 On Plümacher, see Rolf Kieser, *Olga Plümacher-Hünerwadel: Eine gelehrte Frau des neunzehnten Jahrhunderts* (Lenzburger: Lenzburger Ortsburgerkommission, 1990). Kieser's biography is excellent in uncovering the basic biographical facts and in devising a helping bibliography. Unfortunately Kieser, who is not a philosopher, does not discuss or assess Plümacher's philosophical achievements.

4 This was the opinion of Arthur Drews, *Eduard von Hartmanns philosophisches System im Grundriss* (Heidelberg: Carl Winter, 1906), p. 59.

5 O. Plümacher, "Pessimism," *Mind* 4 (1879), 68–89. The article is a critique of James Sully's *Pessimism: A History and a Criticism* (London: Henry King, 1877).

6 Plümacher's husband, Eugen Plümacher, founded a Swiss colony in Grundy County, Tennessee. Plümacher lived there from 1869 to 1881 and then returned to Switzerland. On the Swiss colony there, see Francis Helen Jackson, *The Swiss Colony at Gruetli* (Gruetli-Laager: Grundy County Swiss Historical Society, 2010). Plümacher returned to Tennessee in 1886 in the hope of curing her son's tuberculosis; but he died there in December of that year.

7 Kieser, *Plümacher*, pp. 7, 62–63.

neglected by philosophical historians. It is also noteworthy that neither Taubert nor Plümacher fits the stereotype of the female intellectual, which is someone devoted to progressive causes. Both were conservative, shared Hartmann's hostility to social democracy, and saw themselves as protectors of culture against the masses. The great value of pessimism for Taubert was in discouraging the masses to aspire to greater participation in politics and the goods of life. For many historians, such political views are reason enough to let them rest in the obscurity of the past. But their achievements rise above their politics and deserve recognition for their own sake.

FURTHER READING

The following suggestions for further reading are slanted toward secondary works in English. I have mentioned German works only when every reader should know about them or when there is no scholarship in English on the topic. Unfortunately there are few translations for most of the primary works mentioned in the bibliography. Whenever one is available, it is mentioned.

GENERAL STUDIES

Although there are no studies devoted specifically to the period 1840–1900, there are many concerned with the second half of the nineteenth century. Gerhard Lehmann, *Geschichte der Philosophie*, Band IX: *Die Philosophie des nenzehnten Jahrhunderts* (Berlin: de Gruyter, 1953), is a useful general survey. Otto Siebert's *Geschichte der neueren deutschen Philosophie seit Hegel* (Göttingen: Vanden-hoeck & Ruprecht, 1898) is still valuable because it covers so many figures who have been neglected or forgotten. Two volumes of the Beck *Geschichte der Philosophie* are excellent: Band X, Stefano Poggi and Wolfgang Röd, *Die Philosophie der Neuzeit 4, Positivismus, Socialismus und Spiritualismus im 19. Jahrhundert* (Munich: Beck, 1989); and Band XIII, Rainer Thurnher, Wolfgang Röd, and Heinrich Schmidinger, *Die Philosophie des ausgehenden 19. und des 20. Jahrhunderts 3* (Munich: Beck, 2002). Also still very much worth reading, despite my misgivings, is Karl Löwith's *Von Hegel bis Nietzsche* (Zurich: Europa Verlag, 1941). There is a translation by David E. Green: *From Hegel to Nietzsche: The Revolution in Nineteenth-Century Thought* (New York: Holt, Rinehart and Winston, 1964). Hermann Schnädelbach's *Philosophy in Germany, 1831–1933* (Cambridge: Cambridge University Press, 1984), though having a wider scope, is often illuminating for the second half of the nineteenth century. An excellent anthology is that of Allen Wood and Songsuk Susan Hahn, eds., *The Cambridge History of Philosophy in the Nineteenth Century (1790–1870)* (Cambridge: Cambridge University Press, 2012).

I THE IDENTITY CRISIS OF PHILOSOPHY

The identity crisis of philosophy is a theme of Herbert Schnädel-bach's *Philosophy in Germany, 1831–1933* (Cambridge: Cambridge University Press, 1984). The theme is not pursued consistently or systematically, however. Schnädelbach does not attempt to identify the various conceptions of philosophy and how they were intended to resolve the obsolescence crisis.

Scholarship on Trendelenburg is still in its infancy. There is no translation of his *Logische Untersuchungen* or his other works. The standard intellectual biography of Trendelenburg is by his student Ernst Bratuscheck, *Adolf Trendelenburg* (Berlin: Hensehel, 1873). There is a complete bibliography of his writings in the excellent anthology *Friedrich Adolf Trendelenburgs Wirkung*, ed. Gerald Hartung and Klaus Christian Köhnke (Eutin: Eutiner Landes-bibliothek, 2006), pp. 271–94. I have attempted to provide an intro-duction to Trendelenburg's philosophy in my *Late German Idealism* (Oxford: Oxford University Press, 2013), pp. 11–123.

On the young Hegelians' conception of philosophy, there are many excellent studies. Among them the following are especially recommended: Daniel Brudney, *Marx's Attempt to Leave Philos-ophy* (Cambridge, MA: Harvard University Press, 1998); Harold Mah, *The End of Philosophy and the Origin of "Ideology"* (Berke-ley: University of California Press, 1987); and Warren Breckman, *Marx, The Young Hegelians, and the Origins of Radical Social Theory* (Cambridge: Cambridge University Press, 1999). An excellent in-troduction to the young Hegelian movement is William Brazill's *The Young Hegelians* (New Haven: Yale University Press, 1970). The best account of the origins and course of the neo-Hegelian move-ment is John Edward Toews, *Hegelianism: The Path toward Dia-lectical Humanism, 1805–1841* (Cambridge: Cambridge University Press, 1980).

Recently there has been a surge of interest in Schopenhauer in the Anglophone world. There are several new introductions to his philosophy: Christopher Janaway, *Schopenhauer: A Very Short Introduction* (Oxford: Oxford University Press, 1994); Julian Young, *Schopenhauer* (London: Routledge, 2005); Dale Jacquette, *The*

Philosophy of Schopenhauer (Kingston: McGill-Queens University Press, 2005); and Robert Wicks, *Schopenhauer* (Oxford: Blackwell, 2008). Two excellent recent studies of his metaphysics are Bryan Magee, *The Philosophy of Schopenhauer*, revised and enlarged edition (Oxford: Clarendon Press, 2009); and Christopher Janaway, *Self and World in Schopenhauer's Philosophy* (Oxford: Oxford University Press, 1989).

The standard account of neo-Kantianism is Klaus Christian Köhnke, *Entstehung und Aufstieg des Neukantianismus: Die deutsche Universitätsphilosophie zwischen Idealismus und Positivismus* (Frankfurt: Suhrkamp, 1986). There is an English translation of this book: *The Rise of Neo-Kantianism: German Academic Philosophy between Idealism and Positivism* (Cambridge: Cambridge University Press, 1991). Unfortunately it is not to be recommended, because all notes and graphs from the original edition are omitted. A useful introductory survey of the movement is provided by Hans-Ludwig Ollig, *Der Neu-Kantianismus* (Stuttgart: Metzlar, 1979).

The standard English translation of Dilthey's *Das Wesen der Philosophie* is by S. A. Emery and T. M. Emery, *The Essence of Philosophy* (Chapel Hill: University of North Carolina Press, 1954). The best account in English of Dilthey's philosophy is Michael Ermath, *Wilhelm Dilthey: The Critique of Historical Reason* (Chicago: University of Chicago Press, 1978). A useful introduction to his thought is provided by H. P. Rickman, *Wilhelm Dilthey: Pioneer of the Human Studies* (Berkeley: University of California Press, 1979).

2 THE MATERIALISM CONTROVERSY

There is a recent collection of essays on the materialism controversy, which is volume 1 of *Weltanschauung, Philosophie und Naturwissenschaft im 19 Jahrhundert, Band I: Der Materialismus-Streit*, ed. Kurt Bayertz, Myriam Gerhard, and Walter Jaeschke (Hamburg: Meiner, 2007). Accompanying it is an anthology of original texts, *Der Materialismus Streit*, ed. Kurt Bayertz, Myriam Gerhard, and Walter Jaeschke (Hamburg: Meiner, 2012).

The standard treatment of materialism in Germany is that of Frederick Gregory, *Scientific Materialism in Nineteenth Century Germany* (Dordrecht: Reidel, 1977), which is invaluable and still unsurpassed. Another general account is Annette Wittkau-Horgby, *Materialismus* (Göttingen: Vandenhoeck & Ruprecht, 1998). There is a translation of Lotze's *Mikrokosmus* by Elizabeth Hamilton and E. E. Constance Jones, *Microcosmus: An Essay concerning Man and his Relation to the World* (New York: Scribner & Welford, 1886), 2 vols. Since the Second World War, there has been little secondary literature on Lotze in English. A useful Lotze bibliography is provided by Paul Kuntz as an appendix to his edition of George Santayana's *Lotze's System of Philosophy* (Bloomington: Indiana University Press, 1971), pp. 233–68. The indispensable account of Lotze's philosophy is Reinhardt Pester's *Hermann Lotze* (Würzburg: Königshausen & Nemann, 1997). I have provided an introduction to Lotze's philosophy in my *Late German Idealism* (Oxford: Oxford University Press, 2013), pp. 127–315.

There is an old English translation of Lange's *Geschichte des Materialismus*: *The History of Materialism and Criticism of Its Present Importance*, trans. E. C. Thomas (Boston: James Osgood, 1877), 3 vols. There is also an old English translation of the eighth edition of Büchner's *Kraft und Stoff: Force and Matter*, trans. Frederick Collingwood (London: Trübner & Co., 1864). The English reader is advised that there are twenty-one editions of Büchner's *Kraft und Stoff*, and that these often differ drastically from one another.

3   THE *IGNORABIMUS* CONTROVERSY

There is nothing in English on the *Ignorabimusstreit*, and only recently has its importance been fully recognized. A collection of essays on some aspects of the controversy are provided in *Weltanschauung, Philosophie und Naturwissenschaft im 19. Jahrhundert, Band 3: Der Ignorabimus-Streit*, ed. Kurt Bayertz, Myriam Gerhard, and Walter Jaeschke (Hamburg: Felix Meiner, 2007). It is accompanied by a useful anthology of original sources, *Der Ignorabimus-Streit*, ed. Kurt Bayertz, Myriam Gerhard, and Walter Jaeschke (Hamburg: Meiner, 2012).

4 TRIALS AND TRIBULATIONS OF CLIO

The classic account of the origin of historicism is Friedrich Meinecke's *Die Entstehung des Historismus* (Munich: Oldenbourg, 1965). There is an English translation: *Historism: Rise of a New Historical Outlook*, trans. J. E. Anderson (London: Routledge & Kegan Paul, 1972). I have attempted to provide a new account of the historicist tradition in my *The German Historicist Tradition* (Oxford: Oxford University Press, 2012). Often regarded as a classic treatment of the historicist tradition is Ernst Troeltsch's *Der Historismus und seine Probleme* (Tübingen: Mohr, 1922). It must be said, however, that Troeltsch's massive tome is a *Geschwätz*, a pastiche of separate articles, which only occasionally gives insight.

An older survey of the historicist tradition, now out of date, is given by Georg Iggers, *The German Conception of History*, 2nd rev. ed. (Middletown, CT: Wesleyan University Press, 1983). A more modern survey is Friedrich Jaeger and Jörn Rüsen, *Geschichte des Historismus* (Munich: Beck, 1992).

An excellent account of the intellectual background of historicism in the romantic era is Theodore Ziolkowski's *Clio, the Romantic Muse* (Ithaca: Cornell University Press, 2004). A good account of the eighteenth-century background of the historicist tradition is given by Peter Hanns Reill, *The German Enlightenment and the Rise of Historicism* (Berkeley: University of California Press, 1975).

All new accounts of Ranke should begin with W. P. Fuchs's edition, *Aus Werk und Nachlass* (Munich: Oldenbourg, 1965), 4 vols. A useful anthology and translation of some of Ranke's writings is Roger Wines, *The Secret of World History: Selected Writings on the Art and Science of History* (New York: Fordham, 1981). An excellent account of Ranke's intellectual development is Theodore von Laue's *Leopold Ranke: The Formative Years* (Princeton: Princeton University Press, 1950). Carl Hinrichs's *Ranke und die Geschichtstheologie der Goethezeit* (Göttingen: Musterschmidt, 1954), is still interesting, though dated. Leonard Krieger's *Ranke: The Meaning of History* (Chicago: University of Chicago Press, 1977), though often cited, is very weak on Ranke's philosophical background.

There is a dearth of literature on Wilhelm Windelband, a neglect out of all proportion to his importance. I have tried to address this in chapter 9 of my *The German Historicist Tradition*, pp. 365–92. The same holds for Chladenius, whose importance has only recently been fully recognized. There is a translation of excerpts from his writings in Kurt Mueller-Vollmer, *The Hermeneutics Reader* (New York: Continuum, 1994), pp. 54–71. For a fuller bibliography of writings on and by Chladenius, see *The German Historicist Tradition*, pp. 570–72.

Readers interested in historicism are urged to avoid at all costs Karl Popper's *The Poverty of Historicism* (London: Routledge & Kegan Paul, 1957), which is essentially cold-war rhetoric. Popper's use of the word "historicism" is idiosyncratic and has little to do with the actual historicist tradition, whose proper study Popper did much to impede.

5 THE PESSIMISM CONTROVERSY

There has been little work devoted to the study of the pessimism controversy. The best account is still that of Olga Plümacher, *Der Pessimismus in Vergangenheit und Gegenwart* (1884). A second edition appeared in 1888. For a bibliography of some of the extensive polemical literature at the time, see James Sully, *Pessimism: A History and a Criticism* (New York: Appleton, 1891), pp. xvii–xix. An excellent bibliography, though it covers only the 1870s, is the appendix to Olga Plümacher's *Der Kampf um's Unbewusste* (Berlin: Duncker, 1881), pp. 114–50.

On the neo-Kantian discussion of pessimism, see Klaus Christian Köhnke, *Entstehung und Aufstieg des Neukantianismus* (Frankfurt: Suhrkamp, 1986), pp. 319–44.

There is very little in English or German on Eugen Dühring, an astonishing gap on an obnoxious but important figure.

There is little English literature on Eduard von Hartmann. See Angus Nicholls and Martin Liebscher, *Thinking the Unconscious: Nineteenth Century German Thought* (Cambridge: Cambridge University Press, 2010), which focuses on the theme of the subconscious. The study of N. Darnoi, *The Unconscious and Eduard von Hartmann: A Historico-Critical Monograph* (Hague: Nijhoff, 1968), is unsympathetic to its subject matter and treats it from a Catholic perspective. For recent work on Hartmann, see Jean-Claude Wolf, *Eduard von Hartmann. Ein Philosoph der Gründerzeit* (Würzburg: Königshausen & Neumann, 2006). Also see his anthology *Eduard von Hartmann. Zeitgenosse und Gegenspieler Nietzsches* (Würzburg: Königshausen & Neumann, 2006). Two older studies on Hartmann are Theodor Kappstein, *Eduard von Hartmann. Einführung in seine Gedankenwelt* (Gotha: Perthes, 1907), and Arthur Drews, *Eduard von Hartmanns philosophisches System im Grundriss*, Zweite Ausgabe (Heidelberg: Carl Winter, 1906). There is a translation of Hartmann's *Philosophie des Unbewussten: Philosophy of the Unconscious*, trans. William Chatterton Coupland (London: K. Paul, Trench and Trübner, 1893).

INDEX

alienation, 24, 26
atheism, 4, 5, 54

Bakunin, Michael, 59
Bauer, Bruno, 5, 22, 23, 26, 27, 54
Beneke, Friedrich, 10–11, 16, 36, 41
Büchner, Ludwig: on Christianity,
    73–74, 76; concept of matter, 71–72,
    74, 110–11; on consciousness, 73,
    109; critique of Du Bois-Reymond,
    108–12; critique of teleology, 72–73;
    defense of materialism, 92–94; on
    free will, 73; his model of explana-
    tion, 113; his monism, 109–10; his
    relativism, 76

Chladenius, Johann Martin, 134–36
Cohen, Hermann, 20, 38, 39, 70, 89, 166
Comte, Auguste, 146, 175
crisis of historicism, ix, 145
critique, 5, 16, 17, 18, 22–24, 26, 27, 32, 37,
    54, 73, 91, 143, 179
Czolbe, Heinrich: his critique of ma-
    terialism, 88; his empiricism, 84; and
    Lotze, 85–87; and the materialism
    controversy, 61–62; his naïve realism,
    88; on self-consciousness, 85, 87; his
    sensualism, 84–89

Darwinism, 5, 22, 47, 48, 55, 56, 69,
    95–96, 103
Dilthey, Wilhelm: on autonomy of
    history, 149; concept of philosophy,
    48–51; critique of metaphysics, 50;
    on explanation, 119–21, 123, 148, 152,
    155; on historical critique of reason,
    143–44; on historical objectivity,
    143; on kinds of psychology, 153; on
    limits of science, 121–23; on lived
    experience (*Erlebnis*), 152, 153–54; on

mechanism, 122–23; his naturalism,
    122; on positivism, 149; relationship
    to Schopenhauer, 49–50; on world-
    views, 48–51
Droyson, Johann: critique of posi-
    tivism, 149–50; critique of Ranke,
    140–41; on historical objectivity,
    140–41, 142; his historical relativism,
    142; his liberal nationalism, 142; on
    method of understanding, 148–49;
    and Wilhelm von Humboldt, 148
Du Bois-Reymond, Emil: his concept
    of explanation, 99; on limits of
    science, 100–101; on matter, 131–32; as
    physicalist, 16, 22, 97, 130; on world
    puzzles, 129–30
Dühring, Eugen: anticipations of
    Nietzsche, 173, 184; critique of meta-
    physics, 177–78; critique of Schopen-
    hauer, 178, 182; his ethics, 179–81; on
    infinite, 177–78; on love, 183–84; his
    positivism, 174–76, 178–79

evil, 6, 30, 31, 76, 79, 80, 95, 98, 162, 163,
    173, 176, 182, 194, 195, 207, 215

Feuerbach, Ludwig: his atheism, 4, 5;
    critique of Hegel, 1, 54; historical
    importance, 1, 175; on philosophy,
    18, 19, 22, 27; on religion, 24, 93; his
    Wesen des Christenthums, 24
Fichte, Johann Gottlieb, 9, 11, 15, 32, 81,
    138, 168
Fischer, Kuno, 9, 17, 36, 37, 39, 42, 166,
    172
foundationalism, 15, 37–38
Frauenstädt, Julius: critique of materi-
    alism, 79–80; critique of mechanism,
    83; as disciple of Schopenhauer, 77–
    79; early Hegelianism, 77–78; on

INDEX

Leibniz, Gottfried Wilhelm von, 67, 68, 114, 116

Lotze, Hermann: his critique of Hegel, 1, 54; his historical importance, 1, 10, 16, 44; his idealism, 65, 66, 68; on matter, 64–68; on mechanism, 64, 66; his review of Czolbe, 85–92; his romanticism, 66; his spiritualism, 65, 68; on teleology, 64–66; on value, 64–65, 91; and Wagner, 62–63, 65

Löwith, Karl, 7–8

Marx, Karl, 4, 7, 8, 22, 23, 26, 27, 139, 222

materialism: controversy about, 4, 6, 8, 53–96, 159; definition of, 53, 67, 79, 84; and dogmatism, 92; and empiricism, 84, 86; and enlightenment, 93; and neo-Kantianism, 91–2, 167; and nominalism, 93, 94; and realism, 87–9, 91

materialism, vital, 21, 71–2

mechanism, 22, 55,64–7, 80, 88, 90, 93, 99, 123–4, 130, 168

Meinecke, Friedrich, 8n13, 133, 225

metaphysics, 1, 10, 17, 18, 21, 23, 26–9, 38, 45–7, 49, 50, 64–69, 81, 90, 91, 95, 104–8, 113, 119, 120, 124, 126, 127, 171, 177–9, 207

Meyer, Jürgen Bona, 17, 36, 39, 42, 166, 168, 171, 172, 195, 196, 200, 202, 214

Müller, Johannes, 22, 55, 82, 92, 128

Nägeli, Carl von: his background, 116; his empiricism, 117, 118; on limits of science, 117–20; model of explanation, 118; on natural selection, 48

neo-Kantianism: critique of pessimism, 167–72; its definition of philosophy, 36–39, 40, 43, 51, 158; early neo-Kantians, 10–11, 36; on foundationalism, 37–38; and Hartmann, 185, 193–94; historical importance of, 8, 36, 96; on history, 145; hostility to metaphysics, 32, 169; and materialism, 91–92, 95, 167; obsession with Schopenhauer, 12, 32, 41–43, 167–68; and positivism, 12, 39, 43; role of Fischer and Zeller in, 36;

its theory of value, 44; its turn toward practical, 40–41, 43–44

Niebuhr, Harthold, 25, 137, 138, 150

Nietzsche, Friedrich, 4, 7, 8, 89, 160, 184

normativity, 18, 95, 135, 144, 145, 155

objectivity, historical, 140–45

Pantheism, 4, 5, 53, 54, 76, 78

Paulsen, Friedrich, 38, 39, 40, 166, 168, 169, 170

Plümacher, Olga: as forgotten figure, 218–219; as historian, 218, 226; on aesthetic pleasure, 205–6; on work, 198–99

positivism, 12, 40, 145–50, 174, 175, 176, 179, 221

Proudhon, Pierre-Joseph, 59

Ranke, Leopold von: and critical school of history, 25, 137; critique of Hegel, 138–39; on historical objectivity, 140, 141; his principle of individuality, 138–39, 148

Rathenau, Walter: critique of Du Bois-Reymond, 123; defense of metaphysics, 126–27; on paradigm of explanation, 124; scientific realism, 125; skepticism about truth, 126; on value of science, 124–25, 126–27

Reinhold, Karl Leonhard, 9, 15, 78, 90

Riehl, Alois, 38, 39, 41, 166, 168, 170n15, 171, 172

Rousseau, Jean Jacques, 26, 125, 202

Schaarschmidt, Carl, 40

Schelling, Friedrich Wilhelm Joseph, 9, 11, 16, 32, 47, 66, 68, 80, 81, 138, 139, 185

Schiller, Friedrich, 69, 201

Schleiermacher, Friedrich Daniel, 35, 138, 148

Schopenhauer, Arthur: his historical importance, 11–12, 41–43, 49–50, 158–59; on ideas, 34–35; influence of, 29, 41–43, 49; on method of metaphysics,

GPSR Authorized Representative: Easy Access System Europe - Mustamäe tee
50, 10621 Tallinn, Estonia, gpsr.requests@easproject.com